Practical Spring Cloud Function

Developing Cloud-Native Functions for Multi-Cloud and Hybrid-Cloud Environments

Banu Parasuraman

Apress®

Practical Spring Cloud Function: Developing Cloud-Native Functions for Multi-Cloud and Hybrid-Cloud Environments

Banu Parasuraman
Frisco, TX, USA

ISBN-13 (pbk): 978-1-4842-8912-9   ISBN-13 (electronic): 978-1-4842-8913-6
https://doi.org/10.1007/978-1-4842-8913-6

Managing Director, Apress Media LLC: Welmoed Spahr
Acquisitions Editor: Steve Anglin
Development Editor: Laura Berendson
Coordinating Editor: Gryffin Winkler
Copy Editor: Kezia Endsley

Cover designed by eStudioCalamar

Cover image by Aamyr on Unsplash (www.unsplash.com)

Distributed to the book trade worldwide by Apress Media, LLC, 1 New York Plaza, New York, NY 10004, U.S.A. Phone 1-800-SPRINGER, fax (201) 348-4505, e-mail orders-ny@springer-sbm.com, or visit www.springeronline.com. Apress Media, LLC is a California LLC and the sole member (owner) is Springer Science + Business Media Finance Inc (SSBM Finance Inc). SSBM Finance Inc is a **Delaware** corporation.

For information on translations, please e-mail booktranslations@springernature.com; for reprint, paperback, or audio rights, please e-mail bookpermissions@springernature.com.

Apress titles may be purchased in bulk for academic, corporate, or promotional use. eBook versions and licenses are also available for most titles. For more information, reference our Print and eBook Bulk Sales web page at http://www.apress.com/bulk-sales.

Any source code or other supplementary material referenced by the author in this book is available to readers on GitHub (https://github.com/Apress). For more detailed information, please visit http://www.apress.com/source-code.

Printed on acid-free paper

I would like to dedicate this book to my wife Vijaya and my wonderful children Pooja and Deepika, who stuck with me through the trials and tribulations during the writing of this book. I also dedicate this to my mom, Kalpana Parasuraman.

Table of Contents

About the Author

Banu Parasuraman is a cloud native technologist and a Customer Success Manager (CSM) at IBM, with over 30 years of experience in the IT industry. He provides expert advice to clients who are looking to move to the cloud or implement cloud-native platforms such as Kubernetes, Cloud Foundry, and the like. He has engaged over 25 select companies spread across different sectors (including retail, healthcare, logistics, banking, manufacturing, automotive, oil and gas, pharmaceuticals, and media and entertainment) in the United States, Europe, and Asia. He is experienced in most of the popular cloud platforms, including VMware VCF, Pivotal PCF, IBM OCP, Google GCP, Amazon AWS, and Microsoft Azure. Banu has taken part in external speaking engagements targeted at CXOs and engineers, including at VMworld, SpringOne, Spring Days, and Spring Developer Forum Meetups. His internal speaking engagements include developer workshops on cloud-native architecture and development, customer workshops on Pivotal Cloud Foundry, and enabling cloud-native sales plays and strategies for sales and teams. Lastly, Banu has numerous blogs on platforms such as Medium and LinkedIn, where he promotes the adoption of cloud-native architecture.

About the Technical Reviewer

 **Manuel Jordan Elera** is an autodidactic developer and researcher who enjoys learning new technologies for his own experiments and creating new integrations. Manuel won the Springy Award 2013 Community Champion and Spring Champion. In his little free time, he reads the Bible and composes music on his guitar. Manuel is known as dr_pompeii. He has tech-reviewed numerous books, including *Pro Spring MVC with Webflux* (Apress, 2020), *Pro Spring Boot 2* (Apress, 2019), *Rapid Java Persistence and Microservices* (Apress, 2019), *Java Language Features* (Apress, 2018), *Spring Boot 2 Recipes* (Apress, 2018), and *Java APIs, Extensions, and Libraries* (Apress, 2018). You can read his detailed tutorials on Spring technologies and contact him through his blog at www.manueljordanelera.blogspot.com. You can follow Manuel on his Twitter account, @dr_pompeii.

Acknowledgments

It has been a great privilege to write this book and help you understand real-world implementations of Spring Cloud Function. Thank you for reading it.

After my presentation at SpringOne 2020, I received a message on LinkedIn from Steve Anglin at Apress. Steve asked me if I would be willing to write a book about Spring Cloud Function. I was a bit hesitant at first, given that I was occupied with many client engagements, which were taking up most of my work hours. I was worried that I would not do the subject justice, due to my preoccupation with my clients. But after a long contemplation and a heartfelt discussion with my family, I decided to take it on.

I want to thank Steve Anglin, Associate Editorial Director, for reaching out to me and providing me this opportunity to write a book on Spring Cloud Function.

Mark Powers, the Editorial Operations Manager, was instrumental in helping me bring this book to close. With his incessant prodding and nudging, he helped me reached the finish line. Thanks, Mark.

Manuel Jordan, the technical reviewer, was immensely helpful. His comments kept me honest and prevented me from cutting corners. He helped improve the quality of the solutions that I present in this book. Thanks, Manuel.

I also want to thank Nirmal Selvaraj and others at Apress, who worked to bring this book to fruition.

This book would not be possible without the help of my wife Vijaya and daughters Pooja and Deepika, who provided the much-needed emotional support through this journey.

Introduction

I entered the field of Information Technology (IT) 25 years ago, after spending time in sales and marketing. I was an average programmer and was never into hardcore programming. During my early life in IT, I worked as part of a team that built a baseball simulator for the Detroit Tigers. I helped build a video capture driver for that simulator using C++. Even though this was a great project with a lot of visibility, it was never my real passion to be a hard-core programmer.

I soon gravitated toward solution architecture. This seemed to perfectly tie my marketing skills to my technology skills. I began looking at solutions from a marketing lens. This approach formed the basis for writing this book. Because, what good is a technology if we do not know how to apply it in real life?

Functional programming was an emerging technology. Cloud providers such as AWS, Google, and Azure created serverless environments, with innovations such as Firecracker virtualization techniques, that allowed infrastructure to scale down to zero. This allowed customers to derive huge cost savings by not paying for resources that were not in use and subscribing to a pay-per-use model.

Initially, development of these functions that run on serverless environments were built on either NodeJS or Python. These functions were also vendor-specific. Spring.io developed the Spring Cloud Function framework, which allowed the functions to run in a cloud-agnostic environment. The focus was on the "write once, deploy anywhere" concept. This was a game changer in the cloud functions world.

Prior to writing this book, I was a staunch evangelist of Pivotal Cloud Foundry and Kubernetes. I promoted writing code that was portable. When Knative came into being in 2018 as a joint effort between IBM and Google, I was excited. Knative was designed as a serverless infrastructure on top of Kubernetes and made the serverless infrastructure portable. Combining the power and portability of Spring Cloud Function and Knative, you have a true portable system with zero scale-down capabilities.

This was something that I wanted to write and evangelize about. But I felt that writing about the technology and how it worked would not be that exciting. I wanted to write about how people could use this technology in the real world.

In this book, you will see how to program and deploy real-life examples using Spring Cloud Function. It starts with examples of writing code and deploying to AWS Lambda, Google Cloud Function, and Azure Function serverless environments. It then introduces you to the Knative on Kubernetes environment. Writing code and deploying is not enough. Automating the deployment is key in large-scale, distributed environments. You also see how to automate the CI/CD pipeline through examples.

This books also takes you into the world of data pipelines, AI/ML, and IoT. This book finishes up with real-world examples in oil and gas (IoT), manufacturing (IoT), and conversational AI (retail). This book touches on AWS, the Google Cloud Platform (GCP), Azure, IBM Cloud, and VMware Tanzu.

The code for these projects is provided on GitHub at `https://github.com/banup-kubeforce`. It is also available at `github.com/apress/practical-spring-cloud-function`. This allows you to get up to speed on the technologies. So, after completing this book, you will have hands-on experience with AI/ML, IoT, data pipelines, CI/CD, and of course Spring Cloud Function.

I hope you enjoy reading and coding this book.

CHAPTER 1

Why Use Spring Cloud Function

This chapter explores Spring Cloud Function using a sample use case—an HRM (Human Resources Management) system. The focus is on systems that reside in an enterprise. The chapter touches on the FaaS (Functions as a Service) concept and explains how it is gaining momentum in the enterprise. The chapter also digs deeper into its implementations in the cloud. You will learn about some of the portability issues present at the code and container level and read about concepts such as Knative on Kubernetes, which includes container portability. You will also learn about some high-level implementations of Spring Cloud Function on AWS, GCP, Azure, VMware Tanzu, and Red Hat OpenShift.

1.1. Functions as a Service (FaaS)

FaaS is a revolutionary technology. It is a great boon for developers and businesses. FaaS allows businesses to adapt to rapidly changing business needs by enabling their development teams to develop products and features at a "high" velocity, thereby improving their Mean Time To Market (MTTM). Developers can develop functions without worrying about setting up, configuring, or maintaining the underlying infrastructure. FaaS models are also designed to use just the right quantity of infrastructure and

© Banu Parasuraman 2023
B. Parasuraman, *Practical Spring Cloud Function*,
https://doi.org/10.1007/978-1-4842-8913-6_1

compute time. They also can be scaled to fit exact demand, by focusing on billing for the number of invocations as compared to billing for uptime. FaaS has two parts, as shown in Figure 1-1.

- The function code encapsulates the business logic in any language, such as Java, C#, Python, Node, and so on.

- The underlying container hosts an application server and an operating system.

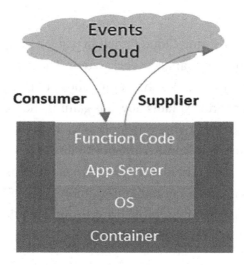

Figure 1-1. *FaaS component architecture*

1.1.1. Implementation of an Enterprise Application

Imagine all the infrastructure needed to run a single payroll application on the cloud. This application may consume only 16GB of RAM and eight vCPUs, but you are charged continuously for the entire duration that the application is active. Using a simple AWS pricing formula, this works out to around $1,000 per year. This cost is for the whole time the application is hosted and active, regardless of use. Of course, you can cost-justify it through a TCO (Total Cost of Ownership) calculation, which helps you determine how your application can bring in revenue or value that compensates for the expense. This revenue-generation model is more suitable to applications that generate revenue for the company, such as an ecommerce site. It is more difficult to prove the value that a supporting application, running in the backend of an enterprise, brings to a company.

1.1.2. Migration ROI for a Portfolio of Application

The value equation gets more complex if you plan to migrate an extensive portfolio of apps in your enterprise.

Let's for a moment assume, as a CTO or CIO of a company, you have a portfolio of about one thousand applications that you plan on migrating to the cloud. The key factors to consider, among the many, include:

- What is the current infrastructure supporting the apps?

- What is the utilization of these apps?

The utilization of apps is an essential factor in determining the value of the application. Consider this—after analyzing the utilization of apps, you find that this portfolio includes the following distribution:

- 10% with 80% utilization

- 40% with 50% utilization

- 50% with 20% utilization

If you calculate the billing cost using an AWS cost calculator, you see that you will spend $1 million per year. This spend is for applications that are critical and highly utilized, as well as for applications that are minimally utilized. This cost is due to the fact that the cloud providers charge for the entire duration the application is active and consuming the infrastructure. The key here is that the infrastructure is fully allocated for the application's life. Imagine how much you could save if the infrastructure was allocated only for the duration that the application was active and serving. This would be a great cost and resource saving approach. Cloud providers have thought through this because they also faced the pressure of finite infrastructure and considered the time needed to provision additional infrastructure.

1.1.3. The Serverless Functions Concept

To work around the problem of finite infrastructure utilization, AWS created Lambda serverless functions. This was a genius invention. Subscribers to this service pay only for the time the application is invoked. The infrastructure is unallocated when it is not invoked. This way, AWS can save on infrastructure by repurposing the infrastructure for other needy applications while transferring the cost savings to the customer. This is a win-win. It's worth considering whether you can apply this same approach to all the enterprise applications in your company today. You would be able to save a lot of money. Also, if you were to bring this technology to the datacenter, you would be able to reap the benefits that AWS realized. Isn't this wonderful?

1.1.4. Applying the Serverless Functions Concept to an Enterprise Application

Let's dig deeper into the concept of functions and how AWS realizes the magic of infrastructure savings. Functions are tiny code pieces with a single input and a single output, and a processing layer (a predicate) acting as the glue. Compare this to enterprise apps, which are designed to do many things. Take a simple payroll system, for example. A payroll system has multiple input interfaces and multiple output interfaces. Here are some of those interfaces:

- Timecard system to get the hours employees worked in a month

- Performance evaluation system

- Peer feedback system

- Inflation adjustment calculator system

- The outgoing interface to the IRS

- The outgoing interface to the medical insurance provider

- An outgoing interface to the internal web portal where employees can download their paystubs

Running this payroll application is not trivial. I have seen such a payroll system use the following:

- Fourteen dedicated middleware application servers

- Two RDBMS database stores

- Two integration tools such as message queues and FTP

- Four dedicated bare-metal servers, with each server configured with 128GB RAM, 32 CPUs, 4TB of HDD, 10TB of vSAN, and the like

The key factor in determining whether this application can be hosted on a serverless functions infrastructure like Lambda is the time it takes for the application to boot up (the startup time or cold start) and the time it takes for the application to shut down (the shutdown time). The faster the startup and shutdown times, the larger the cost savings.

It is also important that these times be quick so that they don't cause disruptions. If you were to research the startup times for large enterprise applications like the payroll application, you would find that it is not pretty. An average startup time is around 15 minutes for all components to come up and another 15 minutes for the application to come down. This would not fly. Imagine if you deployed this application to an AWS Lambda serverless function. Thirty minutes of downtime for each invocation? This will not work. Your users would abandon the application entirely. As you can see, large applications cannot benefit from resource release and resource reassignment because they take a long time to start up and shut down, which would impact the general operation of the application.

Can you make this large payroll application behave in an expected way for serverless functions? The answer is yes. A lot of refactoring is required, but it can be done.

Serverless Function in the Cloud

All cloud providers have now incorporated the serverless functions into their infrastructure offerings. AWS has Lambda Functions, Google has Cloud Functions, and Azure has Azure Functions. These providers, in the quest for making their customers captive, made sure to introduce proprietary elements into their environments. The two components that are essential to run the functions are:

- Serverless function code that serves the functions

- Serverless infrastructure (containers) that supports the code

Why Is It Important for Serverless Functions to be Non-Proprietary?

Enterprises are gravitating toward a multi-cloud, hybrid-cloud approach to their cloud strategy. As you can see in Figure 1-2, the survey of 3,000 global respondents indicated that 76 percent already work in a multi-cloud environment. This means they are not bound to one single cloud provider. The adoption of a multi-cloud strategy alleviates the risk of vendor lock-in.

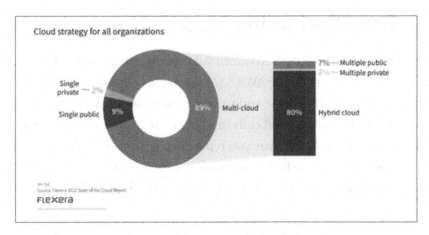

Figure 1-2. *Multi-cloud adoption report*
Source: `https://info.flexera.com/CM-REPORT-State-of-the-Cloud?lead_source=Website%20Visitor&id=Blog`

In a multi-cloud world, it is essential that enterprises subscribe to services that can be easily ported between clouds. This is especially important for commodity services.

FaaS, or serverless functions, have of late become a commodity with all the providers having some services around FaaS. It is therefore imperative that FaaS containers not have proprietary code.

Serverless functions become portable when they do not use proprietary code. Portable serverless functions allow for workload mobility across clouds. If, for instance, AWS Lambda functions are costly and Azure Functions are cheap, enterprises can avail the cost savings and move that Lambda workload to Azure Functions with very little effort.

The subsequent sections discuss in detail these portability issues and explain how you can solve them.

1.2. Code Portability Issues

Listing 1-1 shows the sample AWS Lambda code written in Java. This code was generated using the AWS SAM (Serverless Application Model) template. When observing the code, you can see that the AWS-specific library references and method calls bind the code to AWS. It is not much, but it is potent. In an enterprise, you typically have hundreds if not thousands of pieces of code that you must refactor if you want to move this type of code to another cloud provider. This is a costly affair.

Listing 1-1. Sample Code Using the AWS SAM Framework

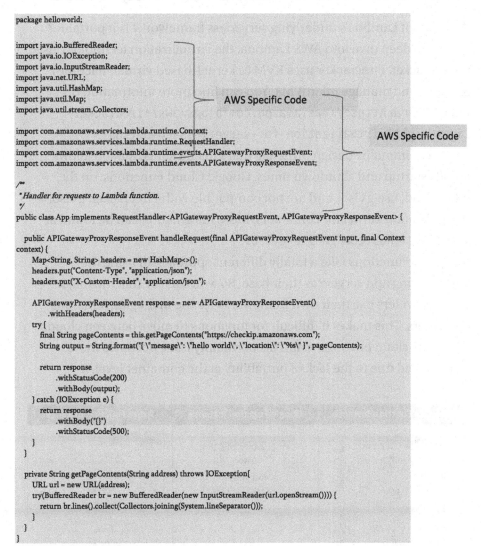

```
package helloworld;

import java.io.BufferedReader;
import java.io.IOException;
import java.io.InputStreamReader;
import java.net.URL;
import java.util.HashMap;
import java.util.Map;                                    AWS Specific Code
import java.util.stream.Collectors;

import com.amazonaws.services.lambda.runtime.Context;
import com.amazonaws.services.lambda.runtime.RequestHandler;    AWS Specific Code
import com.amazonaws.services.lambda.runtime.events.APIGatewayProxyRequestEvent;
import com.amazonaws.services.lambda.runtime.events.APIGatewayProxyResponseEvent;

/**
 * Handler for requests to Lambda function.
 */
public class App implements RequestHandler<APIGatewayProxyRequestEvent, APIGatewayProxyResponseEvent> {

    public APIGatewayProxyResponseEvent handleRequest(final APIGatewayProxyRequestEvent input, final Context
context) {
        Map<String, String> headers = new HashMap<>();
        headers.put("Content-Type", "application/json");
        headers.put("X-Custom-Header", "application/json");

        APIGatewayProxyResponseEvent response = new APIGatewayProxyResponseEvent()
            .withHeaders(headers);
        try {
            final String pageContents = this.getPageContents("https://checkip.amazonaws.com");
            String output = String.format("{ \"message\": \"hello world\", \"location\": \"%s\" }", pageContents);

            return response
                .withStatusCode(200)
                .withBody(output);
        } catch (IOException e) {
            return response
                .withBody("{}")
                .withStatusCode(500);
        }
    }

    private String getPageContents(String address) throws IOException{
        URL url = new URL(address);
        try(BufferedReader br = new BufferedReader(new InputStreamReader(url.openStream()))) {
            return br.lines().collect(Collectors.joining(System.lineSeparator()));
        }
    }
}
```

The following section explores the portability of the underlying serverless container, which impacts how multi-cloud migrations are conducted.

1.2.1. Serverless Container Portability Issue

What about Lambda's underlying serverless framework? Is it portable?

If you deep dive into AWS Lambda, the virtualization technology used is Firecracker. Firecracker uses KVM (a kernel-based virtual machine) to create and manage microVMs. You can find more information on Firecracker at `https://aws.amazon.com/blogs/aws/firecracker-lightweight-virtualization-for-serverless-computing/`.

The minimalist design principle that Firecracker is built on allows for fast startup and shutdown times. Google Cloud Functions, on the other hand, use gVisor and are not compatible with Firecracker. gVisor is an application kernel for containers. More information can be found at `https://github.com/google/gvisor`.

Azure Functions take a totally different approach of using the PaaS offering app service as their base. So, you can see that the major cloud providers use their own frameworks for the managing functions' containers. This makes it difficult for functions to move between clouds in a multi-cloud environment. This portability issue becomes more pronounced due to the lack of portability at the container level.

Figure 1-3. *Serverless architecture comparison*

You can see that the code and containers both differ from the provider and are not easily portable.

In the discussions so far, you have seen the following issues related to FaaS:

- Portability of code

- Portability of the serverless container

- Cold start of the serverless environment

How do you solve these issues?

Enter Spring Cloud Function and Knative. Spring Cloud Function addresses function code portability, and Knative addresses container portability.

Information on Spring Cloud Function is available at `https://spring. io/projects/spring-cloud-function`, and information about Knative is available at `https://knative.dev/docs/`.

The following sections deep dive into each of these topics.

1.3. Spring Cloud Function: Writing Once and Deploying to Any Cloud

As you learned from the earlier discussion, writing functions for AWS Lambda, Google Cloud Functions, or Azure Functions is a proprietary activity. You have to write code specific to a hyperscaler. Hyperscalers refer to large-scale cloud providers like AWS, Google, or Azure, who have a complete mix of hardware and facilities that can scale to 1000s of servers. This is not bad if your strategy is to have a strong single hyperscaler relationship, but over time, when your strategy changes to a hybrid cloud or multi-cloud, you may have to rethink your approach.

A hybrid cloud comprises a private cloud and a public cloud and is managed as one entity. Multi-cloud includes more than one public cloud and does not have a private cloud component.

11

This is where the Spring Cloud Function comes in. The Spring.io team started the Spring Cloud Function project with the following goals:

- Promote the implementation of business logic via functions.

- Decouple the development lifecycle of business logic from any specific runtime target so that the same code can run as a web endpoint, a stream processor, or a task.

- Support a uniform programming model across serverless providers, as well as the ability to run standalone (locally or in a PaaS).

- Enable Spring Boot features (auto-configuration, dependency injection, metrics) on serverless providers.

Source: `https://spring.io/projects/spring-cloud-function`

The key goals are decoupling from a specific runtime and supporting a uniform programming model across serverless providers.

Here's how these goals are achieved:

- Using Spring Boot

- Wrapper beans for Function<T, R> (Predicate), Consumer<T>, and Supplier<T>

- Packaging functions for deployments to target platforms such as AWS Lambda, Azure Functions, Google Cloud Functions, and Knative using adapters

- Another exciting aspect of Spring Cloud Function is that it enables functions to be executed locally. This allows developers to unit test without deploying to the cloud

Figures 1-4 and 1-5 show how you can deploy Spring Cloud Function. When Spring Cloud Function is bundled with specific libraries, it can be deployed to AWS Lambda, Google Cloud Functions, or Azure Functions.

Figure 1-4. *Deploying Spring Cloud Function directly to FaaS environments provided by the cloud providers*

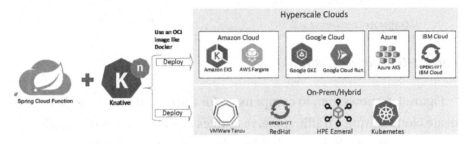

Figure 1-5. *Deploying Spring Cloud Function on Knative serverless configured on Kubernetes environments provided by the cloud providers*

When Spring Cloud Function is containerized on Knative, it can be deployed to any Kubernetes offering, whether on the cloud or on-premises. This is the preferred way to deploy it on hybrid and multi-cloud environments.

1.4. Project Knative and Portable Serverless Containers

Having a portable serverless container is also important. This minimizes the complexity and time required to move between cloud providers. Moving between cloud providers to take advantage of discounted pricing goes a long way toward saving costs. One methodology used is called *cloud bursting* (Figure 1-6). Cloud bursting compensates for the lack of infrastructure on-premises by adding resources to the cloud. This is usually a feature of a hybrid cloud.

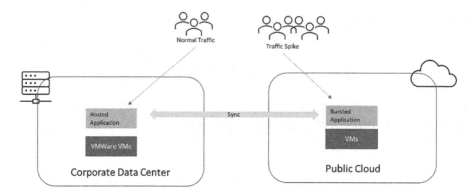

Figure 1-6. *Cloud bursting*

Figure 1-6 shows that, to compensate for the lack of resources in a private cloud during a traffic spike, resources are allocated to the public cloud where the traffic is routed. When the traffic spike goes down, the public cloud resources are removed. This allows for targeted use of costs and resources—that is, it uses additional resources only during the traffic spike period. The burst of activity during an eCommerce event like Cyber Monday is a great example of a traffic spike.

This cannot be easily achieved with just a portable code. You need containers that are also portable. This way, containers can be moved across cloud boundaries to accommodate traffic spikes. In Figure 1-6, you can see that VMs from VMware are used as containers. Since the VMs hosted in the datacenter and hosted in the cloud are similar in construct, cloud bursting is possible.

Applying this to Functions as a Service, you need a new way to make the underlying serverless containers portable.

One such revolutionary approach in the cloud function world is Knative. The next section dives deep into Knative.

1.4.1. Containers, Serverless Platforms, and Knative

What was the need for containers /serverless platforms?

Over the course of the evolution of IT, there has been a need for secure isolation of running processes. In the early 90's, chroot jail-based isolation allowed developers to create and host a virtualized copy of the software system. In 2008 Linux Containers (LXC) was introduced which gave the developers a virtualized environment. In 2011 Cloud Foundry introduced the concept of a container, and with Warden in 2019 container orchestration became a reality. Docker, introduced in 2013, provided containers that can host any operating system. Kubernetes, introduced in 2014, provided the capability to orchestrate containers based on Docker. Finally, Knative, introduced in 2018, extended Kubernetes to enable serverless workloads to run on Kubernetes clusters.

Serverless workloads (Knative) grew out of the need to help developers rapidly create and deploy applications without worrying about the underlying infrastructure. The serverless computing model takes care of provisioning, management, scheduling, and patching and allows cloud providers to develop the "pay only for resources used" model.

With Knative, you can create portable serverless containers that run on any Kubernetes environment. This allows for FaaS to be portable in a multi-cloud or hybrid-cloud environment.

Besides making developers more productive, the serverless environment offers faster deploys (see Figure 1-7). Developers can use the "fail fast and fail often" model and spin up or spin down code and infrastructure faster, which helps drive rapid innovation.

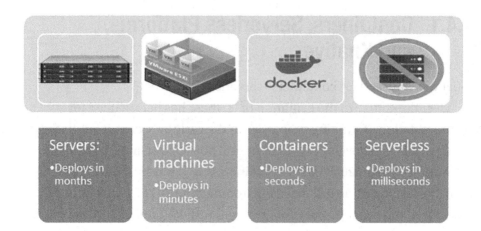

Figure 1-7. *Serverless deploys the quickest*

1.4.2. What Is Knative?

Knative is an extension of Kubernetes that enables serverless workloads to run on Kubernetes clusters. Working with Kubernetes is a pain. The amount of tooling that is required to help developers move their code from the IDE to Kubernetes defeats the purpose of the agility that Kubernetes professes to bring to the environment. Knative automates the process of build packages and deploying to Kubernetes by provider operators that are native to Kubernetes. Hence, the names "K" and "Native".

Knative has two main components:

- *Serving*: Provides components that enable rapid deployment of serverless containers, autoscaling, and point-in-time snapshots

- *Eventing*: Helps developers use event-driven architecture by providing tools to route events from producers to subscribers/sinks

You can read more about Knative at https://Knative.dev/docs.

1.5. Sample Use Case: Payroll Application

Let's look at how you can apply serverless functions to a real-life example.

We introduced the payroll application in the beginning of the chapter, we'll now build on it. Consider a payroll application with the configuration shown in Figure 1-8.

Figure 1-8. *Payroll application components*

Figure 1-9 shows the configuration.

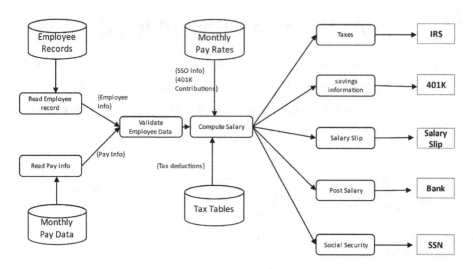

Figure 1-9. *Payroll application flow*

Translating this flow diagram into an actual implementation that can be deployed in a corporate datacenter results in Figure 1-10. You see that the functions are developed as REST APIs that are executed in batch mode. The REST APIs expose SAP ECC payroll modules. These REST APIs are run as batch jobs every 15 days. The databases are hosted on Oracle, and integrations are exposed using IBM API Connect (APIC). Note that this is not an on-demand process and can consume a lot of resources when idle. These REST APIs cannot be easily shut down and started up because a typical time for booting up a SAP NetWeaver component can be anywhere from 2 to 15 minutes, depending on the JVM configuration. These application components must be running constantly to keep the payroll application from breaking down.

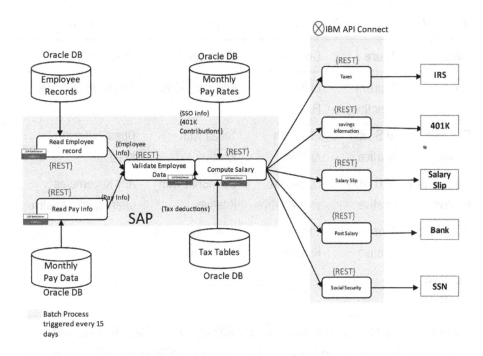

Figure 1-10. *Current payroll architecture*

Using this use case, the following sections explore how you can leverage Spring Cloud Function to modernize and transform this application into a highly efficient, scalable, and portable system.

1.6. Spring Cloud Function Support

The Spring Cloud Function is supported in almost all cloud offerings, as shown in Table 1-1.

Table 1-1. *Spring Cloud Function Support Among Cloud Providers*

AWS	Azure	Google	IBM Cloud	On-Premises
Lambda	Azure Functions	Cloud Functions	IBM Functions	Tanzu with Knative
EKS with Knative	AKS with Knative	GKE with Knative	Tanzu with Knative	OpenShift with Knative
Fargate with Knative	ARO with Knative	OpenShift with Knative	OpenShift with Knative	Any Kubernetes offering with Knative
ROSA with Knative	Tanzu with Knative	Tanzu with Knative	IBM Kubernetes with Knative	
Tanzu with Knative				

Abbreviations: ROSA: Red Hat OpenShift on AWS; ARO: Azure Red Hat OpenShift; EKS: Elastic Kubernetes Services; AKS: Azure Kubernetes Services; GKE: Google Kubernetes Engine

1.6.1. Spring Cloud Function on AWS Lambda on AWS

Transforming an application deployed on-premises to leverage an AWS Lambda environment and be portable requires function code that abstracts away the hard dependencies of AWS Lambda from the implementation and the serverless container. This example uses Spring Cloud Function for the function code framework and Lambda for the container. By writing once using Spring Cloud Function, you can use the DevOps pipeline, discussed in subsequent chapters, to deploy to other serverless environments. Figure 1-11 shows how AWS and its components help realize the payroll application in the cloud.

Now you need to deploy the payroll system on AWS Lambda. The deployment sequence is important, as you need to deploy SAP ECC and Oracle before integrating and then configure API and messaging for the Spring Cloud Function to integrate with SAP. Spring Cloud Function can be created and tested with dummy information, but it needs to be deployed after integration testing with SAP ECC:

1. Deploy SAP ECC on the AWS EC2 instances.

2. Deploy Oracle DB as an RDS instance.

3. Configure the SAP to Oracle integration.

4. Deploy Spring Cloud Function to AWS.

5. Set up the Amazon API Gateway.

6. Set up Amazon SQS for messaging.

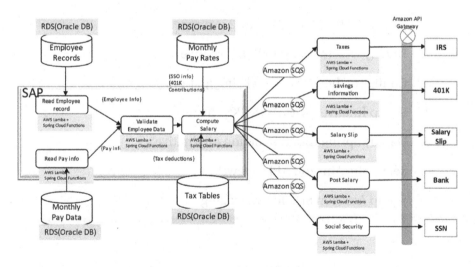

Figure 1-11. *Spring Cloud Function on AWS*

1.6.2. Spring Cloud Function on Knative and EKS on AWS

If you want to implement a truly portable environment in AWS, you can leverage the AWS EKS, which is a Kubernetes platform that AWS offers. You can install Knative in EKS and this will give you a truly portable, serverless container that allows for faster deployment and improved cold starts. It uses appropriate technologies, such as Spring Cloud Function on GraalVMs. GraalVMs uses the AOT (Ahead of Time) compilation technique, which significantly improves execution times. Subsequent sections address GraalVMs and Spring Cloud Function. See Figure 1-12.

Follow this process to deploy the payroll system on Knative hosted on an Azure AKS and ensure that the SAP ECC and Oracle DB are up and integrated. You do this before developing and deploying Spring Cloud Function on Knative:

1. Deploy SAP ECC on AWS EC2 instances.

2. Deploy Oracle DB as an RDS instance.

3. Configure the SAP to Oracle integration.

4. Set up Knative on an AWS EKS cluster.

5. Deploy Spring Cloud Function on Knative.

6. Set up the Amazon API Gateway.

7. Set up Amazon SQS for messaging.

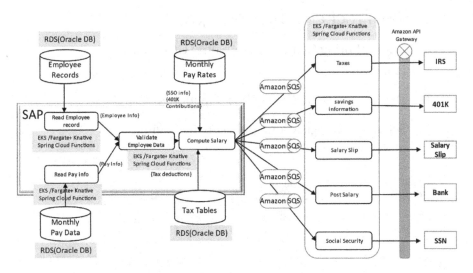

Figure 1-12.   *Spring Cloud Function on Knative on AWS*

1.6.3. Spring Cloud Function on Cloud Functions on GCP

GCP Cloud Functions provide a cloud alternative to AWS Lambda Functions. The GCP offering is newer than Lambda, but with the Anthos strategy, it is gaining a good amount of the function space. Spring.io works closely with Google to make the Spring.io components work seamlessly with the GCP components.

To deploy the payroll system on Cloud Functions on GCP, follow the process outlined here (see Figure 1-13). Ensure that the SAP ECC and Oracle DB are up and integrated before developing and deploying Spring Cloud Function on Cloud Functions:

1. Deploy SAP ECC onto GCE.

2. Deploy Oracle DB on GCE VMs, as there is no AWS RDS-like service on GCP.

3. Configure the SAP to Oracle integration.

4.   Set up a GCP Cloud Function project.

5.   Deploy Spring Cloud Function onto GCP Cloud Functions.

6.   Deploy Apigee on GCP to host function APIs.

7.   Set up the Google Cloud pub/sub messaging platform.

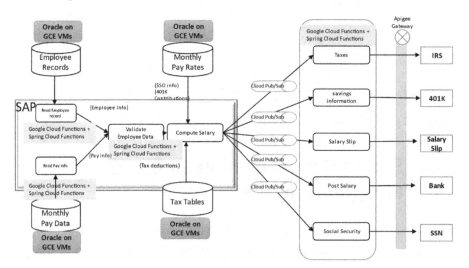

Figure 1-13. *Spring Cloud Function on GCP*

1.6.4. Spring Cloud Function on Knative and GKE on GCP

Knative, as discussed, is a way to make the functions portable. Knative, incidentally, was created by Google. With GCP, you can set up Knative on GKE, which is the Kubernetes engine provided by Google.

To deploy the payroll system on Knative hosted on a GCP GKE, follow the process outlined here (Figure 1-14). Ensure that the SAP ECC and

Oracle DB are up and integrated before developing and deploying Spring Cloud Function on Knative:

1. Deploy SAP ECC as a Docker image onto the GKE cluster.

2. Deploy Oracle DB as a Docker image onto the GKE cluster.

3. Configure the SAP to Oracle integration.

4. Configure a GKE cluster with Knative.

5. Deploy Spring Cloud Function onto Knative.

6. Set up the Apigee API Gateway.

7. Set up RabbitMQ on GKE for messaging.

8. Set up Google cloud pub/sub.

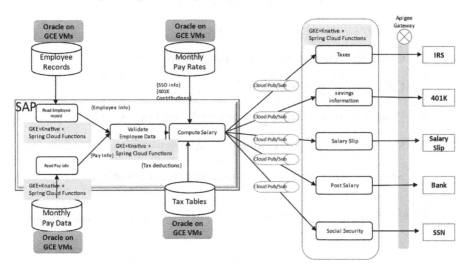

Figure 1-14. *Spring Cloud Function on Knative on GCP*

1.6.5. Spring Cloud Function on Azure Functions on Azure

Spring Cloud Function deployed on Azure Functions is not portable due to the explicit use of an Azure Function Invoker class. While Lambda and Google Cloud Functions require a change to Pom.xml (if you are using Maven), Azure needs an additional class. This makes it less portable. If you have a portfolio of one thousand Spring Cloud Functions in AWS that you need to move to Azure, you have to do a lot of development activity. This is disruptive.

To deploy the payroll system on Azure Functions, follow the process outlined here (see Figure 1-15). Ensure that the SAP ECC and Oracle DB are up and integrated before developing and deploying Spring Cloud Function on Azure Functions:

1. Deploy SAP ECC on Azure VMs.

2. Deploy Oracle DB on Azure VMs.

3. Configure the SAP to Oracle integration.

4. Configure Azure Functions.

5. Deploy Spring Cloud Function on Azure Functions.

6. Set up the Azure API Gateway on Azure.

7. Set up Azure Queue storage on Azure for messaging.

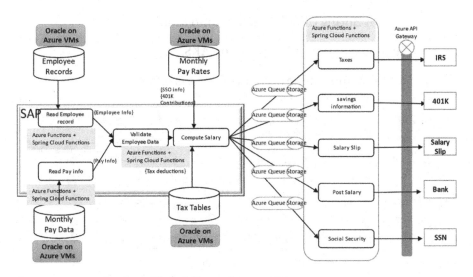

Figure 1-15. *Spring Cloud Function on Azure*

1.6.6. Spring Cloud Function on Knative and AKS on Azure

Knative on Azure AKS is the only option for deploying Spring Cloud Function on Azure that makes it portable. As in any Kubernetes implementation, it requires an implementation of Knative to run the functions. Transforming the payroll application to AKS requires an AKS cluster.

To deploy the payroll system on Knative hosted on an Azure AKS environment, follow the process outlined here (Figure 1-16). Ensure that the SAP ECC and Oracle DB are up and integrated before developing and deploying Spring Cloud Function on Knative:

1. Deploy SAP ECC on Azure VMs.

2. Deploy Oracle DB on Azure VMs.

3. Configure the SAP to Oracle integration.

4. Configure an AKS cluster with Knative.

5. Deploy Spring Cloud Function onto Knative.

6. Set up an Azure API Gateway on AKS.

7. Set up Azure Queue on Azure for messaging.

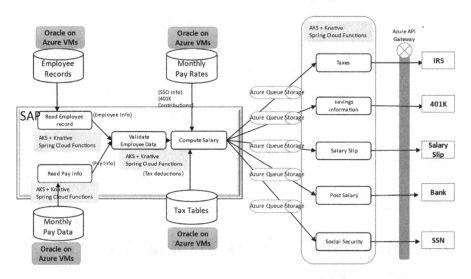

Figure 1-16. *Spring Cloud Function on Knative on Azure*

1.6.7. Spring Cloud Function on VMware Tanzu (TKG, PKS)

VMware Tanzu is an evolution of Pivotal Cloud Foundry (PCF). Those who are familiar with PCF should be aware of the "cf push" experience. It was a one-click provisioning approach and was very popular in the developer community. This is the same experience that Knative provides through its Knative build feature. To transform the payroll application to run on VMware Tanzu, you need the Tanzu Kubernetes grid, also known as TKG. TKG is built using the main branch of Kubernetes code. This can be deployed on-premises and in the cloud and can facilitate a multi-cloud or hybrid-cloud strategy. You can start up an instance of TKG on AWS, Azure, or Google by subscribing to the service in the provider's marketplace.

In a datacenter, you need a collection of servers or a hyper-converged infrastructure like VxRail with PRA (Pivotal Ready Architecture). You also need to upgrade your vSphere to Version 7.

Going back to the payroll application, you need to follow the process outlined here (Figure 1-17). Ensure that the SAP ECC and Oracle DB have been up and integrated before developing and deploying Spring Cloud Function on Knative:

1. Deploy SAP ECC as a Docker image onto TKG.

2. Deploy Oracle DB as a Docker image onto TKG.

3. Configure the SAP to Oracle integration.

4. Configure a TKG cluster with Knative.

5. Deploy Spring Cloud Function onto Knative.

6. Set up a Spring Cloud Gateway on TKG as an API Gateway.

7. Set up RabbitMQ on TKG for messaging.

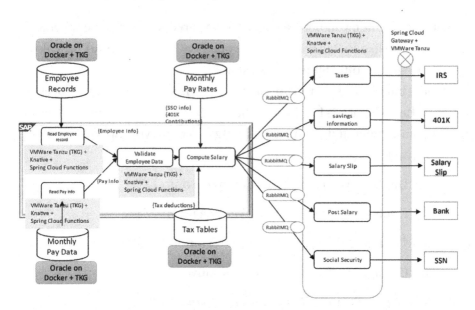

Figure 1-17. *Spring Cloud Function on TKG*

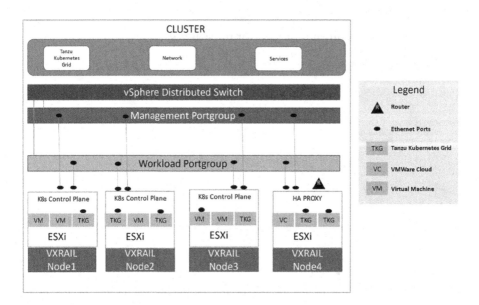

Figure 1-18. *Four-node VxRail P570F cluster for vSphere with Tanzu and HAProxy*

1.6.8. Spring Cloud Function on Red Hat OpenShift (OCP)

Red Hat OpenShift can be an on-premises option for deploying Spring Cloud Function. As in any Kubernetes implementation, it requires an implementation of Knative to run the functions. OpenShift has its own serverless implementation, called OpenShift serverless. Transforming the payroll application to OpenShift requires an OpenShift cluster.

To deploy the payroll system to OpenShift hosted on a VMware vSphere environment, follow the outlined process. First ensure that the SAP ECC and Oracle DB are up and integrated before developing and deploying Spring Cloud Function on Knative:

1. Deploy SAP ECC as a Docker image onto OpenShift cluster.

2. Deploy an Oracle DB as a Docker image onto the OpenShift cluster.

3. Configure the SAP to Oracle integration.

4. Configure an OpenShift cluster with Knative.

5. Deploy Spring Cloud Function onto Knative.

6. Set up a Red Hat 3scale API Gateway on OpenShift.

7. Set up RabbitMQ on TKG for messaging.

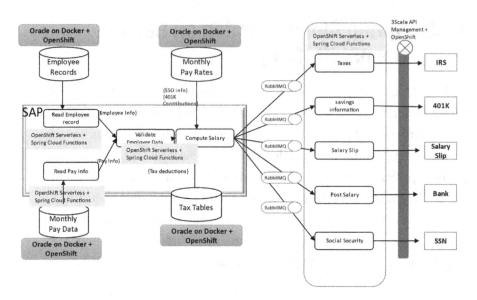

Figure 1-19. *Spring Cloud Function on Red Hat OpenShift*

1.7. Summary

This chapter discussed FaaS environments, Spring Cloud Function, and Knative. You saw that FaaS containers/environments provided by AWS, Google, or Microsoft Azure are not portable, as the underlying components that host the FaaS environment do not have the same architecture, which makes it difficult to move or migrate FaaS containers between cloud providers. You also saw that Spring Cloud Function can abstract the dependent AWS and Google libraries and provide a portable alternative. Spring Cloud Function on Knative can improve developer productivity by "writing once and deploying anywhere." You saw how to apply Spring Cloud Function and Knative to an enterprise payroll application and learned about the various implementation approaches. The next chapter walks through the deployments step-by-step. You will also see how to develop and deploy code to various targets, such as AWS, GCP, Azure, OpenShift, and VMware Tanzu. This will help you understand the power of Spring Cloud Function.

CHAPTER 2

Getting Started with Spring Cloud Function

This chapter discusses how to develop code using Spring Cloud Function and deploy it to environments in the cloud, on-premises (on a premises datacenter), and on your laptop. It includes a step-by-step approach to coding and deploying the function.

A sample payroll use case of inserting salary details and retrieving salary information is provided. Here are some of the common tasks that need to be performed for each of these environments:

1. Set up the IDE for the Spring Boot framework.

2. Add JPA, H2 (this example uses an embedded database to demonstrate the CRUD operations), Spring Cloud Function, and Spring Web Support.

3. Complete the code for `EmployeeFunction`, `EmployeeConsumer`, and `EmployeeSupplier`.

Note that the code remains the same in all environments; the only change you make is to the `pom.xml` file. There is also an introduction to a `FunctionInvoker <Message<String>`, `<String>` class regarding Azure Functions. Azure build looks for this class during the build process. Another difference you will notice with Azure is that you have to use JDK 11 and above to get the Azure templates in the IDE.

© Banu Parasuraman 2023
B. Parasuraman, *Practical Spring Cloud Function*,
https://doi.org/10.1007/978-1-4842-8913-6_2

The common tasks you will perform for Knative and Kubernetes environments such as EKS, AKS, GKE, OpenShift, and Kubernetes grid are the following:

1. Create a Docker image of the code.

2. Set up Knative on all environments.

3. Deploy the code to Knative.

Deployment of Spring Cloud Function to Knative will demonstrate true portability.

You also see how to use a single IDE such as IntelliJ or VS Code to perform all the functions (i.e., building and deploying to the target environments).

I have used multiple devices to set up the local and on-premises Kubernetes environments. I recommend that VMware VMs be used. You can get the VMware workstation player from VMware for free at `https://www.vmware.com/products/workstation-player.html`. You can also use other alternatives, such as Windows Subsystem for Linux (WSL) or Virtual Box.

All the code is available on GitHub at `https://github.com/banup-kubeforce payroll-h2.git`.

Happy coding!

2.1. Setting Up the Spring Boot and Spring Cloud Function Locally

This is a preliminary step that you undertake to determine if the Spring Cloud Function works. This will set the stage for deployment.

Prerequisites:

- An IDE such as IntelliJ, Eclipse, Spring IDE, or Red Hat Code Ready workspace

- Maven or Gradle

- Postman for testing

- Code from GitHub at `https://github.com/banup-kubeforce/payroll.git`

Here are the steps:

Step 1: Create the Spring Boot scaffolding.

Step 2: Create the employee model.

Step 3: Write the consumer.

Step 4: Write the supplier.

Step 5: Write the function.

Step 6: Deploy and run the code locally.

Step 7: Test the function.

I am using IntelliJ, as it makes me more productive with all the capabilities such as plugins for the cloud, Docker, Maven, and so on.

2.1.1. Step 1: Create the Spring Boot Scaffolding

In IntelliJ, create a Spring Boot project using Spring Initializer. Make sure you provide the name and choose JDK 11. Then provide a name and a group name. Click Next to reach the New Project screen, as shown in Figure 2-1.

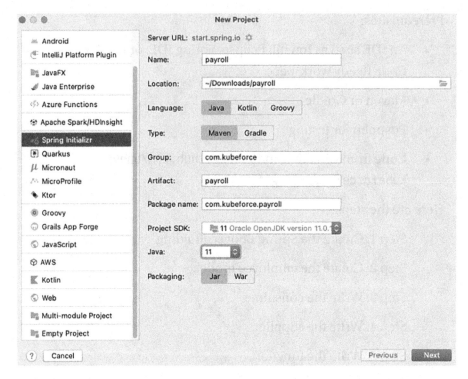

Figure 2-1. *Spring Initializer set up in IntelliJ*

On the next screen, it is important to select Spring Web and Function. If you just choose Function, you will not be able to test the function locally, as the functions will not persist. See Figure 2-2.

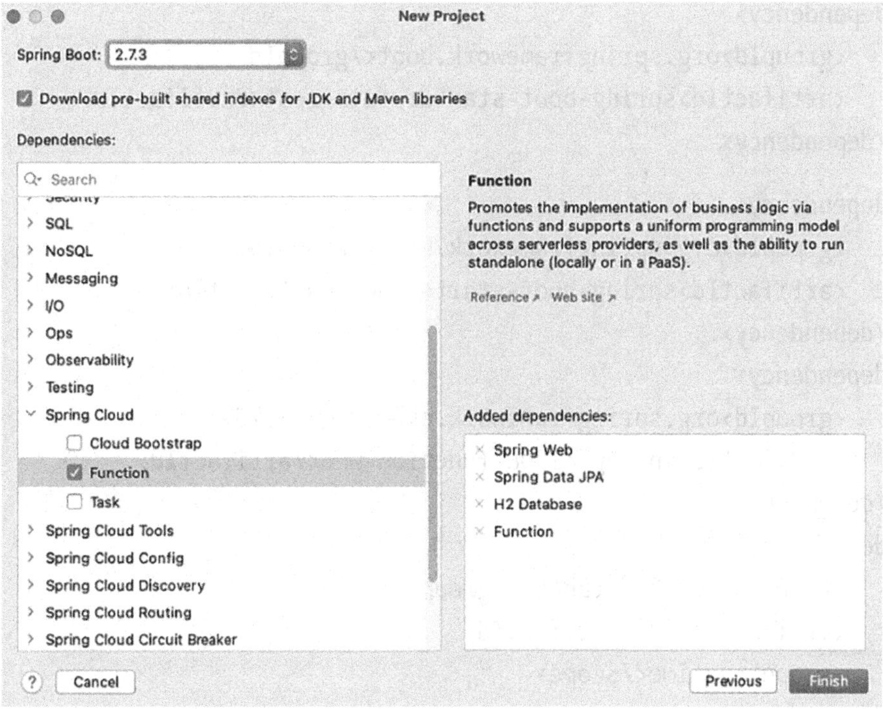

Figure 2-2. *Pick the dependencies for the project*

As you can see from the Added Dependencies section in Figure 2-2, I also included an H2 Database. You can use the database of your choice.

Upon clicking the Finish button, the IDE will create the code bits and take you to the project screen. Alternatively, you can bring the code down from GitHub by cloning the project.

Listing 2-1 shows the pom.xml file with Maven dependencies.

Listing 2-1. pom.xml File with Maven Dependencies

```
<dependency>
    <groupId>org.springframework.boot</groupId>
    <artifactId>spring-boot-starter-data-jpa</artifactId>
</dependency>
```

```xml
<dependency>
    <groupId>org.springframework.boot</groupId>
    <artifactId>spring-boot-starter-data-rest</artifactId>
</dependency>

<dependency>
    <groupId>org.springframework.boot</groupId>
    <artifactId>spring-boot-starter-web</artifactId>
</dependency>
<dependency>
    <groupId>org.springframework.cloud</groupId>
    <artifactId>spring-cloud-function-web</artifactId>
</dependency>
<dependency>
    <groupId>com.h2database</groupId>
    <artifactId>h2</artifactId>
    <scope>runtime</scope>
</dependency>
```

Listing 2-2 shows the `application.properties` file. I included `spring.h2.console.enabled=true` to be able to verify if the database has been populated.

Listing 2-2. application.properties

```
spring.cloud.function.definition=employeeConsumer
spring.datasource.url=jdbc:h2:mem:employee
spring.datasource.driverClassName=org.h2.Driver
spring.datasource.username=sa
spring.datasource.password=
spring.jpa.hibernate.ddl-auto=create
spring.h2.console.enabled=true
```

PayrollApplication.java, as shown Listing 2-3, is the main entry point for the application. It is important to define three beans that represent the consumer, supplier, and function, so that these functions can be accessed after deployment.

If you do not do this, you will not be able to invoke the function.

Listing 2-3. PayrollApplication.java

```
package com.kubeforce.payroll;
import org.springframework.boot.SpringApplication;
import org.springframework.boot.autoconfigure.
SpringBootApplication;
import org.springframework.cloud.function.context.
FunctionalSpringApplication;
import org.springframework.context.annotation.Bean;

@SpringBootApplication
public class PayrollAwsApplication {

    public static void main(String[] args) {SpringApplication.
    run(PayrollApplication.class,args);
        //SpringApplication.run can be used to run the function
        application locally.
        //Change SpringApplication.run to
        FunctionalSpringApplication.run when deploying to a
        serverless platforms
        // such as lambda, knative, etc.
    }
    @Bean
    public EmployeeFunction employeeFunction() {
        return new EmployeeFunction();
    }
```

```
    @Bean
    public EmployeeConsumer employeeConsumer() {
        return new EmployeeConsumer();
    }
    @Bean
    public EmployeeSupplier employeeSupplier() {
        return new EmployeeSupplier();
    }
}
```

Once the scaffolding and code bits are completed, you are ready for the next step, which is to create the model for your employee.

2.1.2. Step 2: Create the Employee Model

The model creates the getters and setters for the ID, name, employee ID, email, and salary.

I created this manually, but you can generate this using the Spring JPA data model generator for data that resides in an RDBM such as Oracle, MYSQL, or SQL Server, or a document database such as MongoDB. The database support for the generation of code using Spring JPA depends on the adapter and can be found at https://docs.spring.io/spring-integration/reference/html/jpa.html#jpa.

The model created in Listing 2-4 allows for CRUD operations into the H2 Database.

Listing 2-4. Employee Entity Model

```
package com.kubeforce.payroll;

import javax.persistence.Entity;
import javax.persistence.GeneratedValue;
import javax.persistence.Id;
import javax.persistence.Table;
```

```
@Entity
@Table(name= "employee")
public class Employee {

        @Id
        @GeneratedValue(generator = "UUID")
        private Long id;

        private String name;

        private int employeeid;

        private String email;

        private String salary;

    public Employee(String name, int employeeIdentifier, String
    email, String salary)
    {
        this.name = name;
        this.employeeid = employeeIdentifier;
        this.email = email;
        this.salary = salary;
    }

    public Employee() {

    }

    public String getName ()
        {
            return name;
        }
        public void setName (String name)
        {
            this.name = name;
        }
```

```java
public int getEmployeeIdentifier ()
{
    return employeeid;
}

public void setCustomerIdentifier (int
employeeIdentifier)
{
    this.employeeid = employeeIdentifier;
}

public String getEmail ()
{
    return email;
}

public void setEmail (String email)
{
    this.email = email;
}

public String getSalary ()
{
    return salary;
}

public void setSalary (String salary)
{
    this.salary = salary;
}

public Long getId ()
{
    return id;
}
```

```
public void setId (Long id)
{
    this.id = id;
}
}
```

Once the model is created/generated, you can proceed with coding the consumer that will write to the database and the supplier that will read from the database.

2.1.3. Step 3: Write the Consumer

In this step, you write the consumer that will write to the database. Here, you expose the function attributes such as name, employeeIdentifier, email, and salary, which enable you to pass the data to the function.

Listing 2-5. Employee Entity Model

```
package com.kubeforce.payroll;

import org.slf4j.Logger;
import org.slf4j.LoggerFactory;
import org.springframework.beans.factory.annotation.Autowired;

import java.util.Map;
import java.util.function.Consumer;

public class EmployeeConsumer implements
Consumer<Map<String,String>> {
    public static final Logger LOGGER = LoggerFactory.
    getLogger(EmployeeConsumer.class);

    @Autowired
    private EmployeeRepository employeeRepository;
```

```
@Override
public void accept (Map<String, String> map)
{
    LOGGER.info("Creating the employee", map);
    Employee employee = new Employee (map.get("name"),
    Integer.parseInt(map.get(
            "employeeIdentifier")), map.get("email"), map.
            get("salary"));
    employeeRepository.save(employee);
}

}
```

2.1.4. Step 4: Write the Supplier

The supplier function in this example allows you to get all the data in the database. You can change it to suit your needs.

Note that you will be using the Spring Data Repositories to interact with the database. This is a common way for both Spring Data REST and Spring Cloud Function.

Listing 2-6. EmployeeSupplier.java

```
package com.kubeforce.payrol;

import org.slf4j.Logger;
import org.slf4j.LoggerFactory;
import org.springframework.beans.factory.annotation.Autowired;
import org.springframework.stereotype.Component;

import java.util.List;
import java.util.function.Supplier;
```

```
@Component
public class EmployeeSupplier implements Supplier
{
    public static final Logger LOGGER = LoggerFactory.
    getLogger(EmployeeSupplier.class);

    @Autowired
    private EmployeeRepository employeeRepository;

    @Override
    public Employee get ()
    {
        List <Employee>employees = employeeRepository.
        findAll();
        LOGGER.info("Getting the employee of our choice - ",
        employees);
        return employees.get(0);
    }
}
```

2.1.5. Step 5: Write the Function

This step is optional, and you can see from the code that you can create
a function definition outside of the consumer and supplier and allow for
getting the data associated with an specific ID. See Listing 2-7.

Listing 2-7. EmployeeFunction.java

```
package com.kubeforce.payroll;

import org.springframework.beans.factory.annotation.Autowired;

import java.util.Optional;
import java.util.function.Function;
```

45

```java
public class EmployeeFunction implements
Function<Long,Employee>  {
    @Autowired
    private EmployeeRepository employeeRepository;

    @Override
    public Employee apply (Long s)
    {
        Optional<Employee> employeeOptional =
        employeeRepository.findById(s);
        if (employeeOptional.isPresent()) {
            return employeeOptional.get();
        }
        return null;
    }
}
```

Once you have developed your code, you can run the function locally. The key step to run this locally is to modify the main class to include:

```java
SpringApplication.run(PayrollApplication.class, args)
```

For deployment to other environments such as Lambda, use:

```java
FunctionalSpringApplication.run(PayrollApplication.class, args)
```

The use of SpringApplication allows you to keep the code up and running so that you can test the function with tools such as Postman.

2.1.6. Step 6: Deploy and Run the Code Locally

In this step, you run the code just like you would for any other Spring Boot code.

Note that the code runs and is available in port 8080.

```
2022-09-20 13:38:15.611 INFO 5144 --- [    main] o.hibernate.annotations.common.Version    : HCANN000001: Hibernate Commons Annotations (5.1.2.Final)
2022-09-20 13:38:15.694 INFO 5144 --- [    main] org.hibernate.dialect.Dialect             : HHH000400: Using dialect: org.hibernate.dialect.H2Dialect
2022-09-20 13:38:16.133 INFO 5144 --- [    main] o.h.e.t.j.p.i.JtaPlatformInitiator        : HHH000490: Using JtaPlatform implementation: [org.hibernate.
2022-09-20 13:38:16.140 INFO 5144 --- [    main] j.LocalContainerEntityManagerFactoryBean  : Initialized JPA EntityManagerFactory for persistence unit 'c
2022-09-20 13:38:16.406 WARN 5144 --- [    main] JpaBaseConfiguration$JpaWebConfiguration  : spring.jpa.open-in-view is enabled by default. Therefore, da
2022-09-20 13:38:17.080 INFO 5144 --- [    main] o.s.c.f.web.mvc.FunctionHandlerMapping    : FunctionCatalog: org.springframework.cloud.function.context.
2022-09-20 13:38:17.138 INFO 5144 --- [    main] o.s.b.w.embedded.tomcat.TomcatWebServer   : Tomcat started on port(s): 8080 (http) with context path ''
2022-09-20 13:38:17.154 INFO 5144 --- [    main] c.kubeforce.payroll.PayrollApplication    : Started PayrollApplication in 4.456 seconds (JVM running for
```

Figure 2-3. *Spring Boot deploy and run*

This allows for the function to be tested by tools such as Postman and curl.

2.1.7. Step 7: Test the Function

You can use curl or Postman to test your function. Here I use Postman. You can download Postman at `https://www.postman.com/downloads/`.

In Postman, choose `POST`, the `http://localhost:8080/employeeConsumer` URL, and the JSON format input.

```
{
  "name": "xxx",
    "employeeIdentifier":"2",
    "email": xxx@yahoo.com,
      "salary":"1000"
}
```

Figure 2-4. *Testing in Postman*

You can test all the three interfaces here, but when you go to Lambda or other environments, you will be restricted to just one interface.

You can also verify if the data has been added by going to the H2 console, as shown in Figure 2-5.

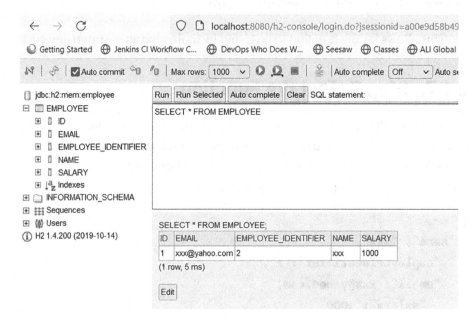

Figure 2-5. *H2 console showing the employee table being updated with the data*

This completes the steps for creating, running, and testing the code of a local function.

In the following sections, you'll see how to use the same code with little to no changes and deploy it to a serverless function container of your choice.

2.2. Setting Up Spring Cloud Function and AWS Lambda

This section discusses deploying the code that you created into AWS Lambda.

You have to do a little bit of tweaking to make the code compatible with Lambda. The tweaking is not too disruptive. Again, going back to real situations where you have over a thousand functions you want to move to AWS, this tweak will not be that significant. Of course, it depends on what cloud provider you are starting to create functions for. Ideally, I have seen enterprises gravitate toward Lambda, but there are enterprises that start with Azure or Google. In any case, making these functions portable across clouds requires a few code changes and some pom.xml changes.

Prerequisites:

- AWS account

- AWS Lambda Function subscription

- AWS CLI (optional)

- Code from GitHub at https://github.com/banup-kubeforce/payroll-aws

<u>Step 1:</u> <u>First follow Steps 1-6 outlined in Section 2.1</u>. The code remains the same for any serverless offerings from the cloud providers.

The change introduced at the code level will be in the main Spring Boot class called PayrollApplication. You will change this:

SpringApplication.run(PayrollApplication.class, args)

to this:

FunctionalSpringApplication.run(PayrollApplication.class, args)

This process is shown in Listing 2-8.

Listing 2-8. PayrollAwsApplication.java

```
package com.kubeforce.payrollaws;

import org.springframework.boot.SpringApplication;
import org.springframework.boot.autoconfigure.
SpringBootApplication;
import org.springframework.cloud.function.context.
FunctionalSpringApplication;
import org.springframework.context.annotation.Bean;

@SpringBootApplication
public class PayrollAwsApplication {

    public static void main(String[] args) {SpringApplication.
    run(PayrollAwsApplication.class,args);
        //SpringApplication.run can be used to run the function
        application locally.
        //Change SpringApplication.run to
        FunctionalSpringApplication.run when deploying to
        serverless platforms
        // such as lambda, knative, etc.
    }
    @Bean
    public EmployeeFunction employeeFunction() {
        return new EmployeeFunction();
    }

    @Bean
    public EmployeeConsumer employeeConsumer() {
        return new EmployeeConsumer();
    }
```

```
@Bean
public EmployeeSupplier employeeSupplier() {
    return new EmployeeSupplier();
}
```

}

The next step is to change the pom.xml file to add the AWS Lambda adapter.

Step 2: Change POM to include AWS dependencies and plugins, as shown in Listing 2-9.

Listing 2-9. The pom.xml File

```xml
<?xml version="1.0" encoding="UTF-8"?>
<project xmlns="http://maven.apache.org/POM/4.0.0"
xmlns:xsi="http://www.w3.org/2001/XMLSchema-instance"
        xsi:schemaLocation="http://maven.apache.org/POM/4.0.0
        https://maven.apache.org/xsd/maven-4.0.0.xsd">
    <modelVersion>4.0.0</modelVersion>
    <parent>
        <groupId>org.springframework.boot</groupId>
        <artifactId>spring-boot-starter-parent</artifactId>
        <version>2.7.3</version>
        <relativePath/> <!-- lookup parent from repository -->
    </parent>
    <groupId>com.kubeforce</groupId>
    <artifactId>payroll-aws</artifactId>
    <version>0.0.1-SNAPSHOT</version>
    <name>payroll-aws</name>
    <description>payroll-aws</description>
    <properties>
        <java.version>11</java.version>
```

```
        <spring-cloud.version>2021.0.1</spring-cloud.version>
        <aws-lambda-events.version>3.9.0</aws-lambda-events.
        version>
    </properties>
    <dependencies>
        <dependency>
            <groupId>org.springframework.boot</groupId>
            <artifactId>spring-boot-starter-data-jpa</
            artifactId>
        </dependency>
        <dependency>
            <groupId>org.springframework.boot</groupId>
            <artifactId>spring-boot-starter-web</artifactId>
        </dependency>
        <dependency>
            <groupId>org.springframework.cloud</groupId>
            <artifactId>spring-cloud-function-web</artifactId>
        </dependency>
        <dependency>
            <groupId>com.amazonaws</groupId>
            <artifactId>aws-lambda-java-core</artifactId>
            <version>1.2.1</version>
            <scope>provided</scope>
        </dependency>
        <dependency>
            <groupId>org.springframework.cloud</groupId>
            <artifactId>spring-cloud-function-adapter-aws</
            artifactId>
        </dependency>
        <dependency>
            <groupId>com.amazonaws</groupId>
            <artifactId>aws-lambda-java-events</artifactId>
```

```
    <version>3.9.0</version>
</dependency>
<dependency>
    <groupId>com.h2database</groupId>
    <artifactId>h2</artifactId>
    <scope>runtime</scope>
</dependency>
<dependency>
    <groupId>org.springdoc</groupId>
    <artifactId>springdoc-openapi-ui</artifactId>
    <version>1.6.11</version>
</dependency>
<dependency>
    <groupId>org.springdoc</groupId>
    <artifactId>springdoc-openapi-webflux-ui
    </artifactId>
    <version>1.6.11</version>
</dependency>

<dependency>
    <groupId>org.springframework.boot</groupId>
    <artifactId>spring-boot-starter-test</artifactId>
    <scope>test</scope>
</dependency>
</dependencies>
<dependencyManagement>
    <dependencies>
        <dependency>
            <groupId>org.springframework.cloud</groupId>
            <artifactId>spring-cloud-dependencies
            </artifactId>
            <version>${spring-cloud.version}</version>
```

```xml
                <type>pom</type>
                <scope>import</scope>
            </dependency>
        </dependencies>
    </dependencyManagement>

    <build>
        <plugins>
            <plugin>
                <groupId>org.apache.maven.plugins</groupId>
                <artifactId>maven-deploy-plugin</artifactId>
                <configuration>
                    <skip>true</skip>
                </configuration>
            </plugin>
            <plugin>
                <groupId>org.springframework.boot</groupId>
                <artifactId>spring-boot-maven-plugin
                </artifactId>
                <dependencies>
                    <dependency>
                        <groupId>org.springframework.boot.
                        experimental</groupId>
                        <artifactId>spring-boot-thin-layout
                        </artifactId>
                        <version>1.0.28.RELEASE</version>
                    </dependency>
                </dependencies>
            </plugin>
```

```
    <plugin>
        <groupId>org.apache.maven.plugins</groupId>
        <artifactId>maven-shade-plugin</artifactId>
        <version>3.2.4</version>
        <configuration>
            <createDependencyReducedPom>false
            </createDependencyReducedPom>
            <shadedArtifactAttached>true
            </shadedArtifactAttached>
            <shadedClassifierName>aws
            </shadedClassifierName>
        </configuration>
    </plugin>
  </plugins>
 </build>

</project>
```

The POM needs to be changed to accommodate the Spring Cloud Function adapter for AWS, Lambda events, and the Maven shade plugin (optional).

These changes will create a package that can be deployed to AWS Lamdba.

Step 3: Package the application into a JAR file to deploy to AWS Lambda. Figure 2-6 shows how to trigger a Maven package run in IntelliJ. Note that payroll-aws-0.0.1-SNAPSHOT-aws.jar is created in the target folder.

Figure 2-6. *Run Maven:package from the IDE*

<u>Step 4:</u> Create a function definition in AWS Lambda.

Log in to AWS and subscribe to AWS Lambda. Information on how to subscribe to Lambda is available at `https://docs.aws.amazon.com/lambda/latest/dg/getting-started.html`.

Create a function defined on the Lambda portal/dashboard, as shown in Figure 2-7.

Upload the JAR file created in Step 3 and provide the settings, as illustrated in Figure 2-7.

Figure 2-7. *AWS lambda dashboard to create a function*

Use the Upload From button, as shown in Figure 2-9, to access the choices for uploading a file.

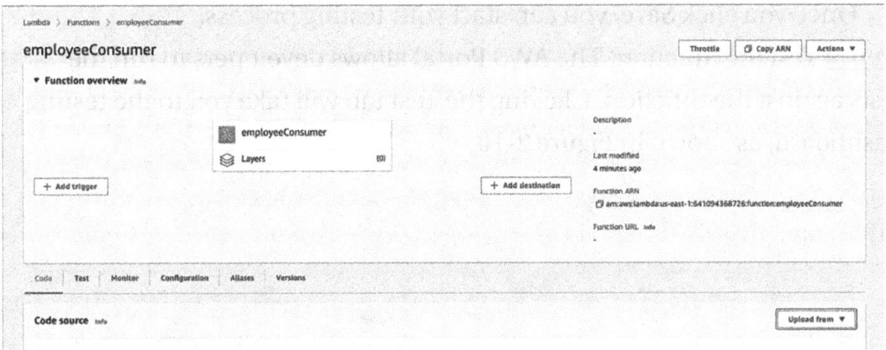

Figure 2-8. *Upload the JAR file into the AWS Lambda dashboard*

Set the handler as shown. The Lambda function handler is the method in your function code that processes events. This will indicate that the Spring Cloud Function adapter will be invoked when the function is called. I used Java 11. Refer to the pom.xml.

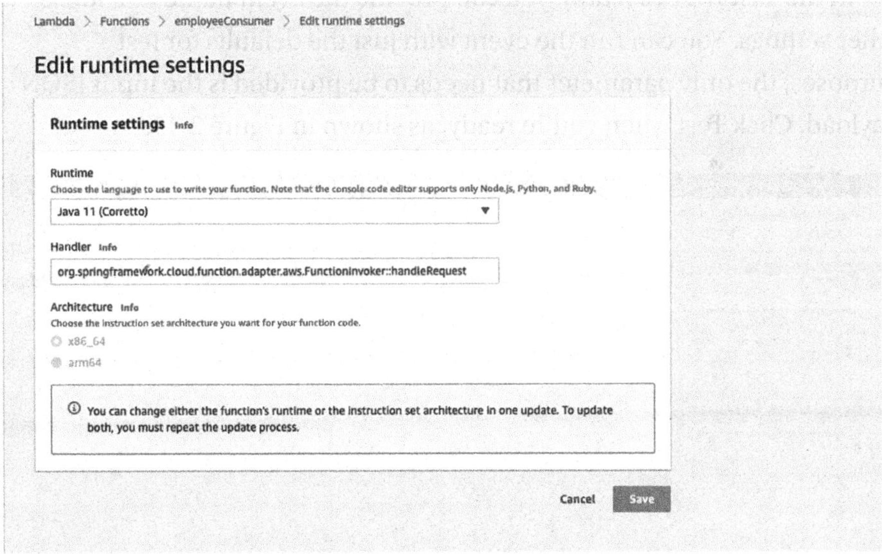

Figure 2-9. *AWS Lambda runtime settings*

Once you click Save, you can start your testing process.

Step 5: Test the function. The AWS Portal allows developers to run the tests against the function. Clicking the Test tab will take you to the testing dashboard, as shown in Figure 2-10.

Figure 2-10. *AWS Lamba Functions Test tab*

The testing dashboard allows you to send a JSON file as an event to trigger the function.

In the Test Event section, you can provide the event name or choose other settings. You can run the event with just the defaults for test purposes; the only parameter that needs to be provided is the input JSON payload. Click Test when you're ready, as shown in Figure 2-11.

Figure 2-11. *Testing the dasboard*

Figure 2-12 shows you the details of the test. Note that the test is successful.

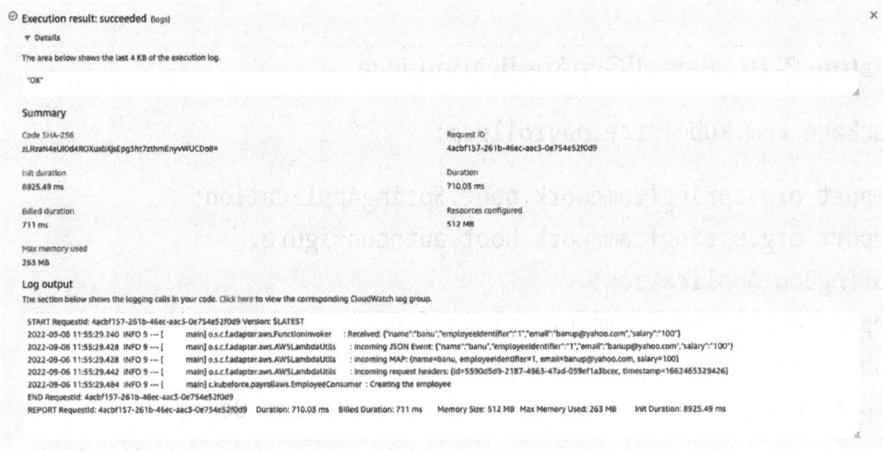

Figure 2-12. AWS Lambda function test results

2.3. Setting Up Spring Cloud Function and Google Cloud Functions

You will use the same example from Section 2.1 and modify it a bit to make it run on Google Cloud Functions. The approach is similar to AWS Lambda, but you will be leveraging Google's libraries.

Prerequisites:

- Google account

- Subscription to Google Cloud Functions

- Google CLI (this is critical as it is a more efficient way than going through the Google Portal)

- Code from GitHub at https://github.com/banup-kubeforce/payroll-gcp

<u>Step 1:</u> Follow Steps 1-6 outlined in Section 2.1. This step is the same as you completed for AWS Lambda. The code is very similar to the AWS code. See Listing 2-10.

Listing 2-10. PayrollGcpApplication.java

```java
package com.kubeforce.payrollgcp;

import org.springframework.boot.SpringApplication;
import org.springframework.boot.autoconfigure.
SpringBootApplication;
import org.springframework.cloud.function.context.
FunctionalSpringApplication;
import org.springframework.context.annotation.Bean;

@SpringBootApplication
public class PayrollGcpApplication {

    public static void main(String[] args) {
        FunctionalSpringApplication.run(PayrollGcpApplication.
        class, args);
    }
    @Bean
    public EmployeeFunction exampleFunction() {
        return new EmployeeFunction();
    }

    @Bean
    public EmployeeConsumer employeeConsumer() {
        return new EmployeeConsumer();
    }
```

```
@Bean
public EmployeeSupplier exampleSupplier() {
    return new EmployeeSupplier();
}
}
```

Step 2: Configure POM. The pom.xml file needs to be modified to include the Spring Cloud Function adapter and any plugins that are specific to GCP. See Listing 2-11.

You will be adding some GCP function-specific dependencies, such as spring-cloud-gcp-starter, spring-cloud-function-adapter-gcp, spring-cloud-gcp-dependencies, and spring-cloud-function-adapter-gcp.

Listing 2-11. The pom.xml File

```xml
<?xml version="1.0" encoding="UTF-8"?>
<project xmlns="http://maven.apache.org/POM/4.0.0"
xmlns:xsi="http://www.w3.org/2001/XMLSchema-instance"
        xsi:schemaLocation="http://maven.apache.org/POM/4.0.0
        https://maven.apache.org/xsd/maven-4.0.0.xsd">
    <modelVersion>4.0.0</modelVersion>
    <parent>
        <groupId>org.springframework.boot</groupId>
        <artifactId>spring-boot-starter-parent</artifactId>
        <version>2.6.5</version>
        <relativePath/> <!-- lookup parent from repository -->
    </parent>
    <groupId>com.kubeforce</groupId>
    <artifactId>payroll-gcp</artifactId>
    <version>0.0.1-SNAPSHOT</version>
    <name>payroll-gcp</name>
    <description>payroll-gcp</description>
```

```xml
<properties>
    <java.version>11</java.version>
    <spring-cloud-gcp.version>3.1.0</spring-cloud-gcp.
    version>
    <spring-cloud.version>2021.0.1</spring-cloud.version>
    <spring-cloud-function.version>4.0.0-SNAPSHOT</spring-
    cloud-function.version>
</properties>
<dependencies>
    <dependency>
        <groupId>org.springframework.boot</groupId>
        <artifactId>spring-boot-starter-data-jpa</
        artifactId>
    </dependency>
    <dependency>
        <groupId>org.springframework.boot</groupId>
        <artifactId>spring-boot-starter-web</artifactId>
    </dependency>
    <dependency>
        <groupId>com.google.cloud</groupId>
        <artifactId>spring-cloud-gcp-starter</artifactId>
    </dependency>
    <dependency>
        <groupId>org.springframework.cloud</groupId>
        <artifactId>spring-cloud-function-web</artifactId>
    </dependency>
    <dependency>
        <groupId>org.springframework.cloud</groupId>
        <artifactId>spring-cloud-function-adapter-gcp</
        artifactId>
```

```
    </dependency>
    <dependency>
        <groupId>com.h2database</groupId>
        <artifactId>h2</artifactId>
        <scope>runtime</scope>
    </dependency>

    <dependency>
        <groupId>org.springframework.boot</groupId>
        <artifactId>spring-boot-starter-test</artifactId>
        <scope>test</scope>
    </dependency>
</dependencies>
<dependencyManagement>
    <dependencies>
        <dependency>
            <groupId>org.springframework.cloud</groupId>
            <artifactId>spring-cloud-dependencies
            </artifactId>
            <version>${spring-cloud.version}</version>
            <type>pom</type>
            <scope>import</scope>
        </dependency>
        <dependency>
            <groupId>com.google.cloud</groupId>
            <artifactId>spring-cloud-gcp-dependencies
            </artifactId>
            <version>${spring-cloud-gcp.version}</version>
            <type>pom</type>
            <scope>import</scope>
        </dependency>
    </dependencies>
</dependencyManagement>
```

```xml
<build>
    <plugins>
        <plugin>
            <artifactId>maven-deploy-plugin</artifactId>
            <configuration>
                <skip>true</skip>
            </configuration>
        </plugin>
        <plugin>
            <groupId>org.springframework.boot</groupId>
            <artifactId>spring-boot-maven-plugin
            </artifactId>
            <configuration>
                <outputDirectory>target/deploy
                </outputDirectory>
            </configuration>
            <dependencies>
                <dependency>
                    <groupId>org.springframework.cloud
                    </groupId>
                    <artifactId>spring-cloud-function-
                    adapter-gcp</artifactId>
                    <version>3.2.2</version>
                </dependency>
            </dependencies>
        </plugin>

        <plugin>
            <groupId>com.google.cloud.functions</groupId>
            <artifactId>function-maven-plugin</artifactId>
            <version>0.9.1</version>
            <configuration>
```

```
                <functionTarget>org.springframework.cloud.
                function.adapter.gcp.GcfJarLauncher
                </functionTarget>
                <port>8080</port>
            </configuration>
        </plugin>
    </plugins>
</build>

</project>
```

Step 3: Build, package, and deploy to Google Cloud Functions. The Google cloud website for this activity is a bit clumsy. You have to zip up your entire directory and upload it. This may not be allowed in some enterprises. I therefore reverted to using the CLI to accomplish this task. See Figure 2-13.

This command must be run from the project root folder:

```
$gcloud functions deploy payroll-gcp --entry-point org.
springframework.cloud.function.adapter.gcp.GcfJarLauncher
--runtime java11 --trigger-http --source target/deploy
--memory 512MB
```

```
banup@Banus-MacBook-Pro payroll-gcp % gcloud functions deploy payroll-gcp --entry-point org.springframework.cloud.function.adapter.gcp.GcfJarLauncher
--runtime java11 --trigger-http --source target/deploy --memory 512MB
Deploying function (may take a while - up to 2 minutes)...⠹

For Cloud Build Logs, visit: https://console.cloud.google.com/cloud-build/builds;region=us-central1/493a8e94-f067-4469-bf4a-ca0e774c2552?project=39446
3569086
Deploying function (may take a while - up to 2 minutes)...done.

availableMemoryMb: 512
buildId: 493a8e94-f067-4469-bf4a-ca0e774c2552
buildName: projects/394463569086/locations/us-central1/builds/493a8e94-f067-4469-bf4a-ca0e774c2552
dockerRegistry: CONTAINER_REGISTRY
entryPoint: org.springframework.cloud.function.adapter.gcp.GcfJarLauncher
httpsTrigger:
  securityLevel: SECURE_OPTIONAL
  url: https://us-central1-theta-totem-240518.cloudfunctions.net/payroll-gcp
ingressSettings: ALLOW_ALL
labels:
  deployment-tool: cli-gcloud
name: projects/theta-totem-240518/locations/us-central1/functions/payroll-gcp
runtime: java11
serviceAccountEmail: theta-totem-240518@appspot.gserviceaccount.com
sourceUploadUrl: https://storage.googleapis.com/uploads-136758024477.us-central1.cloudfunctions.appspot.com/02f7d50e-8fff-43af-ad1d-e1a47a9a2aee.zip
status: ACTIVE
timeout: 60s
updateTime: '2022-09-06T14:10:06.692Z'
versionId: '3'
```

Figure 2-13. *Gcloud CLI execution results*

Once the command has been successfully executed, you can go to your Google Cloud Functions console to see the deployed function. See Figure 2-14.

Figure 2-14. *Cloud Functions dashboard*

Now you can test it to verify that it works.

<u>Step 4:</u> Test the function in GCP. Google provides a way to test from the website itself. You can provide the input in the form of the JSON file, as you did before, and then execute the tests.

Figure 2-15 shows the successful execution of the test.

Figure 2-15. *Cloud Functions testing dashboard*

2.4. Setting Up Spring Cloud Function Azure Functions

You will use the same example from Section 2.1 and modify it a bit to make it run on Azure Functions. You will see that the approach for Azure Functions is different from AWS or Google. You have to add another class called `EmployeeConsumerHandler`, which extends a `FunctionInvoker<I,O>`. This `FunctionInvoker` class is merely a pass through for the `EmployeeConsumer` function.

Prerequisites:

- Azure account

- Subscription to Azure Functions

- Azure Functions CLI. You can download the tools at `https://docs.microsoft.com/en-us/azure/azure-functions/functions-run-local`

- Code from GitHub at `https://github.com/banup-kubeforce/payroll-azure`

<u>Step 1:</u> Follow Steps 1-6 outlined in Section 2.1.

You have to introduce a `FunctionInvoker <I,O>` class, which makes the code non-portable to other cloud providers. While AWS and Google externalize the invocation of the function, as you have seen in previous sections, Azure forces you to provide a handler class that extends a `FunctionInvoker`.

Listing 2-12 introduces the class called `EmployeeConsumerHandler`, which extends `FunctionInvoker`. The input for this `FunctionInvoker` will be a `Map<String,String>`, which will take in the JSON object that is passed. This then gets sent to the `EmployeeConsumer` function, which processes the data.

Listing 2-12. EmployeeConsumerHandler.java

```java
package com.kubeforce.payrollazure;
import com.microsoft.azure.functions.*;
import com.microsoft.azure.functions.annotation.*;
import org.aspectj.weaver.NewConstructorTypeMunger;
import org.springframework.cloud.function.adapter.azure.
FunctionInvoker;

import java.util.List;
import java.util.Map;

import java.util.Optional;
import org.springframework.messaging.Message;
import org.springframework.messaging.support.MessageBuilder;

public class EmployeeConsumerHandler extends FunctionInvoker<Ma
p<String,String>,String  >{

    @FunctionName("employeeConsumer")
    public String execute(
            @HttpTrigger(name = "request", methods =
            {HttpMethod.GET, HttpMethod.POST}, authLevel =
            AuthorizationLevel.ANONYMOUS) HttpRequestMessage<Op
            tional<Map>> request,
                ExecutionContext context) {

    String message = "Successfully inserted: " +request.
    getBody().get().getName();
    return message;
    }

}
```

<u>Step 2:</u> Build and package the function. IntelliJ offers you the ability to execute Maven commands through a Maven window, as shown in Figure 2-16.

You have to run the `maven clean` command before you run the `maven package` command. These commands are under the Lifecycle menu in the Maven window. Run the Maven package to get the deployable JAR file. These JAR files are stored in the target folder in your project directory

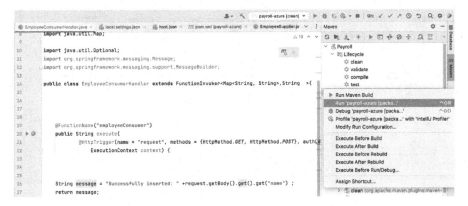

Figure 2-16.   *The Maven package*

Figure 2-17 shows a successful run of the Maven package.

Figure 2-17.   *Azure Functions build and succcessful package*

<u>Step 3:</u> Deploy the function in Azure. You will see some artifacts created in the target folder. `Payroll-azure-0.0.1-SNAPSHOT.jar` is the file you are interested in. This file needs to be deployed to the Azure Cloud.

IntelliJ has a feature/plugin for Azure that you can enable. Once you enable that feature, you can perform Azure Function-based activities from the IDE.

In this case, to start the deploy process, choose Run Azure Functions ➤ Deploy from the Azure Functions list, as shown in Figure 2-18.

Figure 2-18.   *Use Azure Functions, Deploy in Maven to deploy to Azure*

After the function is successfully deployed to the Azure Cloud, you can use the URL provided to runs tests in Postman or proceed to the Azure Functions console to test.

The Azure Functions console is shown in Figure 2-19.

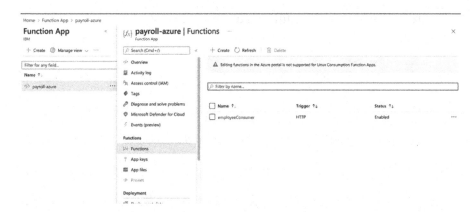

Figure 2-19. *Azure Functions Console*

You will see that the function is deployed in Azure and is running.

Step 4: Test. Clicking the employeeConsumer function will take you to the detail console, as shown in Figure 2-20. Here, you can conduct tests by clicking the Code + Test link. The dashboard has an Input section, where you can specify the JSON in the body, choose the HTTP method as POST (in this example), and click the Run button. You can see the results of the execution in the command console, as shown in Figure 2-21.

Figure 2-20. *Run test with input*

Figure 2-21 shows successful execution of the test.

Figure 2-21. *Successful run of the test*

2.5. Setting Up Locally with Kubernetes and Knative and Spring Cloud Function

This section explores another way to deploy Spring Cloud Function. Kubernetes, as you might be aware, is a portable approach to containerization and running containers. Kubernetes allows you to host containers that are packaged as images and deployed on Kubernetes pods.

Knative is an environment that sits on Kubernetes and can host a function. Chapter 1 explained how the cloud providers created environments such as AWS Lambda that could start up on demand and shut down when a resource is not in use. Similarly, you can create such an on-demand environment with Knative for functions. This section explores how to set up the Knative environment locally, which is difficult with AWS and Google Functions, and deploy and work with your functions locally and on the cloud. This section starts with local deployment and then moves on to the cloud.

You will notice that I used EmployeeSupplier as the function. To do this, you need to prepopulate the H2 database with some data so that you can query the database using the EmployeeSupplier function.

Prerequisites:

- Docker on Mac, Linux, or Windows

- Kind (Kubernetes in Docker)

- Knative serving

- IntelliJ, Eclipse, VS Code, or other IDEs

- Code from GitHub

Here is the process of setting up Kubernetes and Knative and deploying Spring Cloud Function.

Step 1: Set up a Kubernetes cluster locally. In this step, you install a local Kubernetes cluster. You deploy a KIND (Kubernetes IN Docker). Cluster. Of course, you can use Minikube or Minishift to deploy locally.

First, you need Docker.

1. Install Docker.

   I am using a Ubuntu VM since it is a popular Linux offering. The command lines are provided in sequence, so you can follow the process. See Listing 2-13.

Listing 2-13. Install Docker

```
$sudo apt-get update
$sudo apt-get install -y \
    apt-transport-https \
    ca-certificates \
    curl \
    gnupg-agent \
```

```
    software-properties-common
$curl -fsSL https://download.docker.com/linux/ubuntu/gpg | sudo
apt-key add -
$sudo add-apt-repository \
    "deb [arch=amd64] https://download.docker.com/linux/ubuntu \
    $(lsb_release -cs) \
    stable"
$sudo apt-get update
$sudo apt-get install -y docker-ce docker-ce-cli containerd.io
$sudo usermod -aG docker $USER
```

Once you run these commands, you will have a running Docker instance.

   2.   Install Kubectl.

         This step is required, as you need Kubectl to interact
         with the Kubernetes cluster

```
$sudo curl -L "https://storage.googleapis.com/kubernetes-
release/release/`curl -s https://storage.googleapis.com/
kubernetes-release/release/stable.txt`/bin/linux/amd64/kubectl"
-o /usr/local/bin/kubectl
```

Run chmod to make Kubectl executable:

```
$sudo chmod +x /usr/local/bin/kubectl
```

   3.   Install KIND.

```
$sudo curl -L "https://kind.sigs.k8s.io/dl/v0.8.1/kind-
$(uname)-amd64" -o /usr/local/bin/kind
```

Run chmod to make KIND executable:

```
$sudo chmod +x /usr/local/bin/kind
```

Now you have the KIND bits that will allow you to install the cluster and deploy Knative.

Step 2: Configure Knative. In order to configure Knative, you need a KIND cluster. You will create a cluster with custom configuration.

Create a cluster using a configuration file called clusterconfig.yaml. Note that the name of the cluster is "knative". You can name it differently, but you have to use that cluster to deploy Knative; see Listing 2-14.

Listing 2-14. Create clusterconfig.yaml and Run the Create Cluster

```
$cat > clusterconfig.yaml << EOF
kind: Cluster
apiVersion: kind.x-k8s.io/v1alpha4
nodes:
- role: control-plane
  extraPortMappings:
    ## expose port 31380 of the node to port 80 on the host
  - containerPort: 31080
    hostPort: 80
    ## expose port 31443 of the node to port 443 on the host
  - containerPort: 31443
    hostPort: 443
EOF
$kind create cluster --name knative --config clusterconfig.yaml
```

```
Creating cluster "knative" ...
 √ Ensuring node image (kindest/node:v1.18.2) 🖼🖼
 √ Preparing nodes 📦📦
 √ Writing configuration 📜📜
 √ Starting control-plane 🕹️🕹️🕹️
 √ Installing CNI 🔌🔌
 √ Installing StorageClass 💾💾
Set kubectl context to "kind-knative"
You can now use your cluster with:

kubectl cluster-info --context kind-knative
```

Figure 2-22. *Cluster has been successfully created*

To set up Knative, you need to install and configure the following:

- Knative serving (information about Knative serving is available at https://knative.dev/docs/serving)

- Kourier is a lightweight Knative serving ingress and is available at https://github.com/knative-sandbox/net-kourier.

- Magic DNS is a DNS provider and is available at https://knative.dev/docs/install/yaml-install/serving/install-serving-with-yaml/#configure-dns.

Install Knative serving

1. Install the Knative serving components (i.e., crds and core):

```
$ kubectl apply -f https://github.com/knative/serving/releases/
download/knative-v1.6.0/serving-crds.yaml
$ kubectl apply -f https://github.com/knative/serving/releases/
download/knative-v1.6.0/serving-core.yaml
```

2. Set up networking using Kourier:

```
$curl -Lo kourier.yaml https://github.com/knative/net-kourier/
releases/download/knative-v1.6.0/kourier.yaml
```

3. Change the file to use nodePort, as shown in Listing 2-15.

Listing 2-15. Configure nodePort

```
apiVersion: v1
kind: Service
metadata:
```

```
name: kourier
namespace: kourier-system
labels:
  networking.knative.dev/ingress-provider: kourier
spec:
ports:
- name: http2
  port: 80
  protocol: TCP
  targetPort: 8080
  nodePort: 31080
- name: https
  port: 443
  protocol: TCP
  targetPort: 8443
  nodePort: 31443
selector:
  app: 3scale-kourier-gateway
type: NodePort
```

4. Install Kourier.

Install Kourier by running the following command (see Figure 2-23):

```
$ kubectl apply --filename kourier.yaml
```

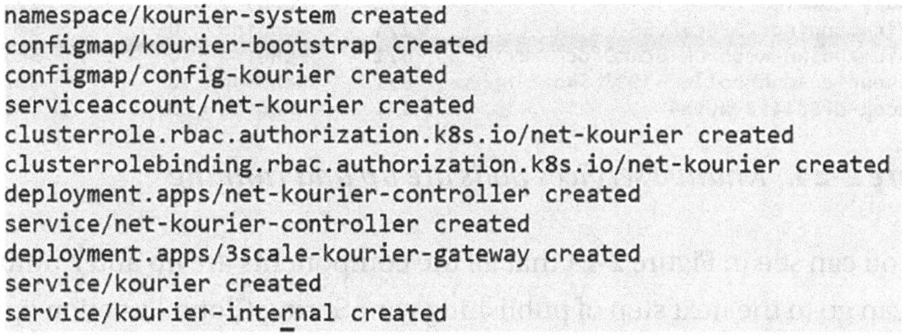

```
namespace/kourier-system created
configmap/kourier-bootstrap created
configmap/config-kourier created
serviceaccount/net-kourier created
clusterrole.rbac.authorization.k8s.io/net-kourier created
clusterrolebinding.rbac.authorization.k8s.io/net-kourier created
deployment.apps/net-kourier-controller created
service/net-kourier-controller created
deployment.apps/3scale-kourier-gateway created
service/kourier created
service/kourier-internal created
```

Figure 2-23. *Kourier is installed successfully*

5. Set Kourier as the default networking layer by
    installing the following patch:

```
$ kubectl patch configmap/config-network \
  --namespace knative-serving \
  --type merge \
  --patch '{"data":{"ingress-class":"kourier.ingress.
  networking.knative.dev"}}'
```

6. Set up a wildcard DNS with sslip.io:

```
$ kubectl apply -f https://github.com/knative/serving/releases/
download/knative-v1.6.0/serving-default-domain.yaml
```

7. Patch with sslip.io:

```
$ kubectl patch configmap/config-domain \
  --namespace knative-serving \
  --type merge \
  --patch '{"data":{"127.0.0.1.sslip.io":""}}'
```

8. Get the status of the pods in the Knative serving:

```
$ kubectl get pods -n knative-serving
```

```
$ kubectl get pods -n knative-serving
NAME                                        READY   STATUS    RESTARTS   AGE
activator-c7d578d94-nts6z                   1/1     Running   0          5m35s
autoscaler-6488988457-z8bw4                 1/1     Running   0          5m35s
controller-6cff4c9d57-ng77h                 1/1     Running   0          5m34s
default-domain-72k45                        1/1     Running   0          22s
domain-mapping-7598c5f659-sbjm4             1/1     Running   0          5m34s
domainmapping-webhook-8c4c9fdc4-mcrv9       1/1     Running   0          5m34s
net-kourier-controller-7997b54d46-hnhsm     1/1     Running   0          5m27s
webhook-df8844f6-hvth4                      1/1     Running   0          5m34s
```

***Figure 2-24.** Knative services pods are up and running*

You can see in Figure 2-24 that all the components are up and running.
You can go to the next step of publishing your Spring Cloud Function app
on Knative.

<u>Step 3:</u> Containerize the app and push it to a repository. Create a Dockerfile with the parameters set shown in Listing 2-16. I used jdk8.

Listing 2-16. The Dockerfile

```
FROM openjdk:8-jdk-alpine
ARG JAR_FILE=target/*.jar
COPY ${JAR_FILE} app.jar
ENTRYPOINT ["java","-jar","/app.jar"]
```

1. Push to Dockerhub. You can use the IDEs Docker features to push it to the Docker registry, as shown in Figure 2-25.

Figure 2-25. *Docker Push from IntellJ*

<u>Step 4:</u> Deploy the app to Knative. You need to create a YAML file for the service. Notice the image that has been used. I pushed a Docker image called "main" that exposes employeeSupplier. You will see that I will use a different image when pushing to other cloud providers. This is to get you acquainted with pushing different images with different exposed endpoints. See Listing 2-17.

Listing 2-17. payroll.yaml

```
apiVersion: serving.knative.dev/v1 # Current version of Knative
kind: Service
metadata:
  name: payroll # The name of the app
  namespace: default # The namespace the app will use
spec:
  template:
    spec:
      containers:
        - image: docker.io/banupkubeforce/
          springcloudfunctions:main # The URL to the image
          of the app
          env:
            - name: TARGET # The environment variable printed
out by the sample app
              value: "employeesupplier"
```

    2.   The next step is to deploy the app to Knative.

Run the following command to install the application with Knative serving:

```
$ kubectl apply -f payoll.yaml
```

Alternatively, you can use a Knative CLI. More information can be found at `https://knative.dev/docs/client/#kubectl`.

`$ kn service create payroll -image docker.io/banupkubeforce/`
`springcloudfunctions:main`

A YAML execution gives you more control over the target environment. Note this URL, as it is required for the testing step. The URL shown here for example is `https://payroll.default.127.0.0.1.sslip.io`.

You can run the following command to get the URL and check if the endpoint is ready for testing.

<u>Step 5:</u> Test . Since `employeeSupplier` queries the database and gets the records, you need to use a GET operation. See Figure 2-26.

Figure 2-26. *Test with Postman*

In this section, you created a KIND-based Kubernetes cluster, configured Knative, and deployed the application. You created a portable image that can be deployed to any Kubernetes cluster that has been configured with Knative.

2.6. Setting Up AWS with EKS and Knative with Spring Cloud Function

This section looks at deploying to an AWS EKS cluster that has Knative configured. You will see similarities to Section 2.5, because you create the cluster, enable Knative, and deploy a Docker image.

Prerequisites:

- AWS subscription (https://aws.amazon.com/)

- AWS CLI, which can be found at https://aws.amazon.com/cli/

- Eksctl CLI (https://eksctl.io/)

- Knative serving (https://knative.dev/docs/serving)

- Knative CLI (https://knative.dev/docs/client/install-kn/)

- IntelliJ, Eclipse, VS Code, or other IDEs

- Code from GitHub

- Docker image registered in the Docker hub

Step 1: Set up a Kubernetes cluster with EKS. Before you run the command in Listing 2-18, ensure that you are properly connected to AWS and have the subscriptions and permissions to create a cluster. Additional information can be found at https://docs.aws.amazon.com/eks/latest/userguide/getting-started.html.

Listing 2-18. cluster.yaml

```
apiVersion: eksctl.io/v1alpha5
kind: ClusterConfig
metadata:
  name: payroll-clstr
```

```
  region: us-east-2
nodeGroups:
 - name: payroll-nodes
   instanceType: m5.large
   desiredCapacity: 3
   volumeSize: 80
```

Create your Amazon EKS cluster using the following command:

```
$eksctl create cluster -f cluster.yaml
```

The process takes 10 to 15 minutes. At the end of the process, you will have created a cluster in EKS. You can verify it in the AWS EKS console in the cloud. See Figure 2-27.

Figure 2-27. *EKS console*

You will see that the dashboard shows the name of the cluster you provided in the Listing 2-18 and the creation of three nodes as set for desiredCapacity in the listing.

Verify that the clusters are up and running (see Figure 2-28). You can do that by running the following command:

```
$kubectl get pods --all-namespaces
```

```
$ kubectl get pods --all-namespaces
NAMESPACE       NAME                       READY   STATUS    RESTARTS   AGE
kube-system     aws-node-8wrln             1/1     Running   0          65s
kube-system     aws-node-vddfw             1/1     Running   0          62s
kube-system     aws-node-vhqd6             1/1     Running   0          65s
kube-system     corédns-5db97b446d-dtxj8   1/1     Running   0          10m
kube-system     coredns-5db97b446d-m4dw4   1/1     Running   0          10m
kube-system     kube-proxy-glv24           1/1     Running   0          62s
kube-system     kube-proxy-qnnx5           1/1     Running   0          65s
kube-system     kube-proxy-vxjwn           1/1     Running   0          65s
```

Figure 2-28. *EKS cluster running successfully*

Step 2: Configure Knative on EKS. In this step, you configure Knative on the EKS cluster you created. See Listing 2-19.

Listing 2-19. Install and Configure Knative

```
$kubectl apply -f https://github.com/knative/serving/releases/
download/knative-v1.4.0/serving-crds.yaml

$kubectl apply -f https://github.com/knative/serving/releases/
download/knative-v1.4.0/serving-core.yaml

$kubectl apply -f https://github.com/knative/net-kourier/
releases/download/knative-v1.4.0/kourier.yaml

$kubectl patch configmap/config-network \
  --namespace knative-serving \
  --type merge \
  --patch '{"data":{"ingress-class":"kourier.ingress.
    networking.knative.dev"}}'

$kubectl --namespace kourier-system get service kourier
$kubectl apply -f https://github.com/knative/serving/releases/
download/knative-v1.4.0/serving-default-domain.yaml
```

NAME	READY	STATUS	RESTARTS	AGE
activator-555b4d79c9-jsl6c	1/1	Running	0	3m59s
autoscaler-567654764f-z7c87	1/1	Running	0	3m59s
controller-744577dddc-rx2vw	1/1	Running	0	3m58s
default-domain--1-wvjzk	0/1	Completed	0	50s
domain-mapping-54bfddd48b-ds7gs	1/1	Running	0	3m58s
domainmapping-webhook-54c4f5f65b-wjcsm	1/1	Running	0	3m58s
net-kourier-controller-6c7bb8b87d-74gzr	1/1	Running	0	3m9s
webhook-7fdb64fc4-qfd2n	1/1	Running	0	3m57s

Figure 2-29. *Knative components running on EKS*

Step 3: Containerize the app with Docker and push it to a repository (optional).

This is an optional step, as you already deployed an image in Section 2.5. You can skip this step and go to Step 4. I used JDK 8 here, but you can use the latest JDK by changing the FROM statement to FROM adoptopenjdk/ openjdk11:latest. See Listing 2-20.

Listing 2-20. The Dockerfile

```
FROM openjdk:8-jdk-alpine
ARG JAR_FILE=target/*.jar
COPY ${JAR_FILE} app.jar
ENTRYPOINT ["java","-jar","/app.jar"]
```

Step 4: Push to the Docker hub. The next step is to push the Docker image to the Dockerhub repository, as shown in Figure 2-30. Be sure to log in to Dockerhub at https://hub.docker.com/ and create a repository and namespace. You will need it for the Docker push.

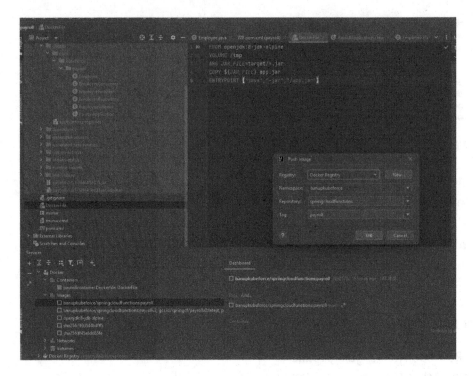

Figure 2-30. Docker push from the IntelliJ IDE

Once the push is successful, you can navigate to Dockerhub to check for the deployment of the image, as shown in Figure 2-31.

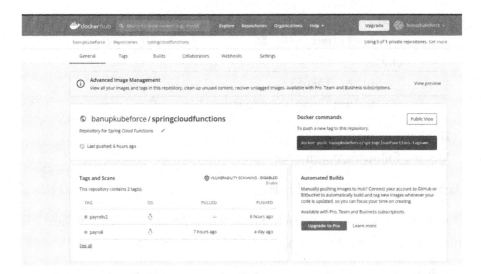

Figure 2-31. *Dockerhub with the deployed image*

<u>Step 5:</u> Deploy the app to Knative on EKS. In this step, you create a YAML file and set the location of the image that you will deploy to Knative.

Create the `payroll.yaml` file and set up the image to be deployed, as shown in Listing 2-21.

Listing 2-21. The payroll.yaml File

```
apiVersion: service.knative.dev/v1
kind: service
metadata:
  name: payroll
spec:
  template:
    spec:
      containers:
        - image: docker.io/banupkubeforce/springcloudfunctions/
          payrollv2
```

```
ports:
  - containerPort: 80
env:
  - name: TARGET
    value: "employeeconsumer"
```

Deploy the app to Knative on EKS.

Run the following command:

```
$ kubectl apply -f payoll.yaml
```

Alternatively, you can use a Knative CLI. More information can be found at https://knative.dev/docs/client/#kubectl.

```
$ kn service create payroll –image docker.io/banupkubeforce/
springcloudfunctions:payrollv2
```

Figure 2-32 shows the result of running the kn cli. A YAML execution gives you more control over the target environment. Note the URL, as it is required for the testing step. The URL shown here for example is https:// payroll.default.13.58.221.247.sslip.io.

You can run the following command to get the URL and check if the endpoint is ready for testing:

```
$ kn services list
```

```
C:\Users\banua\Downloads\EKS>kn service create payroll --image docker.io/banupkubeforce/springcloudfunctions:payrollv2
Creating service 'payroll' in namespace 'default':

  0.045s The Route is still working to reflect the latest desired specification.
  0.054s ...
  0.092s Configuration "payroll" is waiting for a Revision to become ready.
 21.161s ...
 21.162s Ingress has not yet been reconciled.
 21.170s Waiting for load balancer to be ready
 21.364s Ready to serve.

Service 'payroll' created to latest revision 'payroll-00001' is available at URL:
http://payroll.default.13.58.221.247.sslip.io

C:\Users\banua\Downloads\EKS>kn services list
NAME     URL                                           LATEST         AGE  CONDITIONS  READY  REASON
payroll  http://payroll.default.13.58.221.247.sslip.io  payroll-00001  38s  3 OK / 3    True
```

Figure 2-32. *Payroll is deployed successfully*

The URL that you need for testing or posting is `payroll.`
`default.13.58.221.247.sslip.io`

Step 6: Testing. Use the URL you got in Step 5 and run the test. The
URL in this case is `https://payroll.default.13.58.221.247.sslip.io/`
`employeeConsumer`

You can use Postman or curl to run the tests. Figure 2-33 shows the
Postman test results.

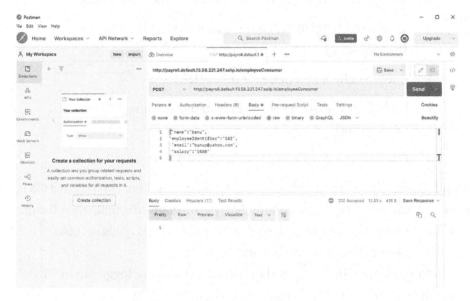

Figure 2-33. *Test Is Postman with the URL*

2.7. Setting Up GCP with Cloud Run/ GKE and Knative with Spring Cloud Function

This section looks at deploying to GCP a GKE cluster that has Knative
configured. You will see similarities to Section 2.5, because you create the
cluster, enable Knative, and deploy a Docker image.

Prerequisites:

- GCP subscription (https://cloud.google.com/)

- The Gcloud CLI, which can be found at https://cloud.google.com/sdk/docs/install

- kubectl (https://kubernetes.io/docs/tasks/tools/)

- Knative serving (https://knative.dev/docs/serving)

- Knative CLI (https://knative.dev/docs/client/install-kn/)

- IntelliJ, Eclipse, VS Code, or other IDEs

- Code from GitHub (optional if you use the image from Dockerhub)

- Docker image registered in the Docker hub

Step 1: Set up a Kubernetes cluster with GKE. In this step, you create a GKE cluster. Make sure you have the sufficient permissions to create the cluster. Additional information can be found at https://cloud.google.com/kubernetes-engine/docs/deploy-app-cluster.

Before running the command ensure, that you have logged in to GCP using the Gcloud CLI. Run the command in Listing 2-22.

Listing 2-22. Create a Cluster in GCP

```
$gcloud container clusters create payroll-clstr \
    --zone=us-central1-a \
    --cluster-version=latest \
    --machine-type=n1-standard-4 \
    --enable-autoscaling --min-nodes=1 --max-nodes=10 \
    --enable-autorepair \
```

```
--scopes=service-control,service-management,compute-rw,
    storage-ro,cloud-platform,logging-write,monitoring-write,
    pubsub,datastore \
--num-nodes=3
```

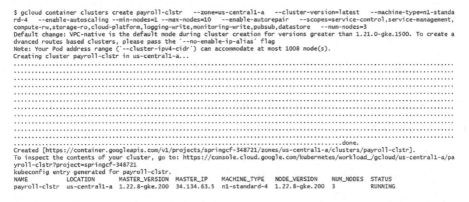

```
$ gcloud container clusters create payroll-clstr   --zone=us-central1-a   --cluster-version=latest   --machine-type=n1-standa
rd-4   --enable-autoscaling --min-nodes=1 --max-nodes=10   --enable-autorepair   --scopes=service-control,service-management,
compute-rw,storage-ro,cloud-platform,logging-write,monitoring-write,pubsub,datastore   --num-nodes=3
Default change: VPC-native is the default mode during cluster creation for versions greater than 1.21.0-gke.1500. To create a
dvanced routes based clusters, please pass the `--no-enable-ip-alias` flag
Note: Your Pod address range (`--cluster-ipv4-cidr`) can accommodate at most 1008 node(s).
Creating cluster payroll-clstr in us-central1-a...
..............................................................................................................................
..............................................................................................................................
..............................................................................................................................
..............................................................................................................................
..............................................................................................................................
..............................................................................................................................
..............................................................................................................................
..............................................................................................................................
..............................................................................................................................
..............................................................................................................................
......................................................................................................done.
Created [https://container.googleapis.com/v1/projects/springcf-348721/zones/us-central1-a/clusters/payroll-clstr].
To inspect the contents of your cluster, go to: https://console.cloud.google.com/kubernetes/workload_/gcloud/us-central1-a/pa
yroll-clstr?project=springcf-348721
kubeconfig entry generated for payroll-clstr.
NAME           LOCATION       MASTER_VERSION  MASTER_IP     MACHINE_TYPE   NODE_VERSION    NUM_NODES   STATUS
payroll-clstr  us-central1-a  1.22.8-gke.200  34.134.63.5   n1-standard-4  1.22.8-gke.200  3           RUNNING
```

Figure 2-34. *Cluster is up and running*

Check the status of the cluster by running the following command:

```
$kubectl get nodes
```

```
$ kubectl get nodes
NAME                                                STATUS   ROLES     AGE      VERSION
gke-payroll-clstr-default-pool-91f90b67-18hx        Ready    <none>    9m28s    v1.22.8-gke.200
gke-payroll-clstr-default-pool-91f90b67-4c9d        Ready    <none>    9m27s    v1.22.8-gke.200
gke-payroll-clstr-default-pool-91f90b67-rnbn        Ready    <none>    9m28s    v1.22.8-gke.200
```

Figure 2-35. *Status of GKE cluster*

Navigate to Google Clouds GKE dashboard to verify the cluster. See
Figure 2-36.

Figure 2-36. *GKE Dashboard on Google Cloud*

<u>Step 2:</u> Configure Knative on GKE. This step is similar to what you did earlier with EKS or local Kubernetes:

1. Install the Knative serving components by running
   the following commands:

```
$kubectl apply -f https://github.com/knative/serving/releases/
download/knative-v1.4.0/serving-crds.yaml
```

```
$kubectl apply -f https://github.com/knative/serving/releases/
download/knative-v1.4.0/serving-core.yaml
```

2. Install the Kourier components required for ingress
   by running the following command:

```
$kubectl apply -f https://github.com/knative/net-kourier/
releases/download/knative-v1.4.0/kourier.yaml
```

3. Configure Kourier for ingress with the following
   command:

```
$kubectl patch configmap/config-network \
  --namespace knative-serving \
  --type merge \
  --patch '{"data":{"ingress-class":"kourier.ingress.
    networking.knative.dev"}}'
```

```
$ kubectl patch configmap/config-network \
>    --namespace knative-serving \
>    --type merge \
>    --patch '{"data":{"ingress-class":"kourier.ingress.networking.knative.dev"}}'
configmap/config-network patched
```

Figure 2-37. *Kourier has been successfully patched*

4. Apply the default domain using the following
    command:

$kubectl apply -f https://github.com/knative/serving/releases/
download/knative-v1.4.0/serving-default-domain.yaml

5. Check the status of the Knative components by
    running the following command:

$kubectl get pods -n knative-serving

```
$ kubectl get pods -n knative-serving
NAME                                          READY   STATUS      RESTARTS   AGE
activator-555b4d79c9-l8p5g                    1/1     Running     0          74s
autoscaler-567654764f-pv4k6                   1/1     Running     0          73s
controller-744577dddc-dlvb7                   1/1     Running     0          73s
default-domain--1-fdczf                       0/1     Completed   0          26s
domain-mapping-54bfddd48b-2rz9d               1/1     Running     0          72s
domainmapping-webhook-54c4f5f65b-kzvd7        1/1     Running     0          72s
net-kourier-controller-6c7bb8b87d-9wwzk       1/1     Running     0          58s
webhook-7fdb64fc4-h2679                       1/1     Running     0          72s
```

Figure 2-38. *Knative services are running successfully*

6. Run the following command to get the Kourier
    ingress information:

$kubectl –namespace kourier-system get service kourier

```
$ kubectl --namespace kourier-system get service kourier
NAME      TYPE           CLUSTER-IP    EXTERNAL-IP    PORT(S)                        AGE
kourier   LoadBalancer   10.36.8.32    34.69.156.24   80:32109/TCP,443:30848/TCP     115s
```

Figure 2-39. *Kourier service status shows an external IP*

Now that you have Knative configured and running, you can proceed to the next step of pushing the app image to Knative.

Step 3: Containerize the app with Docker and push it to a repository (optional).

This is an optional step, as you already deployed an image in Section 2.5. You can skip this step and go to Step 4. I used JDK 8 here, but you can use the latest JDK by changing the FROM statement to FROM adoptopenjdk/ openjdk11:latest, as shown in Listing 2-23.

Listing 2-23. The Dockerfile that Helps Create the Container and Image

```
FROM openjdk:8-jdk-alpine
ARG JAR_FILE=target/*.jar
COPY ${JAR_FILE} app.jar
ENTRYPOINT ["java","-jar","/app.jar"]
```

Step 4: Push to the Docker hub. The next step is to push the Docker image to the Dockerhub repository, as shown in Figure 2-40. Make sure to log in to Dockerhub at https://hub.docker.com/ and create a repository and namespace. You will need it for the Docker push.

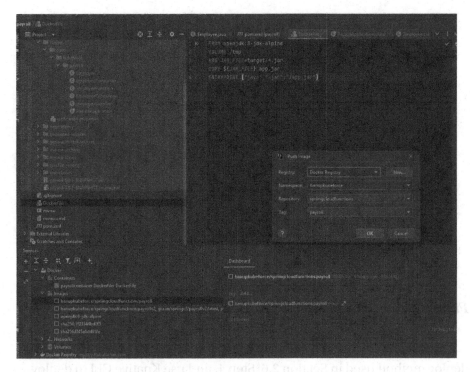

Figure 2-40. *Docker push from the IDE*

Once the push is successful, you can navigate to Dockerhub to check for the deployment of the image, as shown in Figure 2-41.

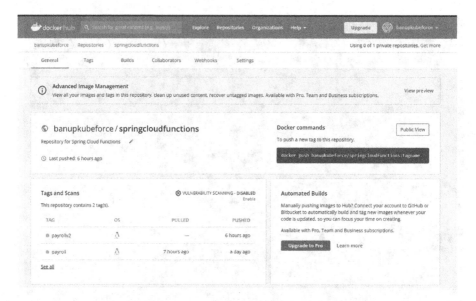

Figure 2-41. *Dockerhub with the deployed image*

Step 5: Deploy the app to Knative on GKE. I skip the Kubectl-based deploy method used in Section 2.6, Step 4, and use Knative CLI to deploy the image. If you need more control over the deployment, you can use the method suggested in Section 2.6, Step 4.

```
$ kn service create payroll -image docker.io/banupkubeforce/
springcloudfunctions:payrollv2
```

Figure 2-42 shows the results of running the kn cli. A YAML execution gives you more control over the target environment. Note the URL, as it is required for the testing step. The URL shown here for example is https://
payroll.default.34.69.156.24.sslip.io.

```
$ kn service create payroll --image docker.io/banupkubeforce/springcloudfunctions:payrollv2
Creating service 'payroll' in namespace 'default':

  0.096s The Route is still working to reflect the latest desired specification.
  0.175s Configuration "payroll" is waiting for a Revision to become ready.
  0.221s ...
 20.810s ...
 20.906s Ingress has not yet been reconciled.
 21.048s Waiting for load balancer to be ready
 21.142s Ready to serve.

Service 'payroll' created to latest revision 'payroll-00001' is available at URL:
http://payroll.default.34.69.156.24.sslip.io
```

Figure 2-42. *Payroll app deployed on GKE with Knative*

Step 6: Test. Use the DNS name provided in Step 5 to test against the following URL:

`https://payroll.default.34.69.156.24.sslip.io/`
`employeeConsumer`

Figure 2-43. *Successful testing with Postman*

Now you have successfully deployed the payroll app on GKE with Knative.

2.8. Setting Up Azure with AKS and Knative with Spring Cloud Function

This section looks at deploying to an Azure AKS cluster that has Knative configured. You will see similarities to Section 2.5, because you create the cluster, enable Knative, and deploy a Docker image.

Prerequisites:

- Azure subscription (`https://portal.azure.com/`)

- Azure CLI, which can be found at `https://docs.microsoft.com/en-us/cli/azure/install-azure-cli`

- kubectl (`https://kubernetes.io/docs/tasks/tools/`)

- Knative serving (`https://knative.dev/docs/serving`)

- Knative CLI (`https://knative.dev/docs/client/install-kn/`)

- IntelliJ, Eclipse, VS Code, or other IDEs

- Code from GitHub (optional if you just use the image from Dockerhub)

- Docker image registered in Docker hub

Step 1: Set up a Kubernetes cluster with AKS. In this step, you create an AKS cluster. Make sure you have the sufficient permissions to create the cluster. Additional information can be found at `https://docs.microsoft.com/en-us/azure/aks/learn/quick-kubernetes-deploy-cli`.

Before running the following command, ensure that you have logged in to Azure using the Azure CLI. Then run the command in Listing 2-24.

Listing 2-24. The Dockerfile

```
az aks create --resource-group $RESOURCE_GROUP \
--name $CLUSTER_NAME \
--generate-ssh-keys \
--kubernetes-version 1.22.6 \
--enable-rbac \
--node-vm-size Standard_DS3_v2
```

Configure your kubeconfig to use the AKS cluster that you created by running the command in Listing 2-25.

Listing 2-25. Set up Kubeconfig

```
$ az aks get-credentials --resource-group payroll-rsg --name
payrollclstr
```

Check the status of the cluster by running the command in Listing 2-26.

Listing 2-26. Check the Status

```
kubectl get nodes
```

```
$ kubectl get nodes
NAME                                  STATUS   ROLES   AGE   VERSION
aks-nodepool1-26576780-vmss000000     Ready    agent   15m   v1.22.6
aks-nodepool1-26576780-vmss000001     Ready    agent   15m   v1.22.6
aks-nodepool1-26576780-vmss000002     Ready    agent   15m   v1.22.6
```

Figure 2-44. *The AKS Cluster is ready*

Step 2: Configure Knative on AKS. This step is similar to what you did earlier with EKS or local Kubernetes.

Install Knative serving:

```
$kubectl apply -f https://github.com/knative/serving/releases/
download/knative-v1.4.0/serving-crds.yaml
```

```
$kubectl apply -f https://github.com/knative/serving/releases/
download/knative-v1.4.0/serving-core.yaml
```

```
$kubectl apply -f https://github.com/knative/net-kourier/
releases/download/knative-v1.4.0/kourier.yaml
```

Configure Kourier for ingress with the following command:

```
$kubectl patch configmap/config-network \
  --namespace knative-serving \
  --type merge \
  --patch '{"data":{"ingress-class":"kourier.ingress.
    networking.knative.dev"}}'
```

```
$ kubectl patch configmap/config-network \
>     --namespace knative-serving \
>     --type merge \
>     --patch '{"data":{"ingress-class":"kourier.ingress.networking.knative.dev"}}'
configmap/config-network patched
```

Figure 2-45. *Kourier ingress is patched*

Apply the default domain using the following command:

```
$kubectl apply -f https://github.com/knative/serving/releases/
download/knative-v1.4.0/serving-default-domain.yaml
```

Check the status of the Knative components by running the following command:

```
$kubectl get pods -n knative-serving
```

Run the command in Listing 2-27 to get the Kourier ingress information.

Listing 2-27. Get the Ingress Information

```
$kubectl –namespace kourier-system get service kourier
```

100

Now that you have the Knative configured and running, you can proceed to the next step of pushing the app image to Knative.

Step 3: Containerize the app with Docker and push it to a repository. Follow Step 3 in Sections 2.5, 2.6, or 2.7 if you choose to create and deploy an image to the Dockerhub repository.

Step 4: Deploy the app to Knative on AKS. Here again, I use the Knative CLI kn to deploy the app, as it convenient for this simple exercise.

Run the command in Listing 2-28.

Listing 2-28. Deploy Payroll Apps

```
$ kn service create payroll -image docker.io/banupkubeforce/spr
ingcloudfunctions:payrollv2
```

Note the URL that is generated. You will use this URL for testing.

```
$ kn service create payroll --image docker.io/banupkubeforce/springcloudfunctions:payrollv2
Creating service 'payroll' in namespace 'default':

  0.056s The Route is still working to reflect the latest desired specification.
  0.097s ...
  0.163s Configuration "payroll" is waiting for a Revision to become ready.
 10.560s ...
 10.653s Ingress has not yet been reconciled.
 10.790s Waiting for load balancer to be ready
 10.981s Ready to serve.

Service 'payroll' created to latest revision 'payroll-00001' is available at URL:
http://payroll.default.20.121.248.21.sslip.io
```

Figure 2-46. *The app is successfully deployed on AKS with Knative*

Step 5: Test. Use the DNS name provided in Step 4 to test against the following URL:

```
https://payroll.default.20.121.248.sslip.io/employeeConsumer
```

Figure 2-47. *Successful test of the payroll example on AKS with Knative*

2.9. Setting Up VMware Tanzu TKG and Knative

As with other Kubernetes offerings, setting up and installing Knative on TKG on your local laptop is pretty straightforward.

VMware released a community edition that can be locally installed. Additional information can be found at `https://tanzucommunityedition.io/download/`.

Prerequisites:

- TKG download (`https://tanzucommunityedition.io/download/`)

- kubectl (`https://kubernetes.io/docs/tasks/tools/`)

- Knative serving (`https://knative.dev/docs/serving`)

- Knative CLI (`https://knative.dev/docs/client/install-kn/`)

- IntelliJ, Eclipse, VS Code, or other IDEs

- Code from GitHub (optional if you just use the image from the Dockerhub)

- Docker image registered in the Docker hub

Here are the steps to configure and deploy Spring Cloud Function on VMware Tanzu:

Step1: Set up TKG locally.

Step2: Create a Kubernetes Cluster for your app.

Step 3: Install Knative on TKG cluster.

Step 4: Deploy the app on Knative.

Step 1: Set up TKG locally. Follow the instructions provided on the website to set up TKG locally. This will give you an unmanaged cluster.

Figure 2-48 shows a successful install.

```
default-local\discovery\standalone\management-cluster.yaml
default-local\discovery\standalone\package.yaml
default-local\discovery\standalone\pinniped-auth.yaml
default-local\discovery\standalone\secret.yaml
default-local\discovery\standalone\unmanaged-cluster.yaml
default-local\distribution\windows\amd64\cli\builder\v0.11.2\tanzu-builder-windows_amd64.exe
default-local\distribution\windows\amd64\cli\cluster\v0.11.2\tanzu-cluster-windows_amd64.exe
default-local\distribution\windows\amd64\cli\codegen\v0.11.2\tanzu-codegen-windows_amd64.exe
default-local\distribution\windows\amd64\cli\conformance\v0.11.0\tanzu-conformance-windows_amd64.exe
default-local\distribution\windows\amd64\cli\diagnostics\v0.11.0\tanzu-diagnostics-windows_amd64.exe
default-local\distribution\windows\amd64\cli\kubernetes-release\v0.11.2\tanzu-kubernetes-release-windows_amd64.exe
default-local\distribution\windows\amd64\cli\login\v0.11.2\tanzu-login-windows_amd64.exe
default-local\distribution\windows\amd64\cli\management-cluster\v0.11.2\tanzu-management-cluster-windows_amd64.exe
default-local\distribution\windows\amd64\cli\package\v0.11.2\tanzu-package-windows_amd64.exe
default-local\distribution\windows\amd64\cli\pinniped-auth\v0.11.2\tanzu-pinniped-auth-windows_amd64.exe
default-local\distribution\windows\amd64\cli\secret\v0.11.2\tanzu-secret-windows_amd64.exe
default-local\distribution\windows\amd64\cli\unmanaged-cluster\v0.11.0\tanzu-unmanaged-cluster-windows_amd64.exe
24 File(s) copied
Installing plugin 'builder:v0.11.2'
    successfully installed 'builder' plugin
Installing plugin 'codegen:v0.11.2'
    successfully installed 'codegen' plugin
Installing plugin 'cluster:v0.11.2'
    successfully installed 'cluster' plugin
Installing plugin 'kubernetes-release:v0.11.2'
    successfully installed 'kubernetes-release' plugin
Installing plugin 'login:v0.11.2'
    successfully installed 'login' plugin
Installing plugin 'management-cluster:v0.11.2'
Warning: Failed to initialize plugin '"management-cluster"' after installation. Downloading TKG compatibility file from 'p
kg/framework-zshippable/tkg-compatibility'
Error: unable to ensure prerequisites: unable to ensure tkg BOM file: failed to download TKG compatibility file from the r
ompatibility image tags: Get "https://projects.registry.vmware.com/v2/": x509: certificate signed by unknown authority
    successfully installed 'management-cluster' plugin
Installing plugin 'package:v0.11.2'
    successfully installed 'package' plugin
Installing plugin 'pinniped-auth:v0.11.2'
    successfully installed 'pinniped-auth' plugin
Installing plugin 'secret:v0.11.2'
    successfully installed 'secret' plugin
Installing plugin 'conformance:v0.11.0'
    successfully installed 'conformance' plugin
Installing plugin 'diagnostics:v0.11.0'
    successfully installed 'diagnostics' plugin
Installing plugin 'unmanaged-cluster:v0.11.0'
    successfully installed 'unmanaged-cluster' plugin
        1 file(s) copied.
"Installation complete!"
"Please add C:\Program Files\tanzu permanently into your system's PATH."
```

Figure 2-48. *Successful installation of TKG bits on a local machine*

<u>Step 2</u>: Create a cluster for your app. Here you create a cluster for the payroll example. Run the following command:

```
$tanzu unmanaged-cluster create payroll
```

You will get a message that the payroll cluster has been completed, as shown in Figure 2-49.

```
.ore package repo status:
:ore package repo status:
:ore package repo status:
:ore package repo status:
:ore package repo status:
:ore package repo status: Reconciling
:ore package repo status: Reconciling
:ore package repo status: Reconciling
:ore package repo status: Reconcile succeeded

Installing CNI
:alico.community.tanzu.vmware.com:3.22.1

Cluster created
```

Figure 2-49. *Successful install of TKG Cluster*

Step 3: Install Knative on the TKG cluster. Run the following command to install kantive-serving on the TKG cluster:

$tanzu package install knative-serving --package-name knative-serving.community.tanzu.vmware.com --version 1.0.0

Step 4: Deploy the app on Knative, as shown in Figure 2-50.

```
$ kn service create payroll --image docker.io/banupkubeforce/springcloudfunction
s:payrollv2
Creating service 'payroll' in namespace 'default':

  0.015s The Route is still working to reflect the latest desired specification.
  0.043s ...
  0.064s Configuration "payroll" is waiting for a Revision to become ready.
 12.517s ...
 12.540s Ingress has not yet been reconciled.
 12.555s Waiting for Envoys to receive Endpoints data.
 12.769s Waiting for load balancer to be ready
 12.988s Ready to serve.

Service 'payroll' created to latest revision 'payroll-00001' is available at URL
:
http://payroll.default.127.0.0.241.nip.io
```

Figure 2-50. *App deployment on TKG with Knative*

Note the URL provided. In this case, it is http://payroll. default.127.0.0.241.nip.io.

<u>Step 5:</u> Test Follow Section 2.5, Step 5 and use Postman or curl to test against the `http://payroll.default.127.0.0.241.nip.io/employeeConsumer` URL.

This completes the successful deployment of Tanzu Kubernetes Grid or TKG.

2.10. Summary

This chapter explained how Spring Cloud Function can be developed and deployed to various target platforms, including AWS Lambda, Google Functions, Azure Functions, and Kubernetes environments such as AWS EKS, Google's GKE, Azure AKS, VMware Tanzu, and the like. With Kubernetes, you were able to use Knative to deploy the same image to all the other Kubernetes flavors without changing the code. Knative ensures that the code is portable across any Kubernetes platform. This is critical, as it ensures movement to any cloud with minimal disruptions. To summarize, you should now have a good understanding of how to build serverless functions with Spring Cloud Function. The next chapter looks at how to automate the deployment process for Spring Cloud Function.

CHAPTER 3

CI/CD with Spring Cloud Function

As you learned in Chapter 2, you can build a Spring Cloud Function and deploy it to multiple environments. You can use various manual methods such as Azure-Function:Deploy, Gcloud CLI, AWS CLI, Kubectl, and Knative CLI. These manual approaches are not sustainable in an enterprise with many different teams, a lot of programmers, and a lot of code. It will be a management nightmare if every team member uses their own method to build and deploy code. Also, as you can see, this process is repeatable. Since it is a repeatable process, there is a chance to leverage automation.

This chapter explores ways to automate the deployment process. It leverages some popular approaches for automating your deploys. It explores GitHub Actions for deploying Lambda, Google Cloud Functions, and Azure Functions and you will integrate with ArgoCD to push to a Kubernetes/Knative environment. While you can use GitHub Actions alone for all environments, that would require custom scripting to push to Kubernetes. ArgoCD has built-in hooks to deploy to Kubernetes, which is the preferred way. More information on GitHub Actions can be found at `https://github.com/features/actions`, and information on ArgoCD can be found at `https://argoproj.github.io/cd/`.

Let's dig a bit deeper into GitHub Actions and ArgoCD.

© Banu Parasuraman 2023
B. Parasuraman, *Practical Spring Cloud Function*,
https://doi.org/10.1007/978-1-4842-8913-6_3

3.1. GitHub Actions

This is a CI/CD platform tightly integrated with GitHub; it allows you to create and trigger workflows from GitHub. So, if you are a fan of GitHub, you will really like this new feature. When you sign up for GitHub, GitHub Actions will automatically be integrated into your project, so you do not have to use a separate tool like Jenkins or Circle CI. Of course, this means that you are restricted to GitHub as your code repository. Creating a workflow is quite straightforward. You can create a workflow directly on the GitHub website by navigating to your project and clicking the New Workflow button in the Actions tab, as shown in the Figure 3-1.

Figure 3-1. *Creating a new GitHub Actions workflow*

Upon clicking New Workflow, as shown in Figure 3-2, you will be taken to the workflow "marketplace," where you can choose from the suggested flows or set up a workflow yourself. Click the Set Up a Workflow Yourself link to start creating a custom workflow.

Figure 3-2. *Workflow marketplace to choose your workflow setup*

The Set Up a Workflow Yourself window, as shown in Figure 3-3, will take you to the page where you can write the script to create your workflow.

Figure 3-3. *Workflow page to create custom workflows*

As you can see in Figure 3-3, the workflow points to a main.yaml file that is created in the .github/workflows directory under your root project folder. You can also create the same file in your IDE and it will show up under the Actions tab once you commit the code. Listing 3-1 shows the sample code created for AWS Lambda.

Listing 3-1. Workflow for Payroll Function to be Deployed on AWS Lambda

```
name: CI

on:
  push:
    branches: [ "master" ]
jobs:
  build-deploy:
    runs-on: ubuntu-latest
    steps:
      - uses: actions/checkout@v2
      - uses: actions/setup-java@v2
        with:
          java-version: '8'
          distribution: 'temurin'
```

```
      cache: maven
- uses: aws-actions/setup-sam@v1
- uses: aws-actions/configure-aws-credentials@v1
  with:
      aws-access-key-id: ${{ secrets.AWS_ACCESS_KEY_ID }}
      aws-secret-access-key: ${{ secrets.AWS_SECRET_
      ACCESS_KEY }}
      aws-region: us-east-2
- name: Build with Maven
  run: mvn -B package --file pom.xml
# sam package
- run: sam package --template-file template.yaml
--output-template-file packaged.yaml --s3-bucket
payrollbucket
```

```
# Run Unit tests- Specify unit tests here
```

```
# sam deploy
    - run: sam deploy --no-confirm-changeset --no-fail-
on-empty-changeset --stack-name payroll-aws --s3-bucket
payrollbucket --capabilities CAPABILITY_IAM --region us-east-2
```

Let's dive deep into the components of the YAML file.

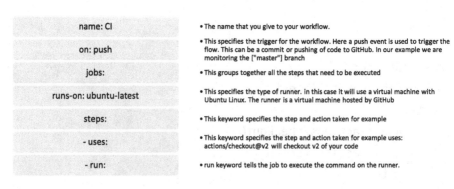

Figure 3-4. *Work flow code elaboration*

This sets up the GitHub Actions workflow and the triggers. Now, every time you commit or push code to this project repository in GitHub, this workflow will execute. Figure 3-5 shows a sample execution of this workflow.

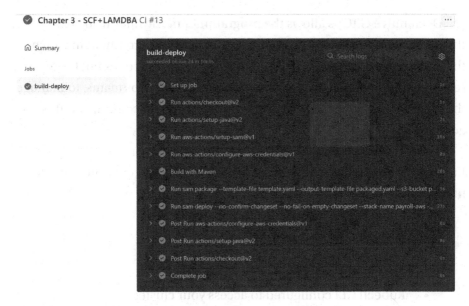

Figure 3-5. *A successful execution of the workflow*

3.2. ArgoCD

While GitHub Actions can push code to serverless environments such as Lambda, it lacks a good graphical representation of code deployed when it comes to the Kubernetes environment. Kubernetes is a orchestrator of containers and has a plethora services that manage deployments. ArgoCD was created for Kubernetes. ArgoCD is a declarative CD (Continuous Delivery) tool, which means application definitions, configurations, and environments can be version controlled. ArgoCD, similar to GitHub

Actions, uses Git repositories as a single source of truth. This is also known as *GitOps*.

Declarative means configuration is guaranteed by a set of facts instead of by a set of instructions.

Declarative GitOps allows the programmer or the ones who created the application to control the configuration of the environment in which the environment will run. This means the programmer does not have to rely on different teams, such as infrastructure or DevOps teams, to manage the pieces of the application. The programmers are in control, and this is a good thing.

ArgoCD set up is mostly programmatic and relies on the underlying Kubernetes configmaps. This is, as you can see, is different from other tools like Jenkins.

Here is how I set up the ArgoCD environment.

Prerequisites:

- A Kubernetes cluster

- Kubectl CLI configured to access your cluster

- ArgoCD CLI installation instructions can be found at `https://argo-cd.readthedocs.io/en/stable/cli_installation/`

Step 1: Create a namespace for ArgoCD.

Run the following command against your Kubernetes cluster:

```
$kubectl create namespace argocd
```

```
$ kubectl create namespace argocd
namespace/argocd created
```

Figure 3-6. *Create an ArgoCD namespace*

Step 2: install ArgoCD.

```
$kubectl apply -n argocd -f https://raw.githubusercontent.com/
argoproj/argo-cd/stable/manifests/install.yaml
```

This will go through a lengthy process to install ArgoCD. Once the installation is successful, you can validate it by using the following command:

```
$kubectl get all -n argocd
```

```
$ kubectl get all -n argocd
NAME                                                     READY   STATUS    RESTARTS   AGE
pod/argocd-application-controller-0                      1/1     Running   0          43s
pod/argocd-applicationset-controller-7f466f7cc-hs61k     1/1     Running   0          44s
pod/argocd-dex-server-54cd4596c4-zd98n                   1/1     Running   0          44s
pod/argocd-notifications-controller-8445d56d96-9mpf4     1/1     Running   0          43s
pod/argocd-redis-65596bf87-sc9fz                         1/1     Running   0          43s
pod/argocd-repo-server-5ccf4bd568-7gjcq                  1/1     Running   0          43s
pod/argocd-server-7dff66c8f8-j8gh8                       1/1     Running   0          43s

NAME                                             TYPE        CLUSTER-IP     EXTERNAL-IP   PORT(S)                       AGE
service/argocd-applicationset-controller         ClusterIP   10.0.32.132    <none>        7000/TCP,8080/TCP             45s
service/argocd-dex-server                        ClusterIP   10.0.221.134   <none>        5556/TCP,5557/TCP,5558/TCP    45s
service/argocd-metrics                           ClusterIP   10.0.156.160   <none>        8082/TCP                      45s
service/argocd-notifications-controller-metrics  ClusterIP   10.0.92.250    <none>        9001/TCP                      45s
service/argocd-redis                             ClusterIP   10.0.67.233    <none>        6379/TCP                      44s
service/argocd-repo-server                       ClusterIP   10.0.15.237    <none>        8081/TCP,8084/TCP             44s
service/argocd-server                            ClusterIP   10.0.26.52     <none>        80/TCP,443/TCP                44s
service/argocd-server-metrics                    ClusterIP   10.0.28.188    <none>        8083/TCP                      44s

NAME                                                READY   UP-TO-DATE   AVAILABLE   AGE
deployment.apps/argocd-applicationset-controller    1/1     1            1           44s
deployment.apps/argocd-dex-server                   1/1     1            1           44s
deployment.apps/argocd-notifications-controller     1/1     1            1           43s
deployment.apps/argocd-redis                        1/1     1            1           43s
deployment.apps/argocd-repo-server                  1/1     1            1           43s
deployment.apps/argocd-server                       1/1     1            1           43s

NAME                                                       DESIRED   CURRENT   READY   AGE
replicaset.apps/argocd-applicationset-controller-7f466f7cc   1         1         1       44s
replicaset.apps/argocd-dex-server-54cd4596c4                 1         1         1       44s
replicaset.apps/argocd-notifications-controller-8445d56d96   1         1         1       43s
replicaset.apps/argocd-redis-65596bf87                       1         1         1       43s
replicaset.apps/argocd-repo-server-5ccf4bd568                1         1         1       43s
replicaset.apps/argocd-server-7dff66c8f8                     1         1         1       43s

NAME                                             READY   AGE
statefulset.apps/argocd-application-controller   1/1     43s
```

Figure 3-7. View the status of an ArgoCD installation

Now you can see that the ArgoCD services are up and running. Notice that an external IP has not been associated with service/argocd-server.

Run the following command to attach a LoadBalancer to the argocd-server:

```
$kubectl patch svc argocd-server -n argocd -p '{"spec":
{"type": "LoadBalancer"}}'
```

Now run the following command:

```
$kubectl get svc -n argocd
```

```
$ kubectl get svc -n argocd
NAME                                      TYPE           CLUSTER-IP        EXTERNAL-IP       PORT(S)                          AGE
argocd-applicationset-controller          ClusterIP      10.0.32.132       <none>            7000/TCP,8080/TCP                2m12s
argocd-dex-server                         ClusterIP      10.0.221.134      <none>            5556/TCP,5557/TCP,5558/TCP       2m12s
argocd-metrics                            ClusterIP      10.0.156.160      <none>            8082/TCP                         2m12s
argocd-notifications-controller-metrics   ClusterIP      10.0.92.250       <none>            9001/TCP                         2m12s
argocd-redis                              ClusterIP      10.0.67.233       <none>            6379/TCP                         2m11s
argocd-repo-server                        ClusterIP      10.0.15.237       <none>            8081/TCP,8084/TCP                2m11s
argocd-server                             LoadBalancer   10.0.26.52        20.119.112.240    80:31517/TCP,443:31175/TCP       2m11s
argocd-server-metrics                     ClusterIP      10.0.28.188       <none>            8083/TCP                         2m11s
```

Figure 3-8. Take note of the external IP of argocd-server

You will see an external IP associated with `argocd-server`. This will allow you to connect to the `argocd-server`.

Before you start to use ArgoCD, you need to change the "admin" user password. You can use Kubectl to read the secret associated with the "admin" user.

Run the following command:

```
$ kubectl -n argocd get secret argocd-initial-admin-secret -o
jsonpath="{.data.password}" | base64 -d; echo
```

$ kubectl -n argocd get secret argocd-initial-admin-secret -o jsonpath="{.data.password}" | base64 -d; echo
lTGVkWKnJIFCvbDp

Figure 3-9. Get the password of the "admin" user

The output of this command is the password for the "admin" user.

You can now log in using the web browser. Then navigate to the 20.119.112.240 URL to change the password.

Log in to ArgoCD with the following command:

```
$argocd login 20.119.112.240
```

```
$ argocd login 20.119.112.240
WARNING: server certificate had error: x509: certificate signed by unknown autho
rity. Proceed insecurely (y/n)? y
Username: admin
Password:
'admin:login' logged in successfully
Context '20.119.112.240' updated
```

Figure 3-10. *Log in to ArgoCD*

You have successfully installed and connected to ArgoCD. Figure 3-11 shows a sample of the ArgoCD UI.

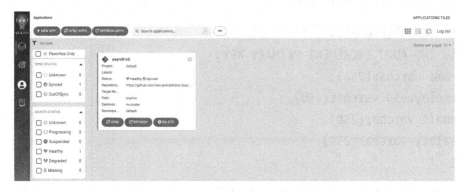

Figure 3-11. *ArgoCD UI showing an app deployed*

Now that you have learned about GitHub Actions and ArgoCD, you can move on to deploying your application and automating the CI/CD process.

3.3. Building a Simple Example with Spring Cloud Function

You will use the same example from Chapter 2, but instead of using the EmployeeConsumer interface, this example uses EmployeeSupplier. In order to do that, you need a prepopulated database. You'll then query the database using a supplier function. You can find the code at https://github.com/banup-kubeforce/payroll-h2.

Here are the required changes.

Step 1: Create scripts to populate the H2 database when the function starts up. Create a schema that creates the employee table. Store the script in a Schema.sql file, as shown in Listing 3-2.

Listing 3-2. Schema.sql

```
DROP TABLE IF EXISTS employee;

CREATE TABLE employee (
 id INT AUTO_INCREMENT PRIMARY KEY,
 name varchar(250),
 employeeid varchar(250),
 email varchar(250),
 salary varchar(250)
);
```

Populate the database with an INSERT statement. Then create a file called Data.sql and store the INSERT statement in it, as shown in Listing 3-3.

Listing 3-3. Data.sql

```
INSERT INTO employee (name, employeeid, email, salary) values
('banu','001','banup@yahoo.com','10000');
```

Add these two files to the resources folder of the main project, as shown in Figure 3-12.

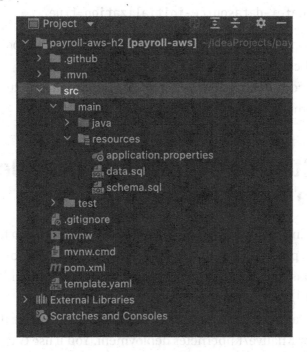

Figure 3-12. *Spring Boot project structure with data.sql and schema.sql*

Modify the Application.properties as follows. Change spring.cloud. function.definition from employeeConsumer to employeeSupplier. This will route function calls to employeeSupplier. See Listing 3-4.

Listing 3-4. Application.properties

```
spring.cloud.function.definition=employeeSupplier
spring.datasource.url=jdbc:h2:mem:employee
spring.datasource.driverClassName=org.h2.Driver
spring.datasource.username=sa
spring.datasource.password=
```

```
spring.h2.console.enabled=true
spring.jpa.database-platform=org.hibernate.dialect.H2Dialect
spring.jpa.defer-datasource-initialization=true
```

Also add `spring.jpa.defer-datasource-initialization=true` to ensure that the data gets populated on startup.

No other code changes are required. It is important to note that the changes you made only affect the configuration file.

3.4. Setting Up a CI/CD Pipeline to Deploy to a Target Platform

As discussed in the introduction of this chapter, you'll use two tools for the CI/CD process. GitHub Actions can be used as a tool for both CI (Continuous Integration) and CD (Continuous Deployment), while ArgoCD is a CD tool.

ArgoCD was designed for Kubernetes, so you can leverage this tool exclusively for Knative/Kubernetes deployment. You'll use GitHub Actions for serverless environments such as Lambda.

Figure 3-13 shows the flow when deploying to serverless environments like AWS Lambda, Google Cloud Functions, and Azure Functions.

The process steps are as follows:

1) Create code and push/commit code to GitHub.

2) GitHub Actions senses the event trigger of the commit and starts the build and deploy process to the serverless environments defined in the actions script.

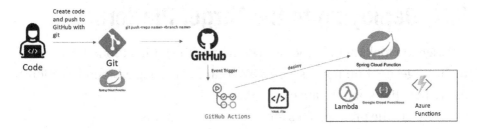

Figure 3-13. *Deploying to serverless functions environments*

Figure 3-13 shows the flow when deploying Spring Cloud Function to a Kubernetes environment with Knative configured.

The process steps are as follows:

1) Create code and push/commit code to GitHub.

2) GitHub Actions senses the event trigger of the commit and starts the build process and deploys the created container image into Docker Hub.

3) ArgoCD polls for changes in GitHub and triggers a "sync." It then retrieves the container image from Docker hub and deploys to Knative on Kubernetes. See Figure 3-14.

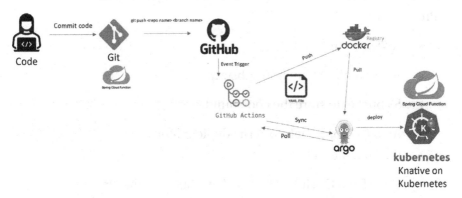

Figure 3-14. *Deploying to a Knative-Kubernetes environment*

3.5. Deploying to the Target Platform

This section looks at the process of deploying the Spring Cloud Function to the target environments such as AWS Lambda, Google Cloud Functions, Azure Functions, and Knative on Kubernetes.

Here are the prerequisites for all the environments:

- GitHub repository with code deployed to GitHub

- Access and connection information to the environments

- All Chapter 2 prerequisites for each of the environments. Refer to Chapter 2 for each environment

- Use the successful deployments of Chapter 2 as a reference for each of the deploys

3.5.1. Deploying to AWS Lambda

Deploying to AWS Lambda requires using a SAM (Serverless Application Model) based GitHub Actions script. This section explains how to use SAM and GitHub Actions. There is no additional coding required.

Prerequisites:

- AWS account

- AWS Lambda Function subscription

- S3 bucket to store the code build

- AWS CLI (optional) to verify deployments through the CLI

- Code from GitHub at `https://github.com/banup-kubeforce/payroll-aws-h2`

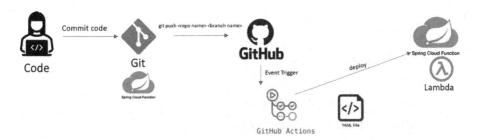

Figure 3-15. *Deploying Spring Cloud Function with GitHub Actions on AWS Lambda*

Step 1: Spring Cloud Function code in GitHub.

Push the code to GitHub. You can bring down code from GitHub at `https://github.com/banup-kubeforce/payroll-aws-h2`. This code can be modified to your specs and deployed to the repository of your choice.

Step 2: Implement GitHub Actions with AWS SAM. AWS SAM (Serverless Application Model) is a framework for building serverless applications. More information can be found at `https://aws.amazon.com/serverless/sam/`.

AWS has a sample SAM-based actions script that is available in the GitHub marketplace that you can leverage. This script will execute the SAM commands.

The action code in Listing 3-5 can be created on the GitHub Actions dashboard or in your IDE

Listing 3-5. Workflow for Payroll Function to be Deployed on AWS Lambda

```
name: CI
on:
  push:
    branches: [ "master" ]
```

```yaml
jobs:
  build-deploy:
    runs-on: ubuntu-latest
    steps:
      - uses: actions/checkout@v2
      - uses: actions/setup-java@v2
        with:
          java-version: '11'
          distribution: 'temurin'
          cache: maven
      - uses: aws-actions/setup-sam@v1
      - uses: aws-actions/configure-aws-credentials@v1
        with:
          aws-access-key-id: ${{ secrets.AWS_ACCESS_KEY_ID }}
          aws-secret-access-key: ${{ secrets.AWS_SECRET_
          ACCESS_KEY }}
          aws-region: us-east-2
      - name: Build with Maven
        run: mvn -B package --file pom.xml
      # sam package
      - run: sam package --template-file template.yaml
      --output-template-file packaged.yaml --s3-bucket
      payrollbucket

# Run Unit tests- Specify unit tests here

# sam deploy
      - run: sam deploy --no-confirm-changeset --no-fail-on-
      empty-changeset --stack-name payroll-aws --s3-bucket
      payrollbucket --capabilities CAPABILITY_IAM --region
      us-east-2
```

The secrets for these two elements can be stored in GitHub secrets:

```
aws-access-key-id: ${{ secrets.AWS_ACCESS_KEY_ID }}
aws-secret-access-key: ${{ secrets.AWS_SECRET_
ACCESS_KEY }}
```

Figure 3-16 shows the place to store configuration secrets for GitHub Actions. It is under the Settings tab.

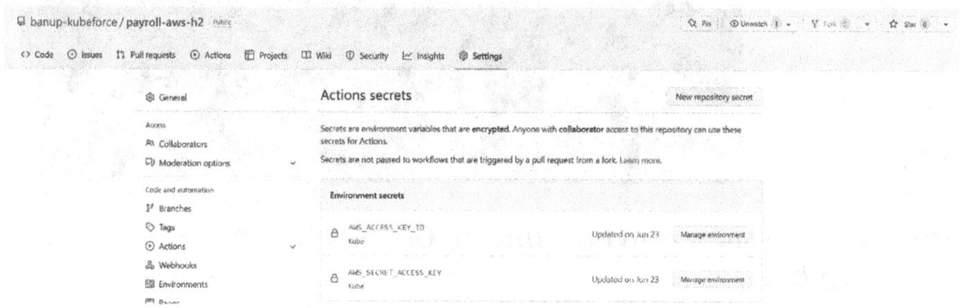

Figure 3-16. *Actions secrets for credentials and configuration*

Step 3: Execute GitHub Actions. Once the workflow is configured, the actions can be triggered from the GitHub console or through a code commit, as defined by the following code in the `sam-pipeline.yaml` file.

```
on:
  push:
    branches: [ "master" ]
```

GitHub Actions execute the steps outlined in the YAML file and deploy the function to AWS Lambda. Figure 3-17 shows a successful run.

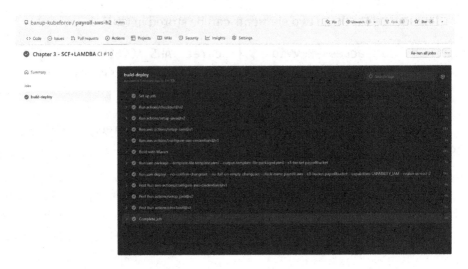

Figure 3-17. *A successful execution of GitHub Actions on*
AWS Lambda

<u>Step 4:</u> Verify that the function is up and running in AWS Lambda.

Figure 3-18. *Function created after execution of GitHub Actions*

Since the `payroll-aws-h2` application exposes `EmployeeSupplier`, you
will do a simple `GET` against the function to see if you get the result of data
that has been inserted into the database on Spring Cloud Function startup.

Figure 3-19. *Testing if the function was successful. See the JSON response*

In Figure 3-19, you can see that the test was successful and see a JSON result of what is in the database.

3.6. Deploying to GCP Cloud Functions

Deploying to GCP Cloud Functions using GitHub Actions is a bit intrusive, as you have to add a `MANIFEST.MF` file to the resources folder. See the code in GitHub.

Prerequisites:

- A GitHub repository with the code. The code at `https://github.com/banup-kubeforce/payroll-gcp-h2.git` can be leveraged

- Google `accountSubscribe` to Google Cloud Functions

- Gcloud CLI is optional if you are just using the GitHub Actions dashboard

Figure 3-20. *GCP and GitHub Actions flow*

Step 1: Spring Cloud Function code in GitHub. Push your code to GitHub. If you have cloned the `https://github.com/banup-kubeforce/payroll-gcp-h2.git` then you have everything that you need to push the code to your repository.

Step 2: Set up Cloud Functions actions.

Set up GitHub actions to run the Cloud Functions command. You have two choices:

- Use `deploy-cloud-functions` runner

- Use `gcloud-cli`

Listing 3-6 shows the GitHub Actions file.

Listing 3-6. Workflow for Payroll Function to be Deployed on GCP Cloud Functions

```
name: Google Cloud Functions

on:
  push:
    branches: [ "master" ]
jobs:
  build-deploy:
    runs-on: ubuntu-latest
    steps:
```

```
- uses: actions/checkout@v2
- uses: actions/setup-java@v2
  with:
    java-version: '11'
    distribution: 'temurin'
    cache: maven
- name: Build with Maven
  run: mvn -B package --file pom.xml

- id: 'auth'
  uses: 'google-github-actions/auth@v0'
  with:
    credentials_json: '${{ secrets.GCP_CREDENTIALS }}'

- name: 'Set up Cloud SDK'
  uses: 'google-github-actions/setup-gcloud@v0'

- name: 'Use gcloud CLI'
  run: 'gcloud functions deploy payroll-gcp --entry-
  point org.springframework.cloud.function.adapter.gcp.
  GcfJarLauncher --runtime java11 --trigger-http --source
  target/deploy --memory 512MB'
```

Note that you will have to store your GCP_CREDENTIALS in the GitHub
Secrets dashboard.

As in the previous example with AWS Lambda, note that the steps to
check out, set up, and build Maven are the same. For the authentication
and deployment, you use the Google Cloud CLI. The Set up Cloud SDK
task will download and set up the Google CLI. You can use the same
command line script that you used when you deployed from a laptop in
Chapter 2.

Step 3: Commit and push code to trigger the GitHub Actions. This trigger is defined in the actions code. In this example, any push or commit to the "master" branch will trigger the GitHub Actions.

```
on:
  push:
    branches: [ "master" ]
```

This can be done on the GitHub Actions website or in the IDE. You can go to GitHub and commit a change by doing a simple modification at the "master" branch. This will start the GitHub Action flow.

Figure 3-21. *GitHub Actions gets triggered by a code commit*

Once the actions successfully complete the job, you can go to the Google Cloud Functions dashboard and test the function. Again, you execute a simple GET against the `EmployeeSupplier` function.

Step 4: Test the function.

Before you test the function, ensure that you pick the function to be invoked from an unauthenticated device such as your laptop. Once you're done testing, remove the privilege to avoid unnecessary invocations.

Figure 3-22. *Allow unauthenticated set for Payroll-gcp-h2*

You can go to the console of your function in the Google Cloud Functions dashboard and execute the test. You do not have to provide any input; simply click the Test the Function button to execute the test. You will see the output of `EmployeeSupplier` in the Output section, as shown in Figure 3-23.

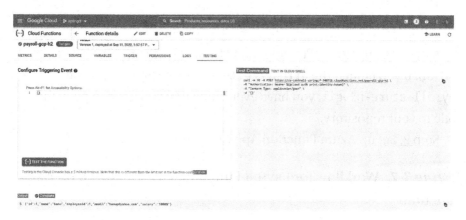

Figure 3-23. *Successful output of the Spring Cloud Function test in GCP Cloud Functions*

3.7. Deploying to Azure Functions

Spring Cloud Function on Azure Functions require a bit of tweaking, as you learned in Chapter 2. This is because the configuration is not externalized, as with AWS Lambda or GCP Cloud Functions. This does not mean that you cannot deploy easily. You have to understand how Azure Function code interprets Spring Cloud Function code and execute. See Chapter 2 for discussions around this issue; make sure that you execute and test locally before pushing to the Azure cloud.

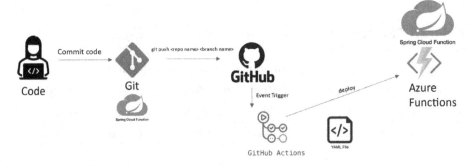

Figure 3-24. *Flow of Spring Cloud Function deployment on Azure*

Step 1: Spring Cloud Function code in GitHub. Push your code to GitHub. If you cloned the `https://github.com/banup-kubeforce/payroll-azure-h2.git`, you have everything that you need to push the code to your repository.

Step 2: Set up Azure Function App Actions. See Listing 3-7.

Listing 3-7. Workflow for Payroll Function to be Deployed on Azure Functions

```
name: Deploy Java project to Azure Function App

on:
  push:
    branches: [ "master" ]

# CONFIGURATION
# For help, go to https://github.com/Azure/Actions
#
# 1. Set up the following secrets in your repository:
#    AZURE_FUNCTIONAPP_PUBLISH_PROFILE
#
# 2. Change these variables for your configuration:
```

```
env:
  AZURE_FUNCTIONAPP_NAME: payroll-kubeforce-new       # set this
  to your function app name on Azure
  POM_XML_DIRECTORY: '.'                              # set this to the
  directory which contains pom.xml file
  POM_FUNCTIONAPP_NAME: payroll-kubeforce-new         # set
  this to the function app name in your local development
  environment
  JAVA_VERSION: '11'                                  # set this to the
  java version to use

jobs:
  build-and-deploy:
    runs-on: ubuntu-latest
    environment: dev
    steps:
    - name: 'Checkout GitHub Action'
      uses: actions/checkout@master

    - name: Setup Java Sdk ${{ env.JAVA_VERSION }}
      uses: actions/setup-java@v1
      with:
        java-version: ${{ env.JAVA_VERSION }}

    - name: 'Restore Project Dependencies Using Mvn'
      shell: bash
      run: |
        pushd './${{ env.POM_XML_DIRECTORY }}'
        mvn clean package
        popd
    - name: 'Run Azure Functions Action'
      uses: Azure/functions-action@v1
      id: fa
```

```
with:
  app-name: ${{ env.AZURE_FUNCTIONAPP_NAME }}
 # package: './${{ env.POM_XML_DIRECTORY }}/target/azure-
    functions/${{ env.POM_FUNCTIONAPP_NAME }}'
   package: './${{ env.POM_XML_DIRECTORY }}/target/azure-
    functions/${{ env.POM_FUNCTIONAPP_NAME }}'
#      package: '${{ env.POM_XML_DIRECTORY }}/target/azure-
    functions/${{ env.POM_FUNCTIONAPP_NAME }}'
 #  package: 'target/azure-functions/${{ env.POM_
    FUNCTIONAPP_NAME }}'
   publish-profile: ${{ secrets.AZURE_FUNCTIONAPP_PUBLISH_
   PROFILE }}
```

Step 3: Execute GitHub Actions. GitHub Actions are executed by this setting in the actions file:

```
on:
  push:
    branches: [ "master" ]
```

Any commit or push to the "master" branch will trigger an execution of GitHub Actions; see Figure 3-25.

Figure 3-25. *Successful deployment of Payroll Spring Cloud Function using GitHub Actions*

After successfully deploying using GitHub actions, you need to verify the deployment in the Azure Functions dashboard; see Figure 3-26.

Figure 3-26. *Azure Functions dashboard showing the function employeeSupplier has been deployed*

Click the `employeeSupplier` link to get to Figure 3-27.

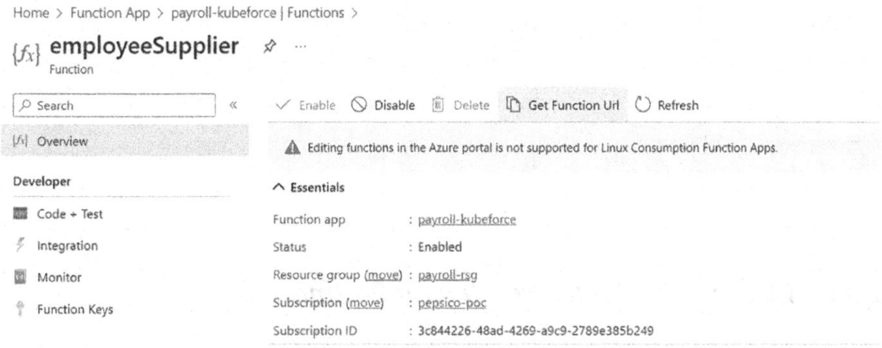

Figure 3-27. *Click the Get Function URL on the employeeSupplier dashboard*

Figure 3-28. *Get the URL of the function*

The URL of the function is `https://payroll-kubeforce.azurewebsites.net/api/employeeSupplier`. Use this URL for testing.

Step 4: Testing. You will use an external testing tool to see if the deployed functions work. The tool you use here is Postman.

You can simply use a `GET` operation to test, as shown in Figure 3-29.

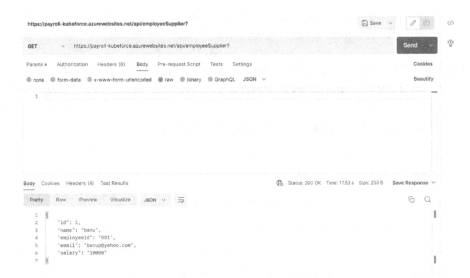

Figure 3-29. *Successful test result with Postman*

This completes the deployment of Spring Cloud Function on Azure Functions using GitHub Actions.

3.8. Deploying to Knative on Kubernetes

The CI/CD for deploying Spring Cloud Function on Knative are similar for every Kubernetes. The only change is the cluster name. This section uses ArgoCD (`http://argoproj.github.io`) for CD even though you can achieve the same result with GitHub Actions. I found GitHub Actions a bit code-intensive. I wanted to separate the CD process and have a good visual tool that shows the deployment. ArgoCD provides a good visual interface.

To have a common repository for all the cloud environments, you'll use Docker hub in this example. Docker hub provides a good interface for managing images and it is popular with developers. If you use ECR, GCR, or ACR, you'll experience vendor lock-in.

The prerequisites for deploying to any Kubernetes platform are the same:

- Get the code from GitHub. You can use `https://github.com/banup-kubeforce/payroll-h2.git` or push your custom code

- A Dockerhub account

- A Dockerfile to push to Dockerhub

- Actions code in your GitHub project

- Access to a Kubernetes Cluster with Knative configured

- ArgoCD up and running

- An app in ArgoCD that is configured to poll the GitHub project

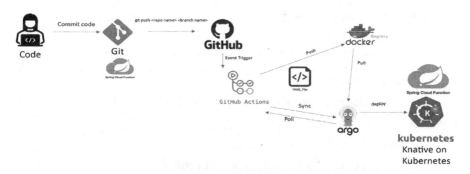

Figure 3-30. *Deployment flow for Spring Cloud Function with GitHub Actions and ArgoCD*

Once you have the prerequisites set up, you can begin configuring an automated CI/CD pipeline. For this example implementation, you'll use the code from GitHub at `https://github.com/banup-kubeforce/payroll-h2.git`.

Step 1: Spring Cloud Function code in GitHub. Push your code to GitHub. You can use the code for `payroll-h2` in GitHub.

Step 2: Create a GitHub Action. Listing 3-8 shows the code for the action.

Listing 3-8. Workflow for Payroll Function Image to be Pushed to Docker Hub

```
name: ci

on:
  push:
    branches:
      - 'main'

jobs:
  docker:
    runs-on: ubuntu-latest
    steps:
      -
        name: Set up QEMU
        uses: docker/setup-qemu-action@v2
      -
        name: Set up Docker Buildx
        uses: docker/setup-buildx-action@v2
      - uses: actions/checkout@v2
      - uses: actions/setup-java@v2
        with:
          java-version: '8'
```

```
    distribution: 'temurin'
    cache: maven

  -

  name: Login to DockerHub
  uses: docker/login-action@
  f054a8b539a109f9f41c372932f1ae047eff08c9
  with:
    username: ${{ secrets.DOCKERHUB_USERNAME }}
    password: ${{ secrets.DOCKERHUB_TOKEN }}

- name: Extract metadata (tags, labels) for Docker1
  id: meta
  uses: docker/metadata-action@98669ae865ea3cffbcbaa878cf
  57c20bbf1c6c38
  with:
    images: banupkubeforce/springcloudfunctions

- name: Build with Maven
  run: mvn -B package --file pom.xml

- name: Build and push Docker image
  uses: docker/build-push-action@
  ad44023a93711e3deb337508980b4b5e9bcdc5dc
  with:
    context: .
    file: ./DockerFile
    push: true
    tags: ${{ steps.meta.outputs.tags }}
    labels: ${{ steps.meta.outputs.labels }}
```

This code creates a Docker image and pushes it to the Docker hub. You can store the username and password as secrets in the GitHub site (see Figure 3-31).

```
username: ${{ secrets.DOCKERHUB_USERNAME }}
password: ${{ secrets.DOCKERHUB_TOKEN }}
```

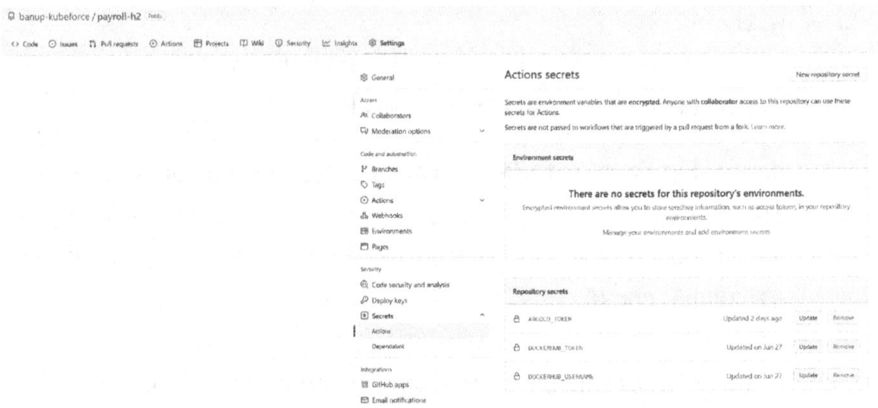

Figure 3-31. *GitHub Secrets store for configurations and credentials*

<u>Step 3:</u> Execute GitHub Actions to build and push the Docker image.

The execution of GitHub Actions can be triggered by a push/commit. The trigger is defined in the GitHub Actions YAML file:

```
on:
  push:
    branches:
      - 'main'
```

Figure 3-32. *Successful run of GitHub Actions*

<u>Step 4:</u> Configure ArgoCD.

Follow the steps outlined in the introduction of this chapter for ArgoCD. You need to connect to your cluster on your local machine before executing this command; see Listing 3-9.

Listing 3-9. ArgoCD Script to Create a Project and Point to the payroll-h2 Repo

```
$ argocd app create payroll-h2 --repo https://github.com/banup-
kubeforce/payroll-h2.git --path knative --dest-server https://
kubernetes.default.svc --dest-namespace default –upsert
```

This will create app `payroll-h2` in ArgoCD, as shown in Figure 3-33.

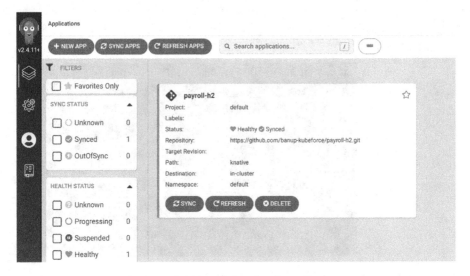

Figure 3-33. *Application payroll-h2 deployed on ArgoCD*

<u>Step 5:</u> Sync the project in Argo CD.

Now that you have created the app and it is pointing to the GitHub repository, make sure you have a connection to the repo, as shown in Figure 3-34. I connected to the repo using HTTPS. This will allow the app to poll for changes and trigger the flow to push the Docker image to the specified Kubernetes environment.

Figure 3-34. *Connect payroll-h2 to the repo using HTTPS*

You can also run a deployment manually by clicking SYNC, as shown in Figure 3-35.

Figure 3-35. *The SYNC button on payroll-h2 app in ArgoCD*

Figure 3-36 shows a successful sync process in ArgoCD.

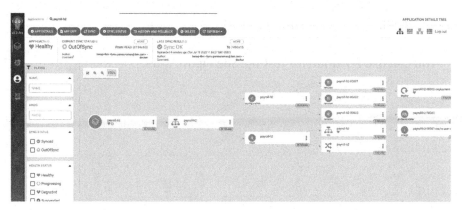

Figure 3-36. *Successful run of the sync showing the deployment flow*

Step 6: Check if the function has been deployed. Navigate to the Kubernetes dashboard on the Azure Portal and verify that the service has been deployed. See Figure 3-37.

Figure 3-37. *Successful deployment of Spring Cloud Function (payroll-h2) on Azure*

Step 7: Testing. The best way to get the URL to test is to connect to the cluster via the command line and get the URL, as explained in Chapter 2.

Run $kn `service list` to get the URL for testing, as shown in Figure 3-38.

```
$ kn service list
NAME        URL                                                LATEST            AGE   CONDITIONS  READY  REASON
payroll-h2  http://payroll-h2.default.40.88.212.153.sslip.io   payroll-h2-00001  39h   3 OK / 3    True
```

Figure 3-38. *URL for testing payroll-h2*

You can use Postman for testing. See Figure 3-39.

146

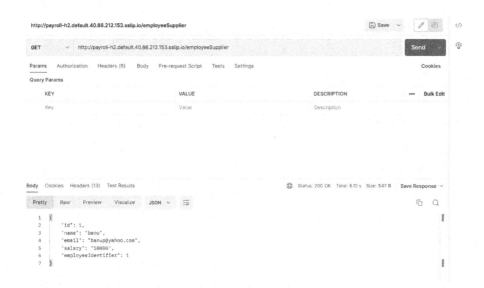

Figure 3-39. *Successful execution of test against payroll-h2 deployed on AKS Knative*

This completes the successful deployment using GitHub Actions and ArgoCD.

3.9. Summary

In this chapter, you learned how to set up some CI/CD tools to create an automated deployment for your Spring Cloud Function.

You learned how to trigger the deployment of functions on Lambda, Google Cloud Functions, and Azure Functions.

You also learned that you can combine the build of Docker images stored in Docker hub and ArgoCD to deploy the image to any Kubernetes cluster that is running Knative.

If you want to achieve "write-once deploy-anywhere," you have to look at using Kubernetes and Knative. Spring Cloud Function is really a portable function.

## CHAPTER 4

Building Event-Driven Data Pipelines with Spring Cloud Function

Spring Cloud Function plays a critical role in the hybrid cloud or on-premises/private cloud space. Building events/data pipelines that span across the local datacenter and the cloud increases complexity due to the firewall boundaries. Data pipelines play an important role when you want to acquire, move, or transform data as it comes (streaming) or when it's offline (batch).

So, what are event data pipelines?

4.1. Data Event Pipelines

Let's look at an example. Say you are driving a car and suddenly you collide with a vehicle. After a few minutes, you get a call from OnStar asking you if you are alright as you were in a collision. How did OnStar know that you were in a collision? All this happens in a flash. Sensors in your vehicle are

B. Parasuraman, *Practical Spring Cloud Function*,
https://doi.org/10.1007/978-1-4842-8913-6_4

triggered by the collision event and begin sending data as streams into the OnStar system. The OnStar system processes the data from numerous other systems and triggers a response in the form of an OnStar operator calling you. The event that triggered the data processing along with the output is the event data pipeline. Figure 4-1 illustrates this process.

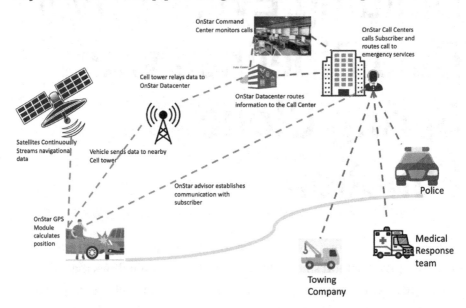

Figure 4-1. *An example event-driven data pipeline implementation for vehicles using OnStar*

All data regarding the incident is collated, processed, analyzed, and sent to various target systems, both internal and external to OnStar. This is an example of event data pipeline.

A data pipeline is a set of processes that takes raw data from disparate sources, and then filters, transforms, and moves the data to target stores, where it can be analyzed and presented in a visually compelling way.

The data can be in the form of streams or batches. Streaming is usually associated with real-time to near real-time data movement and batches are usually scheduled and non-real-time. Figure 4-2 illustrates this.

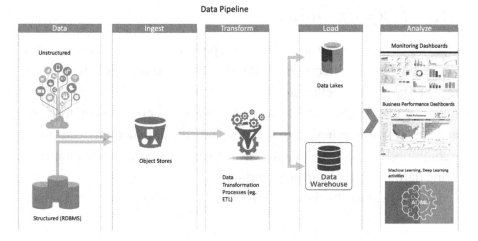

Figure 4-2. *Data pipeline process*

The data can also be unstructured or structured. Unstructured data can be from a multitude of resources, including Internet-based platforms such as Twitter, to an automotive device emanating data.

Structured data usually originates from within the company's applications. This data needs to be combined at a landing zone of object stores. These object stores can be on-premises or in the cloud. Once the data is ingested into the object stores, it is then retrieved and transformed, usually through an ETL process in other datastores such as data lakes or data warehouses. This data is then further analyzed using BI tools such as Power BI and Tableau or further processed with the AI/ML processes.

This whole process—from data ingestion to consumption—is called the data pipeline.

Let's dive a bit deeper into the various sub-processes outlined in the data pipeline process.

4.1.1. Acquire Data

Acquiring data is the first step in the data pipeline process. Here, business owners and data architects decide on what data to use to fulfil the requirements for a specific use case.

For example, in the case of a collision event detection for OnStar, the data needs to be acquired from sensors. This sensor data then needs to be combined with data from internal and external partners, like finance, towing partners, rental partners, and so on.

Table 4-1 shows the data, the type of data, and the sources for a vehicle event-driven pipeline.

Table 4-1. *Data Identification*

Data	Type of Data	Data Source
Sensor	Unstructured (JSON, CSV)	Sensors
Rental info	Relational (RDBMS)	External rental agency
User info	Relational (RDBMS)	OnStar registration
Vehicle info	Relational (RDBMS)	Vehicle data systems
Towing info	Relational (RDBMS)	External towing company

4.1.2. Store/Ingest Data

The data from various sources is acquired and stored as raw data into the store of choice. The method of ingestion can be stream-based or batch-based.

For example, in the case of OnStar, sensor data is streamed at regular intervals or is event-based. Other data, such as rental info, can either be batch based or on-demand query driven. The raw datastore can be an S3 object store hosted in the cloud or on-premises.

4.1.3. Transform Data

The data that is stored raw in the object store is then processed. The process may include converting or transforming unstructured data into structured data and storing it in an RDBMS database.

For example, in OnStar, partner data and internal data will be combined and transformed into a common data model. The sensor data will also be transformed into an RDBMS format.

4.1.4. Load Data

Once the data is transformed, it is then loaded into a single or multiple databases with a common schema. This schema is based on a predefined data model specific to the use case. The target datastore can be a data lake or another RDBMS store. Here again, it depends on the type of analysis that needs to be done.

For example, if this an OLTP type of analysis, the data needs to be processed and sent to requesting systems quickly. This would require an RDBMS store. Data that needs to be available for reporting and research can be stored in a data lake.

4.1.5. Analyze Data

During this sub-process, the data that is stored in a data lake or RDBMs will be analyzed using tools such as Tableau, Power BI, or a dedicated web page for reporting.

In the case of OnStar, data that is stored in the data lake will be analyzed using Tableau or Power BI, while the data that needs immediate attention will be analyzed by a custom dashboard or reporting interface on the web.

Spring Cloud Function plays an integral role in the whole process, especially when combined with tools such as Spring Cloud Data Flow, AWS Glue, Azure Data Factory, Google's data flow, and so on. You will dive deep into these tools in this chapter.

4.2. Spring Cloud Function and Spring Cloud Data Flow and Spring Cloud Streams

Spring Cloud Data Flow (SCDF) is a Spring.io-based product that supports the creation and deployment of a data pipeline. It supports batch and event-driven data, which makes it versatile. SCDF pipelines can be built programmatically or wired up through a GUI. It is heavily based on the Spring Framework and Java, which makes it very popular among Spring developers.

Figure 4-3 shows a sample dashboard of SCDF with a simple data pipeline that has a source, a processor, and a sink. You can drag-and-drop from the available components to build the pipeline. You can also build your custom source, processors, and sinks and deploy them for use within your enterprise.

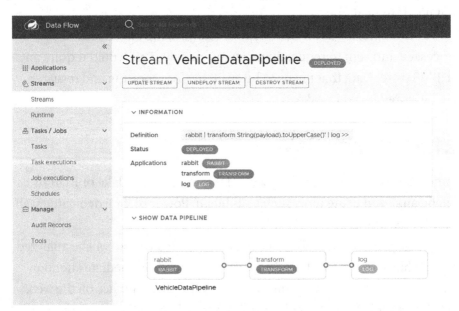

Figure 4-3. *A sample graphical representation of a data pipeline in SCDF*

As you can see from the dashboard, you can build stream-based or batch-based (task) data pipelines and manage these through a single dashboard.

SCDF, unlike other the data pipeline tools available in the cloud, can be deployed in a Kubernetes, Docker, or Cloud Foundry environment, making it a portable tool for data pipeline development and deployment.

4.2.1. Spring Cloud Function and SCDF

Spring Cloud Function and SCDF are perfectly matched, as they are built out of the same framework, Spring. You can deploy Spring Cloud Function as a source, processor, sink, or as a trigger for the pipeline. Since the data pipelines are usually invoked sporadically for processing data, you can optimize utilization of resources and costs with a Spring Cloud Function.

Let's look at a sample implementation of Spring Cloud Function with SCDF.

In this example, you will build a simple data pipeline using RabbitMQ as a source, do a simple transformation, and store the messages in a log. You will publish sample vehicle information into a RabbitMQ topic called VehicleInfo and do a simple transformation, then store it in a log file.

RabbitMQ ➤ Transform ➤ Log

Prerequisites:

- SCDF deployed on Kubernetes or locally in Docker

- Kubernetes or Docker

- A RabbitMQ cluster/instance

- A queue to publish messages

- Code from GitHub at https://github.com/banup-kubeforce/SCDF-Rabbit-Function.git

155

Additional prerequisites for each environment can be found at
`https://dataflow.spring.io/docs/installation`
Step 1: Installing Spring Cloud Data Flow.

- Local machine: Docker Compose is an easy way to
  get an instance of Spring Cloud Data Flow up and
  running. The details of the installation are available at
  `https://dataflow.spring.io/docs/installation/`
  `local/docker/`

- Kubernetes: Instructions for installing this on
  Kubernetes are available at`https://dataflow.spring.`
  `io/docs/installation/kubernetes/`.

For this example, I used an existing cluster that I created in Chapter 2
and ran the following `helm` command to install the SCDF, which results in
the output shown in Figure 4-4.

```
$helm install scdf bitnami/spring-cloud-dataflow -n scdf-system
--set server.service.type=LoadBalancer --set server.service.
loadBalancerIP=${ingress} --set server.ingress.enabled=true
--set server.ingress.server.host=scdf.${ingress}.xip.io
```

```
NAME: scdf
LAST DEPLOYED: Tue Sep 13 14:00:11 2022
NAMESPACE: scdf-system
STATUS: deployed
REVISION: 1
TEST SUITE: None
NOTES:
CHART NAME: spring-cloud-dataflow
CHART VERSION: 12.0.4
APP VERSION: 2.9.4

** Please be patient while the chart is being deployed **

Spring Cloud Data Flow chart was deployed enabling the following components:

- Spring Cloud Data Flow server
- Spring Cloud Skipper server
```

Figure 4-4. *Successful execution of a helm chart for SCDF*

Once the command runs successfully, as shown in Figure 4-4, you can check the status by running kubectl get pods. You can also get the external IP with the kubectl get svc commands, as shown in Figures 4-5 and 4-6.

```
$kubectl get pods -n scdf-system
```

```
NAME                                                        READY  STATUS    RESTARTS  AGE
scdf-mariadb-0                                              1/1    Running   0         4m37s
scdf-rabbitmq-0                                            1/1    Running   0         4m37s
scdf-spring-cloud-dataflow-server-ddddd86fd-2kmrw          1/1    Running   0         4m37s
scdf-spring-cloud-dataflow-skipper-695b97cf6c-qp5tz        1/1    Running   0         4m37s
```

Figure 4-5. *Get the external IP of the SCDF*

```
$kubectl get svc -n scdf-system
```

```
banup@Banus-MacBook-Pro kubernetes % kubectl get svc -n scdf-system
NAME                     TYPE         CLUSTER-IP      EXTERNAL-IP   PORT(S)
scdf-mariadb             ClusterIP    10.0.124.125    <none>        3306/TCP
scdf-rabbitmq            ClusterIP    10.0.109.15     <none>        5672/TCP,
scdf-rabbitmq-headless   ClusterIP    None            <none>        4369/TCP,
```

Figure 4-6. *Get the status of SCDF*

You can now access SCDF using the external IP. For example, http://20.241.228.184:8080/dashboard

The next step is to add applications. Spring provides a standard set of templates that you can use to build your pipeline.

Step 2: Add Applications to your SCDF Instance

Use the Add Application(s) button to create some starter apps that you can use to create a data pipeline; see Figures 4-7 and 4-8.

Figure 4-7. *Add application view in SCDF*

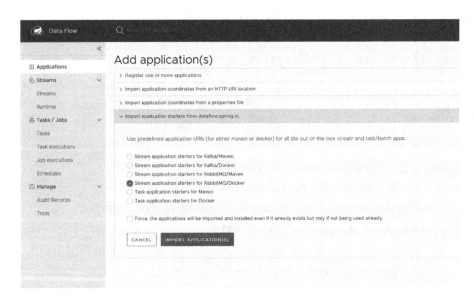

Figure 4-8. *Pick the starters of your choice. If SDCF is deployed in Kubernetes, pick Docker based starters*

Figure 4-8 shows you the options to add applications that are custom built through the Registering One or More Applications option. You import the application coordinates from an HTTP URI or use a properties file. There is also an option to import some prebuilt starters from Spring.

Furthermore, you can choose starters that are Maven- or Docker-based or RabbitMQ- or Kafka-based. RabbitMQ and Kafka are used as backbone messaging systems for internal SCDF components and not for external use. When deploying to a Kubernetes cluster, you have to choose a Docker-based starter. When deploying locally in a Docker environment, you can choose between Maven and Docker-based starters.

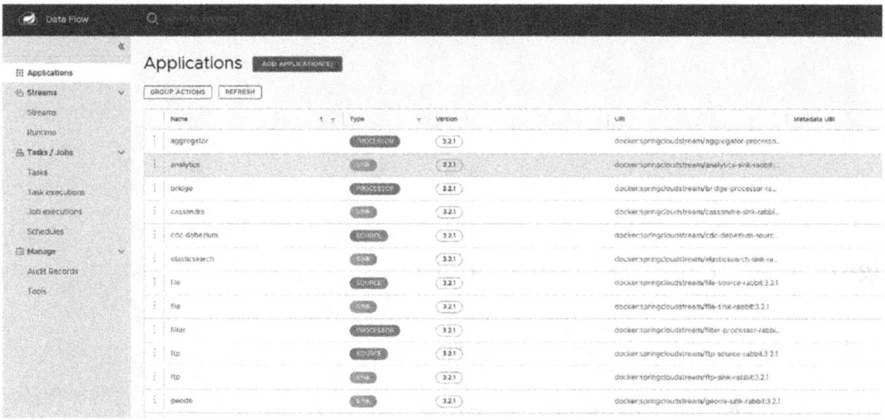

Figure 4-9. *Prebuilt templates are installed in SCDF*

Figure 4-9 shows prebuilt templates with the Docker images URI. SCDF is running on a Kubernetes environment, so the prebuilt images have a Docker URI.

These prebuilt templates come in three categories—source, processor, and sink. They allow you to wire up a data pipeline without the need for coding. If you want a custom component, you can follow the examples in https://dataflow.spring.io/docs/stream-developer-guides/.

The next step is to create a stream using the starter templates you loaded.

159

<u>Step 3</u>: Create a Stream

The Streams dashboard allows you to wire up a data pipeline. Click the Create Streams button to start the process, as shown in Figure 4-10.

Figure 4-10. *The Streams dashboard*

Then perform the following steps:

1. **Pick the source.**

This example uses a RabbitMQ as the source, so pick Rabbit from the available options, as shown in Figure 4-11.

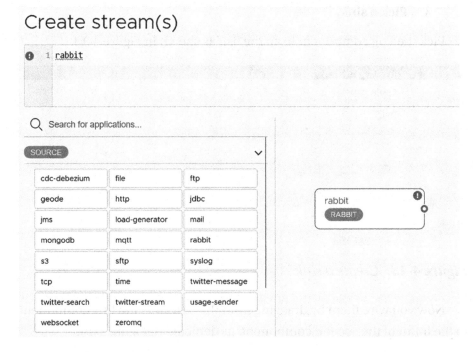

Figure 4-11. *Create a source*

2. **Pick a processor.**

Pick the Transform component from the list, as shown in Figure 4-12.

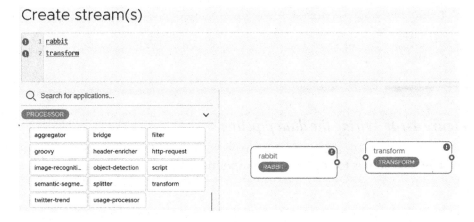

Figure 4-12. *Create a processor*

3. **Pick a sink.**

Pick the Log component from the list, as shown in Figure 4-13.

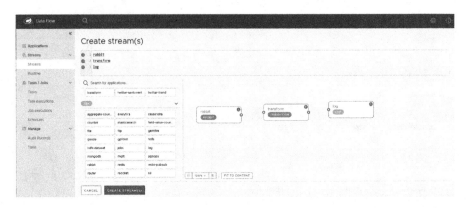

Figure 4-13. *Create a sink*

Now you wire them by dragging from the output of the first component to the input of the second component, as depicted in Figure 4-14.

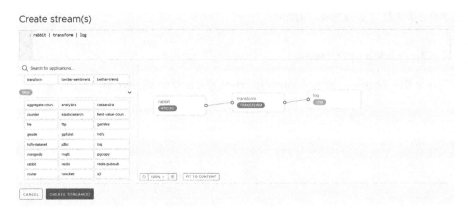

Figure 4-14. *Wiring the data pipeline*

The next step is to configure the pipeline.

4.   **Configure RabbitMQ.**

You have to point the Rabbit source to your RabbitMQ instance. There are three categories in the form to populate. Open and fill in the appropriate fields. I used username, password, port, host, and queue, as shown in Figure 4-15.

Figure 4-15. *Set the properties for rabbit*

Click Update once you're done with the configuration.

5.   **Configure the transform.**

In this example, you simply transform the incoming string to uppercase. Note that you have to use SpEL (Spring Expression Language). More information on SpEL Is available at `https://docs.spring.io/ spring-framework/docs/3.0.x/reference/expressions.html`. See Figure 4-16.

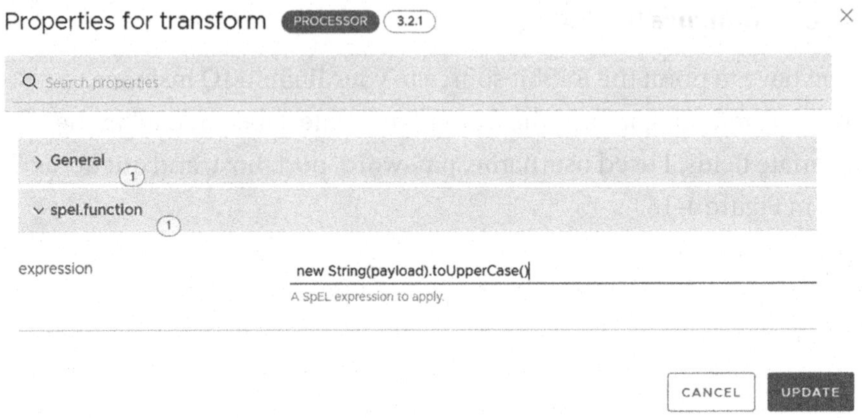

Properties for transform   PROCESSOR   3.2.1   ×

Q Search properties

> General
      1

∨ spel.function
            1

expression   new String(payload).toUpperCase()
                                  A SpEL expression to apply.

                                                              CANCEL   UPDATE

Figure 4-16. *Set the transform properties*

6.   **Configure the sink.**

In this case, you just use a simple log. No configuration is required. See
Figure 4-17.

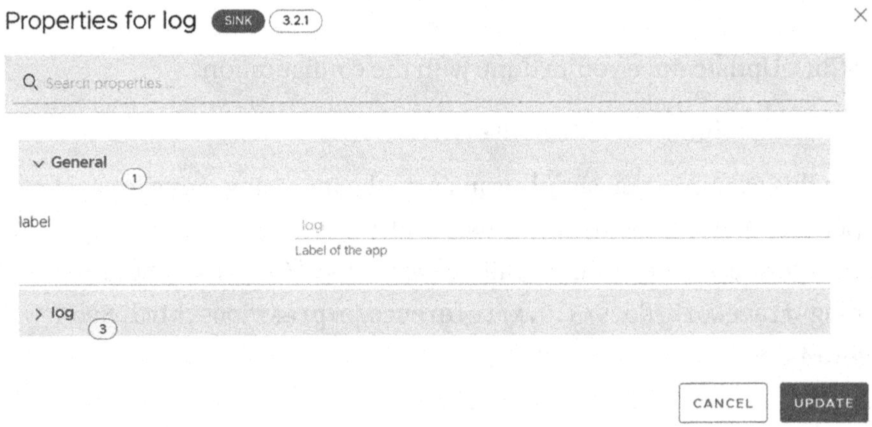

Properties for log   SINK   3.2.1   ×

Q Search properties

∨ General
      1

label   log
                                  Label of the app

> log
    3

                                                              CANCEL   UPDATE

Figure 4-17. *Setting properties for the log*

7. **Wire up the data pipeline.**

Once you wire up, you will get a data pipeline. This will also show a Stream DSL (Domain Specific Language) expression that you can save and reuse using a SCDF shell or dashboard, as shown in Figure 4-18.

```
rabbit --password=pa55word --port=5672 --host=20.40.208.246
--username=banup --queues=VehicleInfo | transform
--expression='new String(payload).toUpperCase()' |log
```

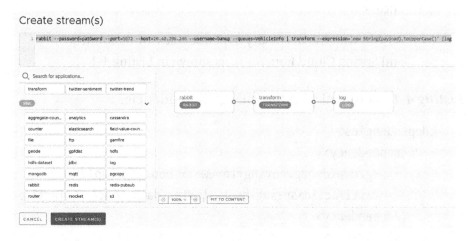

Figure 4-18. *Wire up the data pipeline*

The pipeline can be triggered by an external Spring Cloud Function on Lambda or using Google Cloud Functions, and so on. See Figure 4-19.

8. **Deploy the stream**

Figure 4-19. *Successful deployment of a data pipeline*

<u>Step 4:</u> Create a function to publish data to RabbitMQ

Here, you create a Spring Cloud Function to publish the data to start the data-pipeline process.

The components that you will create are as follows:

- SenderConfig

- QueueSender

- SenderFunction

Prerequisites:

- A POM with the necessary dependencies for RabbitMQ and Spring Cloud Functions, as shown in Listing 4-1.

Listing 4-1. pom.xml with RabbitMQ Dependencies

```
<dependencies>
    <dependency>
        <groupId>org.springframework.boot</groupId>
        <artifactId>spring-boot-starter-data-jpa</artifactId>
    </dependency>
    <dependency>
        <groupId>org.springframework.boot</groupId>
        <artifactId>spring-boot-starter-web</artifactId>
    </dependency>
    <dependency>
        <groupId>org.springframework.boot</groupId>
        <artifactId>spring-boot-starter-amqp</artifactId>
    </dependency>
    <dependency>
        <groupId>org.springframework.cloud</groupId>
        <artifactId>spring-cloud-function-web</artifactId>
    </dependency>
```

```
<dependency>
    <groupId>org.springframework.boot</groupId>
    <artifactId>spring-boot-starter-test</artifactId>
    <scope>test</scope>
</dependency>
</dependencies>
<dependencyManagement>
    <dependencies>
        <dependency>
            <groupId>org.springframework.cloud</groupId>
            <artifactId>spring-cloud-dependencies
            </artifactId>
            <version>${spring-cloud.version}</version>
            <type>pom</type>
            <scope>import</scope>
        </dependency>
    </dependencyManagement>
```

Add the RabbitMQ server and configuration references to the application.properties file, as in Listing 4-2.

Listing 4-2. application.properties

```
spring.cloud.function.definition=senderFunction
spring.rabbitmq.host=20.40.208.246
spring.rabbitmq.port=5672
spring.rabbitmq.username=banup
spring.rabbitmq.password=pa55word

queue.name=VehicleInfo
```

1. **Create the SenderConfig Component**

This is a simple setter for the queue name. You can expand this to include other RabbitMQ configurations. This is the entity definition (see Listing 4-3).

Listing 4-3. application.properties

```
package com.kubeforce.scdffunctiontigger;

import org.springframework.amqp.core.Queue;
import org.springframework.beans.factory.annotation.Value;
import org.springframework.context.annotation.Bean;
import org.springframework.context.annotation.Configuration;

@Configuration
public class SenderConfig {

    @Value("${queue.name}")
    private String message;

    @Bean
    public Queue queue() {
        return new Queue(message, true);
    }

}
```

2. **Create the QueueSender Component**

You use a RabbitTemplate from the springframework amqp library to define the connection to the RabbitMQ instance (see Listing 4-4).

Listing 4-4. QueueSender.java

```
package com.kubeforce.scdftrigger;

import org.springframework.amqp.core.Queue;
import org.springframework.amqp.rabbit.core.RabbitTemplate;
import org.springframework.beans.factory.annotation.Autowired;
import org.springframework.stereotype.Component;

@Component
public class QueueSender {

    @Autowired
    private RabbitTemplate rabbitTemplate;

    @Autowired
    private Queue queue;

    public void send(String order) {
        rabbitTemplate.convertAndSend(this.queue.
        getName(), order);
    }
}
```

3. **Wrap the Sender in Spring Cloud Function framework**

This example uses the queueSender to send the data (see Listing 4-5).

Listing 4-5. SenderFunction.java

```
package com.kubeforce.scdftrigger;
import org.springframework.beans.factory.annotation.Autowired;
import java.util.function.Function;
```

```java
public class SenderFunction implements
Function<String,String> {
    @Autowired
    private QueueSender queueSender;
    @Override
    public String apply(String s) {
        queueSender.send("Vehicle:SUV,Make:Ford,Model:Edge,
        Year:2021");
        return "ok. done";
    }
}
```

Step 5: Test the function using Postman

Use the GET function on Postman and provide the URL to the senderFunction.

You should get the result shown in this image.

Check the RabbitMQ queue for any messages.

Now you have a function that can post messages to a RabbitMQ topic. The SCDF data pipeline will be listening to the queue and will start processing.

You can also look at the logs associated with each of the components to monitor the status of the data pipeline, as shown in Figure 4-20.

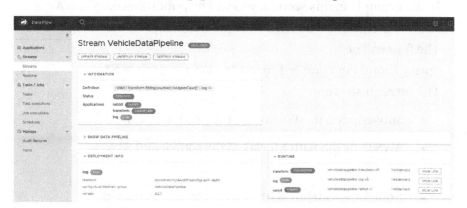

Figure 4-20. *Details of the VehicleDataPipeline stream*

You have seen how to create a data pipeline in SCDF that monitors a topic in RabbitMQ. You created a Spring Cloud Function that posts messages into the RabbitMQ topic. Spring Cloud Function can also be deployed as a source in SCDF; more information on how to develop code for SCDF is available on the SCDF site.

4.3. Spring Cloud Function and AWS Glue

AWS Glue works very similarly to Spring Cloud Data Flow in that you can wire up a data pipeline that has a source, processor, and sink. More information can be found at `https://us-east-2.console.aws.amazon.com/gluestudio/home?region=us-east-2#/`.

Spring Cloud Function can participate in the data pipeline process as a trigger, or simply by integrating with one of the components in the data pipeline.

For example, if you have AWS Kinesis as a source and you need to get data from a vehicle, you can have Spring Cloud Function stream the data that it gets into AWS Kinesis.

In the example in this section, you will be publishing data into AWS Kinesis and then kick off an AWS Glue job manually.

The flow will be:

Spring Cloud Function ➤ Kinesis ➤ AWS Glue Job ➤ S3

The prerequisites are:

- Subscription to AWS, AWS Glue job, Kinesis, and S3

- AWS Glue job with Kinesis as the source and S3 as the target

- Code from GitHub at `https://github.com/banup-kubeforce/Kinesis_trigger.git`

It is assumed that you have some knowledge of AWS Glue, as we do not delve into the details of this product. The focus is on creating the Spring Cloud Function.

4.3.1. Step 1: Set Up Kinesis

You can get to Kinesis at `https://us-east-1.console.aws.amazon.com/`
`kinesis/home?region=us-east-1#/home`.

Once you subscribe to Kinesis, you can begin creating the data stream.
Make sure you select on-demand (see Figure 4-21), as this will save you
some money.

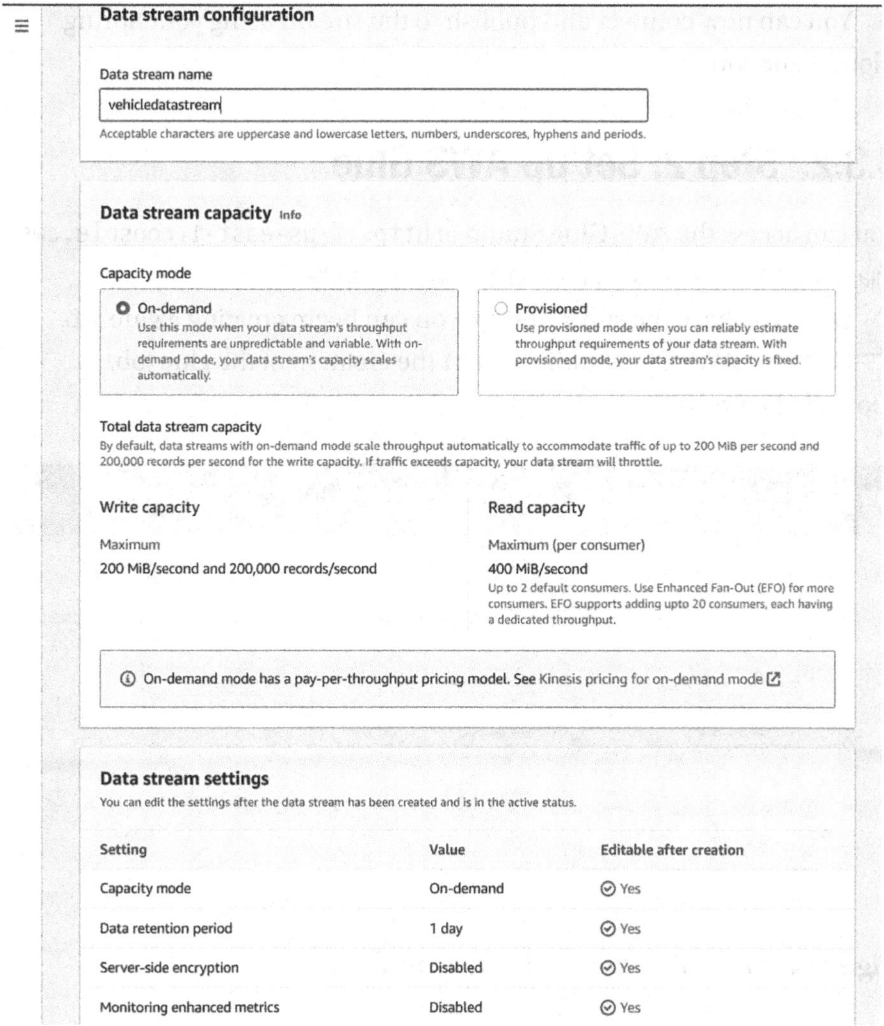

Figure 4-21. *Create a vehicledatastream in AWS Kinesis*

Figure 4-22. *vehicledatastream is active*

You can now connect and publish to the stream using your Spring Cloud Function.

4.3.2. Step 2: Set Up AWS Glue

You can access the AWS Glue Studio at `https://us-east-1.console.aws. amazon.com/gluestudio/home?region=us-east-1#/`.

Once you have the subscription, you can begin creating a glue job.

Go to the AWS Glue Studio to start the creation of the glue job, as shown in Figure 4-23.

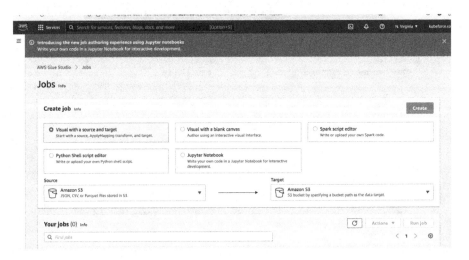

Figure 4-23. *AWS Glue Studio, Create a Job*

Create a job called `vehicledatapipeline`. Use Amazon Kinesis as the source and Amazon S3 as the target. Ensure that you set the proper configurations for each of these components.

The job shown in Figure 4-24 will read Amazon Kinesis shards and post the data into Amazon S3.

Figure 4-24. *Configure Kinesis and S3 integration*

Now you have a job in AWS Glue that you can trigger manually or via a function.

4.3.3. Step 3: Create a Function to Load Data into Kinesis

1: Set the application properties. Make sure that you provide the stream name. AWS information has to be set, as shown in Listing 4-6.

Listing 4-6. application.properties

```
spring.cloud.function.definition=producerFunction
#use your aws credentials here
aws.access_key =
aws.secret_key =
aws.region = us-east-2
```

#use your stream name that you have created
aws.stream_name = vehicledatastream

2: Add the kinesis dependencies. Make sure to add the necessary libraries. The latest version of producer has some bugs, so I used the working version, as shown in Listing 4-7.

Listing 4-7. pom.xml dependecies

```
<dependency>
    <groupId>com.amazonaws</groupId>
    <artifactId>amazon-kinesis-client</artifactId>
    <version>1.14.1</version>

</dependency>
<dependency>
    <groupId>com.amazonaws</groupId>
    <artifactId>amazon-kinesis-producer</artifactId>
    <version>0.13.1</version>
</dependency>
<dependency>
    <groupId>com.amazonaws</groupId>
    <artifactId>amazon-kinesis-client</artifactId>
    <version>1.14.1</version>
</dependency>
```

3: Create the model. This is a simple model for tracking a vehicle's detail. See Listing 4-8.

Listing 4-8. TrackDetail.java

```
public class TrackDetail {
    private String vehicleId;
    private String driverId;
    private String driverName;
```

```java
public String getVehicleId() {
    return vehicleId;
}

public void setVehicleId(String vehicleId) {
    this.vehicleId = vehicleId;
}

public String getDriverId() {
    return driverId;
}

public void setDriverId(String driverId) {
    this.driverId = driverId;
}

public String getDriverName() {
    return driverName;
}

public void setDriverName(String driverName) {
    this.driverName = driverName;
}

}
```

4: Create the Kinesis producer. This interface is nice to have; see Listing 4-9.

Listing 4-9. ProducerService.java

```java
public interface ProducerService {

    public void putDataIntoKinesis(String payload) throws
    Exception;
    public void stop();

}
```

5: Create the producer implementation. The implementation provided in Listing 4-10 sets the method for posting to Kinesis.

Listing 4-10. ProducerServiceImpl.java

```java
import com.amazonaws.auth.AWSStaticCredentialsProvider;
import com.amazonaws.auth.BasicAWSCredentials;
import com.amazonaws.services.kinesis.producer.*;
import com.google.common.util.concurrent.FutureCallback;
import com.google.common.util.concurrent.Futures;
import com.google.common.util.concurrent.ListenableFuture;
import org.slf4j.Logger;
import org.slf4j.LoggerFactory;
import org.springframework.beans.factory.annotation.Value;
import org.springframework.stereotype.Service;

import java.io.UnsupportedEncodingException;
import java.nio.ByteBuffer;
import java.util.concurrent.ExecutorService;
import java.util.concurrent.Executors;
import java.util.concurrent.atomic.AtomicLong;

@Service
public class ProducerServiceImpl implements ProducerService {

    private static final Logger LOG = LoggerFactory.
    getLogger(ProducerServiceImpl.class);

    @Value(value = "${aws.stream_name}")
    private String streamName;

    @Value(value = "${aws.region}")
    private String awsRegion;

    @Value(value = "${aws.access_key}")
    private String awsAccessKey;
```

```java
@Value(value = "${aws.secret_key}")
private String awsSecretKey;

private KinesisProducer kinesisProducer = null;

// The number of records that have finished (either
   successfully put, or failed)
final AtomicLong completed = new AtomicLong(0);

private static final String TIMESTAMP_AS_PARTITION_KEY =
        Long.toString(System.currentTimeMillis());

public ProducerServiceImpl() {
    this.kinesisProducer = getKinesisProducer();
}

private KinesisProducer getKinesisProducer() {
    if (kinesisProducer == null) {

        BasicAWSCredentials awsCreds = new BasicAWSCredenti
        als("AKIAZKRBTXXLPA3V2RW5", "kUqeO3bJyHEGziMO9ru83/
        yU5vulbYagqHXmM4zG");

        KinesisProducerConfiguration config = new
        KinesisProducerConfiguration();
        config.setRegion("us-east-2");
        config.setCredentialsProvider(new AWSStaticCredenti
        alsProvider(awsCreds));
        config.setMaxConnections(1);
        config.setRequestTimeout(6000); // 6 seconds
        config.setRecordMaxBufferedTime(5000); // 5 seconds

        kinesisProducer = new KinesisProducer(config);
    }

    return kinesisProducer;
}
```

```java
@Override
public void putDataIntoKinesis(String payload) throws
Exception {

    FutureCallback<UserRecordResult> myCallback = new Futur
    eCallback<UserRecordResult>() {

        @Override
        public void onFailure(Throwable t) {

            // If we see any failures, we will log them.
            int attempts = ((UserRecordFailedException)
            t).getResult().getAttempts().size() - 1;
            if (t instanceof UserRecordFailedException) {
                Attempt last =
                        ((UserRecordFailedException)
                        t).getResult().getAttempts().
                        get(attempts);
                if (attempts > 1) {
                    Attempt previous =
                    ((UserRecordFailedException)
                    t).getResult().getAttempts()
                            .get(attempts - 1);
                    LOG.error(String.format(
                            "Failed to put record - %s
                            : %s. Previous failure -
                            %s : %s",
                            last.getErrorCode(), last.
                            getErrorMessage(),
                            previous.getErrorCode(),
                            previous.getErrorMessage()));
                } else {
```

```java
            LOG.error(String.format("Failed to put
            record - %s : %s.",
                    last.getErrorCode(), last.
                    getErrorMessage()));
        }

    }
    LOG.error("Exception during put", t);
}

@Override
public void onSuccess(UserRecordResult result) {

    long totalTime = result.getAttempts().stream()
            .mapToLong(a -> a.getDelay() +
            a.getDuration()).sum();

    LOG.info("Data writing success. Total time
    taken to write data = {}", totalTime);

    completed.getAndIncrement();
    }
};

final ExecutorService callbackThreadPool = Executors.
newCachedThreadPool();

ByteBuffer data = null;

try {
    data = ByteBuffer.wrap(payload.getBytes("UTF-8"));
} catch (UnsupportedEncodingException e) {
    e.printStackTrace();
}
```

```java
        // wait until unfinished records are processed
        while (kinesisProducer.getOutstandingRecordsCount()
        > 1e4) {
            Thread.sleep(1);
        }

        // write data to Kinesis stream
        ListenableFuture<UserRecordResult> f =
                kinesisProducer.addUserRecord(streamName,
                TIMESTAMP_AS_PARTITION_KEY, data);

        Futures.addCallback(f, myCallback, callbackThreadPool);

    }

    @Override
    public void stop() {
        if (kinesisProducer != null) {
            kinesisProducer.flushSync();
            kinesisProducer.destroy();
        }

    }

}
```

6: Create the producer function. This is the critical function that will be exposed to post data into Kinesis; see Listing 4-11.

Listing 4-11. ProducerFunction.java

```java
import com.fasterxml.jackson.core.JsonProcessingException;
import com.fasterxml.jackson.databind.ObjectMapper;
import org.springframework.beans.factory.annotation.Autowired;

import java.util.function.Function;
```

```java
public class ProducerFunction implements
Function<TrackDetail,String> {
    @Autowired
    private ProducerService producerService;
    @Override
    public String apply(TrackDetail trackDetail) {
        ObjectMapper mapper = new ObjectMapper();
        String data = "";
        try {
            data = mapper.writeValueAsString(trackDetail);
            producerService.putDataIntoKinesis(data);
        } catch (JsonProcessingException e) {
            e.printStackTrace();
        } catch (Exception e) {
            e.printStackTrace();
        }
        return "Saved data into Kinesis successfully!";
    }
}
```

7: Run the function; see Figure 4-25.

```
2022-09-15 14:02:49.574  INFO 3048 --- [           main] o.s.b.w.embedded.tomcat.TomcatWebServer  : Tomcat started on port(s): 8080 (http) with context path ''
2022-09-15 14:02:49.581  INFO 3048 --- [           main] c.e.kinesis_scf.KinesisScfApplication    : Started KinesisScfApplication in 1.847 seconds (JVM running for 2
2022-09-15 14:02:53.763  INFO 3048 --- [nio-8080-exec-1] o.a.c.c.C.[Tomcat].[localhost].[/]       : Initializing Spring DispatcherServlet 'dispatcherServlet'
2022-09-15 14:02:53.764  INFO 3048 --- [nio-8080-exec-1] o.s.web.servlet.DispatcherServlet        : Initializing Servlet 'dispatcherServlet'
2022-09-15 14:02:53.764  INFO 3048 --- [nio-8080-exec-1] o.s.web.servlet.DispatcherServlet        : Completed initialization in 0 ms
2022-09-15 14:02:58.970  INFO 3048 --- [pool-4-thread-1] c.e.kinesis_scf.ProducerServiceImpl      : Data writing success. Total time taken to write data = 5053
```

Figure 4-25. *Successful run of the function*

8: Test with Postman. Run a POST-based test against ProducerFunction to publish data into Kinesis.

Add text that introduces and gives context to Figure 4-26.

Figure 4-26. Postman test

You will get a message that the data is saved.

9: Check Kinesis for data. This information can be found on the Kinesis dashboard under Monitoring, as shown in Figure 4-27.

Figure 4-27. Kinesis dashboard showing the data metrics

10: Run Glue manually. From the Glue Studio, start the process by clicking Run, as shown in Figure 4-24.

Figure 4-28. *The Glue job run*

The job starts to run, as shown in Figure 4-28. Check the s3 bucket for any data.

In this section, you learned how to create a Spring Cloud Function that can post data into AWS Kinesis that is part of the data pipeline. You learned that you can publish data into Kinesis and trigger the AWS Glue pipeline manually, but I also encourage you to explore other ways you can implement Spring Cloud Function for AWS Glue, such as creating and deploying triggers. More information on how to create AWS Glue triggers in Spring is available at https://docs.aws.amazon.com/sdk-for-java/latest/developer-guide/examples-glue.html.

4.4. Spring Cloud Function and Google Cloud Dataflow

Google Cloud Dataflow is very similar to Spring Cloud Data Flow, in that it allows you to wire up a data pipeline with a source, processor, and sink. The Dataflow product is easier to develop with. You can read about Dataflow and its capabilities at https://cloud.google.com/dataflow.

For the example in this section, you will create a dataflow that includes cloud pub/sub:

Spring Cloud Function ➤Dataflow {Cloud Pub/Sub ➤ Cloud Storage}

Prerequisites:

- Subscription to Google Data Flow

- A cloud pub/sub instance

- A cloud storage bucket

- Code from GitHub at `https://github.com/banup-kubeforce/GooglePubSub`

Step 1: Create and configure a cloud pub/sub instance.

Before coming to this step, ensure that you are subscribed to cloud pub/sub. Also ensure that you have proper subscriptions to the APIs.

Navigate to Cloud Pub/Sub console in your subscription to create a topic. See Figure 4-29.

Figure 4-29. *Cloud Pub/Sub with a topic*

Step 2: Create and configure a bucket in cloud storage. Create a cloud storage instance and bucket. I created a bucket called `vehiclebucket1` to store the file coming from cloud pub/sub; see Figure 4-30.

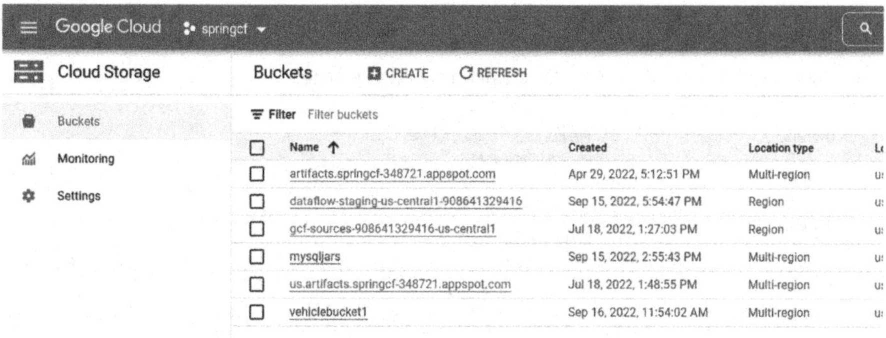

Figure 4-30. *Google Cloud Storage with vehiclebucket1*

Now you are ready to build the Dataflow data pipeline.

Step 3: Create a data pipeline. Navigate to the Dataflow dashboard and create a pipeline. I created a pipeline using a prebuilt template.

1: Pick the template

This example uses the Pub/Sub to Text Files on Cloud Storage template, as shown in Figure 4-31.

Figure 4-31.   *Create a data pipeline from the template*

2: Set the parameters for pub/sub and cloud storage.

You will be able to pick the topic that you created in Step 1 and the bucket in Step 2. See Figure 4-32.

Figure 4-32. *Complete the parameters set up for Dataflow*

3: Verify the creation of the data pipeline.

You can see from Figure 4-33 that a data pipeline has been created.

Figure 4-33. *Successful creation of vehicledatapipeline*

An associated job will also be created, as shown in Figure 4-34.

Figure 4-34. *An associated job is created*

You can find a graphical representation of the job by drilling further into the URL of the job, as shown in Figure 4-35.

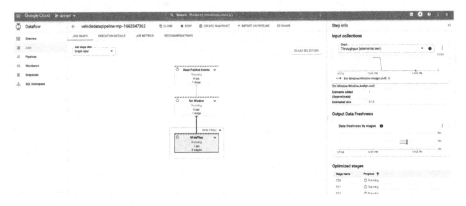

Figure 4-35. *Execution of the pipeline*

Figure 4-36. *The bucket shows the posted document*

<u>Step 4:</u> Create the Spring Cloud Function.

In this Spring Cloud Function, you create the following classes:

- `MessageEntity` class to formulate the message

- `TrackDetail` class as the entity class

- `PubSubPublisher` class that subscribes to the topic and publishes data

- `ProducerFunction` class to implement the Spring Cloud Function

Prerequisites:

- Maven dependencies

You need to add `spring-cloud-gcp-starter-pubsub` and `spring-integration-core` in addition to `spring-cloud-function-web`; see Listing 4-12.

Listing 4-12. Maven Dependencies

```
<dependencies>
    <dependency>
        <groupId>org.springframework.boot</groupId>
        <artifactId>spring-boot-starter-web</artifactId>
    </dependency>
    <dependency>
        <groupId>org.springframework.cloud</groupId>
        <artifactId>spring-cloud-function-web</artifactId>
    </dependency>
    <!-- [START pubsub_spring_boot_starter] -->
    <!-- [START pubsub_spring_integration] -->
    <dependency>
        <groupId>com.google.cloud</groupId>
        <artifactId>spring-cloud-gcp-starter-pubsub
        </artifactId>
        <version>3.3.0</version>
    </dependency>
    <!-- [END pubsub_spring_boot_starter] -->
    <dependency>
        <groupId>org.springframework.integration</groupId>
        <artifactId>spring-integration-core</artifactId>
    </dependency>
    <!-- [END pubsub_spring_integration] -->
    <dependency>
```

```xml
    <dependency>
        <groupId>org.springframework.boot</groupId>
        <artifactId>spring-boot-starter-test</artifactId>
        <scope>test</scope>
    </dependency>
  </dependencies>
```

The Application.properties file is shown in Listing 4-13.

Listing 4-13. application.properties

```
spring.cloud.function.definition=producerFunction
spring.cloud.gcp.project-id=springcf-348721
spring.cloud.gcp.credentials.location=file:C://Users//banua//
Downloads//application_default_credentials.json

pubsub.topic=projects/springcf-348721/topics/vehicletopic
```

1: Create the MessageEntity **class.**
    Store the message with a timestamp, as shown in Listing 4-14.

Listing 4-14. MessageEntity.java

```java
package com.kubeforce.googlepubsub;

import java.time.LocalDateTime;

public class MessageEntity {

    private final LocalDateTime timestamp;
    private final String message;

    public MessageEntity(LocalDateTime timestamp, String
    message) {
        this.timestamp = timestamp;
        this.message = message;
    }
```

```java
public LocalDateTime getTimestamp() {
    return timestamp;
}

public String getMessage() {
    return message;
}
}
```

2: Create the TrackDetail **class.**

The TrackDetail class will have three fields—vehicleId, driverId, and driverName; see Listing 4-15.

Listing 4-15. TrackDetail.java

```java
package com.kubeforce.googlepubsub;

public class TrackDetail {
    private String vehicleId;
    private String driverId;
    private String driverName;

    public String getVehicleId() {
        return vehicleId;
    }

    public void setVehicleId(String vehicleId) {
        this.vehicleId = vehicleId;
    }

    public String getDriverId() {
        return driverId;
    }
```

```
public void setDriverId(String driverId) {
    this.driverId = driverId;
}

public String getDriverName() {
    return driverName;
}

public void setDriverName(String driverName) {
    this.driverName = driverName;
}
```

3: Create the PubSubPublisher.

The PubSubPublisher will use the topic defined in application.
properties to send messages; see Listing 4-16.

Listing 4-16. PubSubPublisher.java

```
package com.kubeforce.googlepubsub;

import com.google.cloud.spring.pubsub.core.PubSubTemplate;

import org.springframework.beans.factory.annotation.Value;
import org.springframework.stereotype.Component;

@Component
public class PubSubPublisher {

    private final String topic;
    private final PubSubTemplate pubSubTemplate;
    public PubSubPublisher(
            @Value("${pubsub.topic}") String topic,
            PubSubTemplate pubSubTemplate) {
        this.topic = topic;
        this.pubSubTemplate = pubSubTemplate;
    }
```

```
public void publish(String payload) {
    pubSubTemplate.publish(topic, payload);
  }
}
```

4: Create the Spring Cloud Function.

The ProducerFunction will use the topic defined in application. properties to send messages. See Listing 4-17.

Listing 4-17. ProducerFunction.java

```
package com.kubeforce.googlepubsub;

import com.fasterxml.jackson.core.JsonProcessingException;
import com.fasterxml.jackson.databind.ObjectMapper;
import org.springframework.beans.factory.annotation.Autowired;

import java.time.LocalDateTime;
import java.util.function.Function;

public class ProducerFunction implements
Function<TrackDetail,String> {
    @Autowired
    private PubSubPublisher publisher;

    @Override
    public String apply(TrackDetail trackDetail) {
        ObjectMapper mapper = new ObjectMapper();
        String data = "";
        try {
            data = mapper.writeValueAsString(trackDetail);

            MessageEntity entity = new
            MessageEntity(LocalDateTime.now(), data);
            publisher.publish(data);
```

```
        } catch (JsonProcessingException e) {
            e.printStackTrace();
        } catch (Exception e) {
            e.printStackTrace();
        }
        return "Saved data into Kinesis successfully!";
    }
}
```

5: Run the application and test if a message is published to Cloud Pub/Sub.

Go to the Pub/Sub console in your Google Cloud console and verify that the message has been posted; see Figure 4-37.

Figure 4-37. *The message has been posted in Cloud Pub/Sub*

6: Verify is the message has been loaded into Cloud Storage.

Navigate to the Cloud Storage console in your Google Cloud to verify that the message has been loaded; see Figure 4-38.

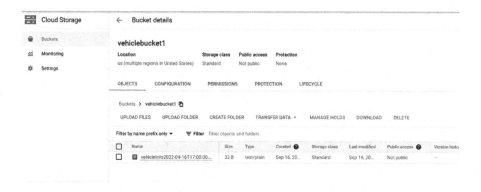

Figure 4-38. *The message is loaded into Cloud Storage*

In this section, you learned how to use Spring Cloud Function to trigger a Google Cloud Dataflow-based data pipeline.

4.5. Summary

This chapter explained how to create dataflow and data pipelines, whether on-premises using SCDF or in the cloud. For the cloud, you can use SCDF or cloud-native tools.

Spring Cloud Function is versatile and can be used in the context of data pipelines as a trigger or as part of the flow.

With AWS Glue and Google Data Flow, you saw that you can use Spring Cloud Function as a trigger for the flows. This requires some additional coding by adding some relevant libraries and invoking the flow.

Upcoming chapters discuss other use cases of Spring Cloud Function.

## CHAPTER 5

AI/ML Trained Serverless Endpoints with Spring Cloud Function

This chapter looks at how Spring Cloud Function can be leveraged in AI/ML. You learn about the AI/ML process and learn where Spring Cloud Function fits in the process. You also learn about some of the offerings from the cloud providers, such as AWS, Google, and Azure.

Before delving into the details of Spring Cloud Function implementation, you need to understand the AI/ML process. This will set the stage for implementing Spring Cloud Function.

5.1. AI/ML in a Nutshell

AI/ML is gaining popularity, as it is being offered by almost all cloud providers. For AI/ML to work properly, it is important to understand the process behind it. See Figure 5-1.

© Banu Parasuraman 2023
B. Parasuraman, *Practical Spring Cloud Function*,
https://doi.org/10.1007/978-1-4842-8913-6_5

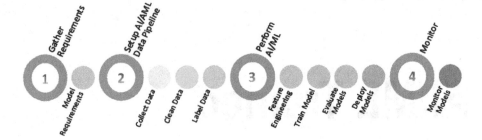

Figure 5-1. *ML lifecycle*

Let's dig deeper into the process depicted in Figure 5-1 and see what is accomplished.

1) Gathering requirements

- Model requirements

This is an important step in the AI/ML process. This determines the ultimate success or failure of the AI/ML model activity. The requirements for models must match the business objectives.

- What is the return on investment (ROI) expected from this activity?

- What are the objectives? Examples may include reduce manufacturing costs, reduce equipment failures, or improve operator productivity.

- What are the features that need to be included in the model?

- In character recognition, it can be histograms counting the number of black pixels along horizontal and vertical directions, the number of internal holes, and so on.

- In speech recognition, it can be recognizing phonemes.

- In computer vision, it can be a lot of features such as objects, edges, shape size, depth, and so on.

2) Setting up the data pipeline

- Data collection

  i.   What datasets to integrate

  ii. What are the sources

  iii. Are the datasets available

- Data cleaning: This activity involves removing inaccurate or noisy records from the dataset. This may include fixing spelling and syntax errors, standardizing datasets, removing empty fields, and removing duplicate data. 45 percent of a data scientist's time is spent on cleaning data (https://analyticsindiamag.com/data-scientists-spend-45-of-their-time-in-data-wrangling/).

- Data labeling: Tagging or labeling raw data such as images, videos, text, audio, and so on, is an important part of the AI/ML activity. This makes the data meaningful and allows the machine learning model to identify a particular class of objects. This helps a lot in the supervised learning activities such as image classification, image segmentation, and so on.

3) Performing the AI/ML tasks

- Feature engineering: This refers to all activities that are performed to extract and select features for machine learning models. This includes the use of domain knowledge to select and transform the most relevant variables from raw data to create predictive models. The goal of feature engineering is to improve the performance of machine learning algorithms. The success or failure of the predictive model is determined by feature engineering and ensure that the model will be comprehensible to humans.

- Train model: In this step the machine learning algorithm is fed with sufficient training data to learn from. The training model dataset consists of sample output data and the corresponding sets of input data that influence the output. This is a iterative process that takes the input data through the algorithm and correlates it against the sample output. The result is then used to modify the model. This iterative process is called "model fitting" until the model precision meets the goals.

- Model evaluation: This process involves using metrics to understand the model's performance, including its strengths and weaknesses. For example, doing a classification prediction, the metrics can include true positives, true negatives, false positives, and false negatives. Other derived metrics can be accuracy, precision, and recall. Model evaluation allows you to determine how well the model is doing, the usefulness of the model, how additional model training will improve performance, and whether you should include more features.

- Deploy model: This process involves deploying a model to a live environment. These models can then be exposed to other processes through the method of model serving. The deployment of models can involve a process of storing the models in a store such as Google Cloud Storage.

4) Monitoring the AI/ML models

In this process, you want to make sure that the model is working properly and that the model predictions are effective. The reason you need to monitor model is that models may degrade over time due to these factors:

- Variance in deployed data

- Variance refers to the sensitivity of the learning algorithms to the training dataset. Every time you try to fit a model, the output parameters may vary ever so slightly, which will alter the predictions. In a production environment where the model has been deployed, these variances may have a significant impact if they're not corrected in time.

- Changes in data integrity

- Machine learning data is dynamic and requires tweaking to ensure the right data is supplied to the model. There are three types of data integrity problems—missing values, range violations, and type mismatches. Constant monitoring and management of these types of issues is important for a good operational ML.

- Data drift

- Data drift occurs when the training dataset does not match the data output in production.

- Concept drift

- Concept drift is the change in relationships between input and output data over time. For example, when you are trying to predict consumer purchasing behavior, the behavior may be influenced by factors other than what you specified in the model. factors that are not explicitly used in the model prediction are called hidden contexts.

Let's evaluate these activities from a compute perspective. This will allow us to determine what kind of compute elements we can assign to these process

Some of the activities in this process are short lived and some are long running process. For example, deploying models and accessing the deployed models is a short lived process. While Training models and model evaluation require both a manual and programmatic intervention and will take a lot of processing time.

Table 5-1 shows the type of compute that can be applied to the processes. Some of the processes are manual.

Table 5-1. *Where to Use Spring Cloud Function in the AI/ML Process*

AI/ML Process	Human	Compute	
		Spring Cloud Function (Short Run)	Batch (Long Run)
Model requirements	Human/ manual process		
Collect data		Integration triggers, data pipeline sources or sinks	Data pipeline process-Transformation
Data cleaning		Integration triggers	Transformation process
Data labeling		Tagging discrete elements-updates, deletes	Bulk tagging
Feature engineering	Manual		
Train model		Trigger for training	Training process
Model evaluation	Manual	Triggers for evaluation	Bulk evaluation
Deploy models Monitoring models		Model serving, model alerts	Bulk storage

AI/ML processes require varying compute and storage requirements. Depending on the model size, the time taken to train, the complexity of the model, and so on, the process may require different compute and storage at different times. So, the environment should be scalable. In earlier days, AI/ML activities were conducted with a fixed infrastructure, through over-allocated VMs, dedicated bare metal servers, or parallel or

205

concurrent processing units. This made the whole process costly and it was left to companies with deep pockets to be able to conduct proper AI/ML activities.

Today, with all the cloud providers providing some level of AI/ML activities through an API or SaaS approach, and with the ability to pay per use or pay as you go, companies small and big have begun to utilize AI/ML in their compute activities.

Paradigms such as cloud functions make it even easier to take advantage of a scalable platform offered by the cloud. Activities such as model storage and retrieval can be done on demand with cloud functions. Serving pre-trained models is easy through cloud functions and these models can be made available to any client without the need to install client libraries. Here are some of the advantages of cloud functions in AI/ML:

- Codeless inference makes getting started easy

- Scalable infrastructure

- No management of infrastructure required

- Separate storage for the model, which is very convenient for tracking versions of the model and for comparing their performance

- Cost structure allows you to pay per use

- Ability to use different frameworks

5.1.1. Deciding Between Java and Python or Other Languages for AI/ML

Most of the popular frameworks such as TensorFlow are written in Python, so the models' outputs are also Python based. Therefore, it's easy for anyone working on AI/ML to code in Python. See Figure 5-2.

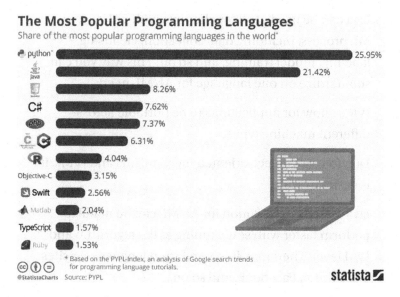

The Most Popular Programming Languages

Share of the most popular programming languages in the world*

python*	25.95%
Java	21.42%
	8.26%
C#	7.62%
php	7.37%
C	6.31%
R	4.04%
Objective-C	3.15%
Swift	2.56%
Matlab	2.04%
TypeScript	1.57%
Ruby	1.53%

* Based on the PYPL-Index, an analysis of Google search trends for programming language tutorials.

@StatistaCharts   Source: PYPL

statista

Figure 5-2. AI/ML language popularity

It is very important to understand that the popularity of a language does not equate to it being a good, robust, secure language for use in AI/ML.

There are several reasons to choose Java over Python or R:

- Enterprises have standardized on Java, so they prefer to have their AI/ML platform written in Java to ease the integration into existing systems.

- Apache.org , the open source community for Java, is very robust and has many libraries and tools that have been tuned toward speed of compute, data processing, and so on. Tools such as Hadoop, Hive, and Spark are integral to the AI/ML process. Developers can easily use these tools and libraries in their java code.

- Java can be used at all touchpoints in the AI/ML process, including data collection, cleansing, labeling, model training, and so on. This way you can standardize on one language for AI/ML needs.

- JVMs allow for applications to be portable across different machine types.

- Due to Java's object-oriented mechanisms and JVMs, it is easier to scale.

- Java-based computation for AI/ML can be made to perform faster with some tuning at the algorithm and JVM level. Therefore, it is a preferred language for sites like Twitter, Facebook, and so on.

- Java is a strong typing programming language, meaning developers must be explicit and specific about variables and types of data.

- Finally, production codebases are often written in Java. If you want to build an enterprise-grade application, Java is the preferred language.

Since Java is a preferred enterprise language for AI/ML, we can safely say that Spring Cloud Function is a better framework to use when developing enterprise-grade functions for AI/ML.

This chapter explores the different offerings from the different cloud providers and explains how you can use Spring Cloud Function with these offerings.

5.2. Spring Framework and AI/ML

A lot of frameworks have been developed in Java that can be leveraged using the Spring Framework. The latest of these frameworks was developed by AWS and is called DJL (Deep Java Library). This library can integrate with PyTorch, TensorFlow, Apache MXNet, ONNX, Python, and TFLite based models.

One of the important capabilities that you need is model serving, where you can leverage Spring Cloud Function to serve trained models, and DJL provides this capability out of the box. It's called djl-serving.

Spring Cloud Function is unique in its ability to transcend the on-premises and cloud, especially in the realm of AI/ML. Even though cloud has become popular, not all companies have fully transitioned to the cloud. Most of them in fact have adopted a hybrid approach. Some of the applications and data still reside in the company-owned datacenters or are co-hosted in datacenters operated by third-party service providers. AI/ML activities revolving the data that is residing in the datacenters will need to have models that are trained and stored and be served using cloud functions that can be hosted in the datacenter. Cloud functions hosted in the datacenter are nearer to their data and therefore have better performance than cloud functions that are hosted in the cloud and access models that are trained and stored in the on-premises datacenters. This is where Spring Cloud Function can help serve models on-premises. See Figure 5-3.

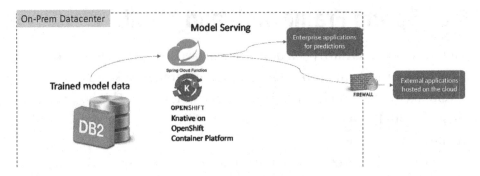

Figure 5-3. *On-premises and Spring Cloud Function deployment for model serving*

5.3. Model Serving with Spring Cloud Function with DJL

Before you explore the cloud provider's option, it's a good idea try this out locally. To do that, you need a framework installed and access to a good tensor model and an image. The framework that you use in this example is called djl-serving.

5.3.1. What Is DJL?

Deep Java Library (DJL) https://docs.djl.ai/ is a high-level, engine-agnostic Java framework for deep learning. It allows you to connect to any framework like TensorFlow or PyTorch and conduct AI/ML activities from Java.

DJL has also great hooks to Spring Boot and can easily be invoked through the Spring Framework. DJL acts as an abstraction layer across frameworks and makes it easy to interact with those frameworks, as shown in Figure 5-4.

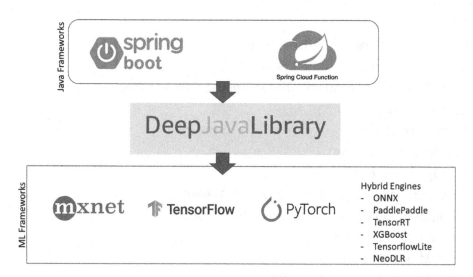

Figure 5-4. *Deep Java Library (DJL) layers*

There are many components in DJL that are useful to look at, but the DJL serving is interesting.

Run the following commands to get the dj1-serving bits. Then unzip the file into your directory of choice and set the path to the serving.bat located at ~\serving-0.19.0\bin\serving.bat. This will allow you to execute serving from anywhere on your machine.

```
curl -O https://publish.djl.ai/djl-serving/serving-0.19.0.zip
unzip serving-0.19.0.zip
```

Listing 5-1 shows a sample run of dj1-serving with a TensorFlow model.

Listing 5-1. djl-serving Run with a Tensorflow Model

```
# Load a TensorFlow model from TFHub

C:\Users\banua>serving -m "resnet=https://tfhub.dev/tensorflow/
resnet_50/classification/1"
[INFO ] - Starting djl-serving: 0.19.0 ...
```

```
[INFO ] -
Model server home: C:\Users\banua
Current directory: C:\Users\banua
Temp directory: C:\Users\banua\AppData\Local\Temp\
Command line:
Number of CPUs: 16
Max heap size: 8114
Config file: N/A
Inference address: http://127.0.0.1:8080
Management address: http://127.0.0.1:8080
Default job_queue_size: 1000
Default batch_size: 1
Default max_batch_delay: 300
Default max_idle_time: 60
Model Store: N/A
Initial Models: resnet=https://tfhub.dev/tensorflow/resnet_50/
classification/1
Initial Workflows: N/A
Netty threads: 0
Maximum Request Size: 67108864
[INFO ] - Initializing model: resnet=https://tfhub.dev/
tensorflow/resnet_50/classification/1
[INFO ] - Downloading https://publish.djl.ai/tensorflow-2.7.0/
win/cpu/api-ms-win-core-synch-l1-2-0.dll.gz ...
[INFO ] - Downloading https://publish.djl.ai/tensorflow-2.7.0/
win/cpu/api-ms-win-core-file-l1-2-0.dll.gz ...
[INFO ] - Downloading https://publish.djl.ai/tensorflow-2.7.0/
win/cpu/THIRD_PARTY_TF_JNI_LICENSES.gz ...
[INFO ] - Downloading https://publish.djl.ai/tensorflow-2.7.0/
win/cpu/api-ms-win-core-file-l1-1-0.dll.gz ...
[INFO ] - Downloading https://publish.djl.ai/tensorflow-2.7.0/
win/cpu/api-ms-win-crt-environment-l1-1-0.dll.gz ...
```

```
[INFO ] - Downloading https://publish.djl.ai/tensorflow-2.7.0/
win/cpu/api-ms-win-core-synch-l1-1-0.dll.gz ...
[INFO ] - Downloading https://publish.djl.ai/tensorflow-2.7.0/
win/cpu/api-ms-win-core-string-l1-1-0.dll.gz ...
[INFO ] - Downloading https://publish.djl.ai/tensorflow-2.7.0/
win/cpu/api-ms-win-core-memory-l1-1-0.dll.gz ...
[INFO ] - Downloading https://publish.djl.ai/tensorflow-2.7.0/
win/cpu/msvcp140.dll.gz ...
[INFO ] - Downloading https://publish.djl.ai/tensorflow-2.7.0/
win/cpu/api-ms-win-core-util-l1-1-0.dll.gz ...
[INFO ] - Downloading https://publish.djl.ai/tensorflow-2.7.0/
win/cpu/api-ms-win-core-datetime-l1-1-0.dll.gz ...
[INFO ] - Downloading https://publish.djl.ai/tensorflow-2.7.0/
win/cpu/vcruntime140.dll.gz ...
[INFO ] - Downloading https://publish.djl.ai/tensorflow-2.7.0/
win/cpu/concrt140.dll.gz ...
[INFO ] - Downloading https://publish.djl.ai/tensorflow-2.7.0/
win/cpu/api-ms-win-core-sysinfo-l1-1-0.dll.gz ...
[INFO ] - Downloading https://publish.djl.ai/tensorflow-2.7.0/
win/cpu/ucrtbase.dll.gz ...
[INFO ] - Downloading https://publish.djl.ai/tensorflow-2.7.0/
win/cpu/api-ms-win-core-interlocked-l1-1-0.dll.gz ...
[INFO ] - Downloading https://publish.djl.ai/tensorflow-2.7.0/
win/cpu/api-ms-win-core-processenvironment-l1-1-0.dll.gz ...
[INFO ] - Downloading https://publish.djl.ai/tensorflow-2.7.0/
win/cpu/api-ms-win-core-file-l2-1-0.dll.gz ...
[INFO ] - Downloading https://publish.djl.ai/tensorflow-2.7.0/
win/cpu/tensorflow_cc.dll.gz ...
[INFO ] - Downloading https://publish.djl.ai/tensorflow-2.7.0/
win/cpu/libiomp5md.dll.gz ...
[INFO ] - Downloading https://publish.djl.ai/tensorflow-2.7.0/
win/cpu/vcomp140.dll.gz ...
```

```
[INFO ] - Downloading https://publish.djl.ai/tensorflow-2.7.0/
win/cpu/api-ms-win-core-timezone-l1-1-0.dll.gz ...
[INFO ] - Downloading https://publish.djl.ai/tensorflow-2.7.0/
win/cpu/jnitensorflow.dll.gz ...
[INFO ] - Downloading https://publish.djl.ai/tensorflow-2.7.0/
win/cpu/api-ms-win-crt-convert-l1-1-0.dll.gz ...
[INFO ] - Downloading https://publish.djl.ai/tensorflow-2.7.0/
win/cpu/api-ms-win-core-errorhandling-l1-1-0.dll.gz ...
[INFO ] - Downloading https://publish.djl.ai/tensorflow-2.7.0/
win/cpu/api-ms-win-core-namedpipe-l1-1-0.dll.gz ...
[INFO ] - Downloading https://publish.djl.ai/tensorflow-2.7.0/
win/cpu/api-ms-win-crt-math-l1-1-0.dll.gz ...
[INFO ] - Downloading https://publish.djl.ai/tensorflow-2.7.0/
win/cpu/api-ms-win-crt-locale-l1-1-0.dll.gz ...
[INFO ] - Downloading https://publish.djl.ai/tensorflow-2.7.0/
win/cpu/api-ms-win-crt-heap-l1-1-0.dll.gz ...
[INFO ] - Downloading https://publish.djl.ai/tensorflow-2.7.0/
win/cpu/api-ms-win-core-profile-l1-1-0.dll.gz ...
[INFO ] - Downloading https://publish.djl.ai/tensorflow-2.7.0/
win/cpu/LICENSE.gz ...
[INFO ] - Downloading https://publish.djl.ai/tensorflow-2.7.0/
win/cpu/api-ms-win-crt-utility-l1-1-0.dll.gz ...
[INFO ] - Downloading https://publish.djl.ai/tensorflow-2.7.0/
win/cpu/api-ms-win-core-heap-l1-1-0.dll.gz ...
[INFO ] - Downloading https://publish.djl.ai/tensorflow-2.7.0/
win/cpu/api-ms-win-core-localization-l1-2-0.dll.gz ...
[INFO ] - Downloading https://publish.djl.ai/tensorflow-2.7.0/
win/cpu/api-ms-win-core-debug-l1-1-0.dll.gz ...
[INFO ] - Downloading https://publish.djl.ai/tensorflow-2.7.0/
win/cpu/api-ms-win-core-processthreads-l1-1-1.dll.gz ...
[INFO ] - Downloading https://publish.djl.ai/tensorflow-2.7.0/
win/cpu/api-ms-win-core-libraryloader-l1-1-0.dll.gz ...
```

```
[INFO ] - Downloading https://publish.djl.ai/tensorflow-2.7.0/
win/cpu/api-ms-win-crt-time-l1-1-0.dll.gz ...
[INFO ] - Downloading https://publish.djl.ai/tensorflow-2.7.0/
win/cpu/api-ms-win-core-rtlsupport-l1-1-0.dll.gz ...
[INFO ] - Downloading https://publish.djl.ai/tensorflow-2.7.0/
win/cpu/api-ms-win-crt-runtime-l1-1-0.dll.gz ...
[INFO ] - Downloading https://publish.djl.ai/tensorflow-2.7.0/
win/cpu/api-ms-win-crt-stdio-l1-1-0.dll.gz ...
[INFO ] - Downloading https://publish.djl.ai/tensorflow-2.7.0/
win/cpu/api-ms-win-core-console-l1-1-0.dll.gz ...
[INFO ] - Downloading https://publish.djl.ai/tensorflow-2.7.0/
win/cpu/vcruntime140_1.dll.gz ...
[INFO ] - Downloading https://publish.djl.ai/tensorflow-2.7.0/
win/cpu/api-ms-win-core-processthreads-l1-1-0.dll.gz ...
[INFO ] - Downloading https://publish.djl.ai/tensorflow-2.7.0/
win/cpu/api-ms-win-core-handle-l1-1-0.dll.gz ...
[INFO ] - Downloading https://publish.djl.ai/tensorflow-2.7.0/
win/cpu/api-ms-win-crt-filesystem-l1-1-0.dll.gz ...
[INFO ] - Downloading https://publish.djl.ai/tensorflow-2.7.0/
win/cpu/api-ms-win-crt-multibyte-l1-1-0.dll.gz ...
[INFO ] - Downloading https://publish.djl.ai/tensorflow-2.7.0/
win/cpu/api-ms-win-crt-string-l1-1-0.dll.gz ...
2022-09-21 12:09:38.465035: I external/org_tensorflow/
tensorflow/core/platform/cpu_feature_guard.cc:151] This
TensorFlow binary is optimized with oneAPI Deep Neural Network
Library (oneDNN) to use the following CPU instructions in
performance-critical operations:  AVX2
To enable them in other operations, rebuild TensorFlow with the
appropriate compiler flags.
[INFO ] - initWorkers for resnet (cpu()): -1, -1
[INFO ] - Loading model resnet on cpu()
```

```
2022-09-21 12:09:38.595923: I external/org_tensorflow/
tensorflow/cc/saved_model/reader.cc:43] Reading SavedModel
from: C:\Users\banua\.djl.ai\cache\repo\model\undefined\ai\djl\
localmodelzoo\ffdb59c80e9d66dc0ce00e409e06e710
2022-09-21 12:09:38.641647: I external/org_tensorflow/
tensorflow/cc/saved_model/reader.cc:107] Reading meta graph
with tags { serve }
2022-09-21 12:09:38.641933: I external/org_tensorflow/
tensorflow/cc/saved_model/reader.cc:148] Reading
SavedModel debug info (if present) from: C:\Users\banua\.
djl.ai\cache\repo\model\undefined\ai\djl\localmodelzoo\
ffdb59c80e9d66dc0ce00e409e06e710
2022-09-21 12:09:38.837590: I external/org_tensorflow/
tensorflow/cc/saved_model/loader.cc:210] Restoring
SavedModel bundle.
2022-09-21 12:09:39.330251: I external/org_tensorflow/
tensorflow/cc/saved_model/loader.cc:194] Running initialization
op on SavedModel bundle at path: C:\Users\banua\.djl.
ai\cache\repo\model\undefined\ai\djl\localmodelzoo\
ffdb59c80e9d66dc0ce00e409e06e710
2022-09-21 12:09:39.746608: I external/org_tensorflow/
tensorflow/cc/saved_model/loader.cc:283] SavedModel load for
tags { serve }; Status: success: OK. Took 1150043 microseconds.
[INFO ] - scanning for plugins...
[INFO ] - plug-in folder not exists:C:\Users\banua\plugins
[INFO ] - 0 plug-ins found and loaded.
[INFO ] - Initialize BOTH server with: NioServerSocketChannel.
[INFO ] - BOTH API bind to: http://127.0.0.1:8080
[INFO ] - Model server started.
```

On the initial run, the model you specified will be loaded:

```
"resnet=https://tfhub.dev/tensorflow/resnet_50/
classification/1"
```

On subsequent runs, the model server will be available at port 8080 at `http://localhost:8080`.

This example provides an image of kitten and it will try to recognize the kitten by providing output with probabilities:

```
$curl -O https://resources.djl.ai/images/kitten.jpg
```

This will show the image in Figure 5-5.

Figure 5-5. *Image of a kitten for the model to predict*

Next, run the following and you will see the output with probabilities.

You provide the djl-serving instance that is running at `http://localhost:8080/predictions` with the kitten image that is located in the current directory, and you get a response shown in Figure 5-6, which shows that the image is probably a tabby cat. The probability is 0.4107377231121063. This is close.

```
banup@gram01:~$ curl -X POST http://localhost:8080/predictions/resnet18_v1 -T kitten.jpg
[
  {
    "className": "n02123045 tabby, tabby cat",
    "probability": 0.4107377231121063
  },
  {
    "className": "n02124075 Egyptian cat",
    "probability": 0.29393628239631653
  },
  {
    "className": "n02123159 tiger cat",
    "probability": 0.19337038695812225
  },
  {
    "className": "n02123394 Persian cat",
    "probability": 0.04586182162165642
  },
  {
    "className": "n02127052 lynx, catamount",
    "probability": 0.009115186519920826
  }
]
```

Figure 5-6. *DJL results for the image*

Next, you see how you can use DJL to create a Spring Cloud Function to serve models.

5.3.2. Spring Cloud Function with DJL

For this example, we borrow an example from DJL called pneumonia detection. This sample is available at https://github.com/ deepjavalibrary/djl-demo/tree/master/pneumonia-detection.

This example uses an Xray image from https://djlai.s3.amazonaws. com/resources/images/chest_xray.jpg.

218

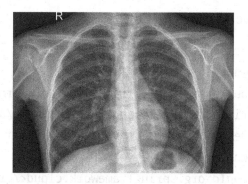

Figure 5-7. *Xray image provided to the saved_model*

It predicts using a model from `https://djl-ai.s3.amazonaws.com/resources/demo/pneumonia-detection-model/saved_model.zip`.

The Spring Cloud Function you create will take an image, load the model, and provide a prediction, as in the cat example.

Prerequisites:

- DJL libraries

- A model: `https://djl-ai.s3.amazonaws.com/resources/demo/pneumonia-detection-model/saved_model.zip`

- The URL of the image to analyze: `https://djl-ai.s3.amazonaws.com/resources/images/chest_xray.jpg`

<u>Step 1:</u> Create the Spring Cloud Function with DJL framework. Add dependencies to the Hadoop file.

Add the DJL highlighted dependencies along with `spring-cloud-function-web` and GCP dependencies, as shown in Listing 5-2.

Listing 5-2. Dependencies for DJL

```
<dependencies>
<dependency>
    <groupId>org.springframework.boot</groupId>
    <artifactId>spring-boot-starter-web</artifactId>
</dependency>
<dependency>
    <groupId>org.springframework.cloud</groupId>
    <artifactId>spring-cloud-function-web</artifactId>
</dependency>
<!-- https://mvnrepository.com/artifact/ai.djl/bom -->
<dependency>
    <groupId>ai.djl</groupId>
    <artifactId>bom</artifactId>
    <version>0.12.0</version>
    <type>pom</type>
</dependency>
<dependency>
    <groupId>ai.djl</groupId>
    <artifactId>api</artifactId>
    <version>0.12.0</version>
</dependency>
<dependency>
    <groupId>ai.djl.tensorflow</groupId>
    <artifactId>tensorflow-api</artifactId>
    <version>0.12.0</version>
</dependency>
<dependency>
    <groupId>ai.djl.tensorflow</groupId>
    <artifactId>tensorflow-engine</artifactId>
    <version>0.12.0</version>
```

```
    </dependency>
    <dependency>
        <groupId>ai.djl.tensorflow</groupId>
        <artifactId>tensorflow-native-auto</artifactId>
        <version>2.4.1</version>
        <scope>runtime</scope>
    </dependency>

    <dependency>
        <groupId>org.projectlombok</groupId>
        <artifactId>lombok</artifactId>
        <optional>true</optional>
    </dependency>
```

Step 2: Create the Spring Cloud Function.

Now create an XRAYFunction that stores a model from the URL provided: https://djl-ai.s3.amazonaws.com/resources/demo/pneumonia-detection-model/saved_model.zip. See Listing 5-3.

Listing 5-3. XRAYFunction.java

```
package com.kubeforce.djlxray;

import ai.djl.inference.Predictor;
import ai.djl.modality.Classifications;
import ai.djl.modality.cv.Image;
import ai.djl.modality.cv.ImageFactory;
import ai.djl.modality.cv.translator.
ImageClassificationTranslator;
import ai.djl.modality.cv.util.NDImageUtils;
import ai.djl.repository.zoo.Criteria;

import ai.djl.repository.zoo.ZooModel;
import ai.djl.translate.Translator;
```

```
import lombok.SneakyThrows;
import org.slf4j.Logger;
import org.slf4j.LoggerFactory;

import java.io.IOException;
import java.util.Arrays;
import java.util.List;
import java.util.Map;
import java.util.function.Function;

public class XRAYFunction implements
Function<Map<String,String>, String> {

    private static final Logger logger = LoggerFactory.getLogger
    (XRAYFunction.class);
    private static final List<String> CLASSES =
    Arrays.asList("Normal", "Pneumonia");
    String imagePath;
    String savedModelPath;

    @SneakyThrows
    @Override
    public String apply(Map<String, String> imageinput) {
            imagePath= imageinput.get("url");
            savedModelPath = imageinput.get("savedmodelpath");
            Image image;
            try {
                image = ImageFactory.getInstance().
                fromUrl(imagePath);
            } catch (IOException e) {
                throw new RuntimeException(e);
            }
            Translator<Image, Classifications> translator =
                    ImageClassificationTranslator.builder()
```

```
                            .addTransform(a -> NDImageUtils.
                            resize(a, 224).div(255.0f))
                            .optSynset(CLASSES)
                            .build();
            Criteria<Image, Classifications> criteria =
                    Criteria.builder()
                            .setTypes(Image.class,
                            Classifications.class)
//                            .optModelUrls("https://djl-ai.
                            s3.amazonaws.com/resources/demo/
                            pneumonia-detection-model/saved_
                            model.zip")
                            .optModelUrls(savedModelPath)
                            .optTranslator(translator)
                            .build();

        try (ZooModel<Image, Classifications> model =
        criteria.loadModel();
            Predictor<Image, Classifications> predictor =
            model.newPredictor()) {
            Classifications result = predictor.
            predict(image);
            logger.info("Diagnose: {}", result);
            return result.toJson();
        }

    }
}
```

Step 3: Test locally. Run the Spring Cloud Function and invoke the endpoint http://localhost:8080/xrayFunction

Provide input:

```
{
"url":"https://djl-ai.s3.amazonaws.com/resources/images/chest_
xray.jpg",
"savedmodelpath":https://djl-ai.s3.amazonaws.com/resources/
demo/pneumonia-detection-model/saved_model.zip
}
```

This is executed in Postman, as shown in Figure 5-8.

Figure 5-8. Testing with a POST in Postman

Upon invoking the function, the model is downloaded and then loaded into memory. This takes about a minute to load, after which it comes back with a successful message. The model took 802066 microseconds (80 seconds) to load, and this is critical for your function calls, as you will have to accommodate for this model-loading time. See Figure 5-9.

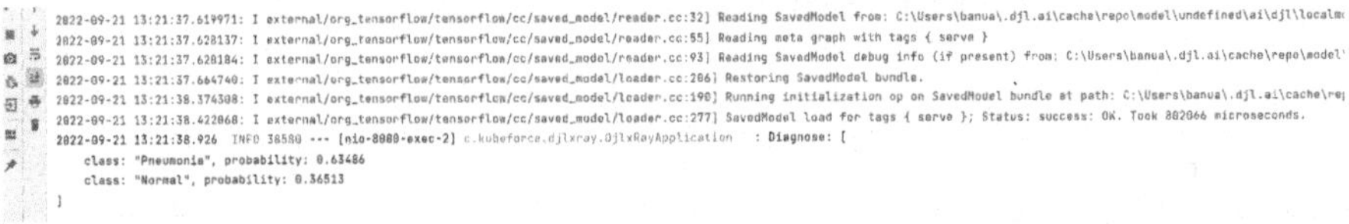

Figure 5-9. Prediction results from the image evaluation

This section successfully demonstrated that Spring Cloud Function can act as a model server in AI/ML. This is a critical function, as you can move the loading and serving of models from traditional servers to a function-based, "pay-per-use" model.

You also learned how to use deep learning Java libraries in your functions. You can deploy this Spring Cloud Function to any cloud, as shown in Chapter 2.

5.4. Model Serving with Spring Cloud Function with Google Cloud Functions and TensorFlow

This section explores the model serving on Google. It uses TensorFlow, which is a Google product from AI/ML and explains how to build and save an AI model with datasets such as MNIST (`https://en.wikipedia.org/wiki/MNIST_database`).

5.4.1. TensorFlow

TensorFlow was developed by Google and is an open source platform for machine learning. It is an interface for expressing and executing machine learning algorithms. The beauty of TensorFlow is that a model expressed in TensorFlow can be executed with minimal changes on mobile devices, laptops, or large-scale systems with multiple GPUs and CPUs. TensorFlow is flexible and can express a lot of algorithms, including training and inference algorithms for deep neural networks, speech recognition, robotics, drug discovery, and so on.

In Figure 5-9, you can see that TensorFlow can be deployed to multiple platforms and has many language interfaces. Unfortunately, TensorFlow is written in Python, so most of the models are written and deployed in Python. This poses a unique challenge for enterprises who have standardized on Java.

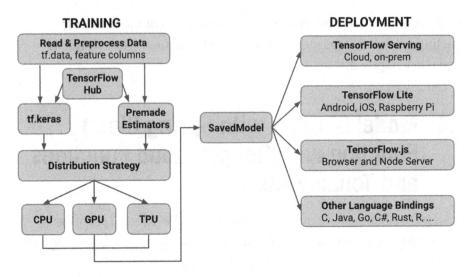

Figure 5-10. *TensorFlow components*[1]

Even though TensorFlow is written in Python, there are lots of frameworks written in Java that work on a saved model.

Let's look at how you can work with TensorFlow on the Google Cloud platform.

Google Cloud provides different approaches to working on models. You can use a container- or Kubernetes-based approach, an SaaS-based approach, or a Cloud Functions-based approach. Each has advantages and disadvantages. Google has published a good guide for you to pick the right platform for your needs, as shown in Table 5-2.

---

[1]Source: https://blog.tensorflow.org/2019/01/whats-coming-in-tensorflow-2-0.html

Table 5-2. *Google and AI/ML Environment[2]*

Feature	Compute Engine	AI Platform Predictions	Cloud Functions
ML frameworks Installation	Pre-loaded TensorFlow and other frameworks when using Deep Learning Images or Deep Learning Containers	Pre-loaded TensorFlow and other frameworks	Installation of libraries is required Libraries are installed via *requirements.txt*
Configuration	Minimal	Simple via UI, CLI or YAML file	Requires developing server code
Infrastructure management	Required	Not required	Not required
Scalability	Scalable infrastructure	Scalable infrastructure via configuration	Scalable infrastructure
Framework support	Latest ML frameworks supported	Pre-defined ML versions supported for inference	Any ML framework for inference
Environment	Production	Production	Experimentation

As you can see from Table 5-2, cloud functions are recommended for experimentation. Google recommends Compute Engine with TF Serving, or its SaaS platform (AI Platform) for predictions for production deployments.

The issue with this approach is that a function-based approach is more than just an experimentation environment. Functions are a way of saving on cost while exposing the serving capabilities for predictions through APIs. It is a serverless approach, so enterprises do not have to worry about scaling.

---

[2] Source: https://cloud.google.com/blog/products/ai-machine-learning/how-to-serve-deep-learning-models-using-tensorflow-2-0-with-cloud-functions

5.4.2. Example Model Training and Serving

In this section you see how to train an AI model locally and upload it to Google Cloud Storage. You will then download the model and test an image through a Cloud Function API. You will use a model that is based on MNIST. More about MNIST can be found at `https://en.wikipedia.org/wiki/MNIST_database`.

In this example, you develop the model in Python and then expose the model through Spring Cloud Function using DJL; see Figure 5-11.

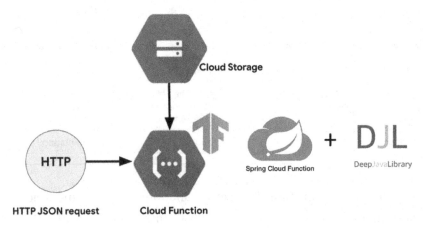

Figure 5-11. *Spring Cloud Function with DJL and TensorFlow*

You use the same example outlined at `https://cloud.google.com/blog/products/ai-machine-learning/how-to-serve-deep-learning-models-using-tensorflow-2-0-with-cloud-functions`. This will allow you to concentrate more on the Spring Cloud Function code that you will be creating rather than the actual implementation in Python.

You will then serve the model using Spring Cloud Function.

Step 1: Install TensorFlow.

```
python3 -m pip install tensorflow
```

<u>Step 2:</u> Create a project. Create a project called MNIST and then create a main.py file with the code in Listing 5-4. I used PyCharm to run this code.

On your Mac, make sure to run this command before running the code; otherwise you will get a certificate error. The code tries to download packages from googleapis:

```
open /Applications/Python\ 3.7/Install\ Certificates.command
```

I ran main.py and the whole process took me 13 minutes. At the end of it, I was able to get two model files as output.

Listing 5-4. main.py

```
from __future__ import absolute_import
from __future__ import division
from __future__ import print_function
from __future__ import unicode_literals

import tensorflow as tf

from tensorflow.keras.layers import Dense, Flatten, Conv2D
from tensorflow.keras import Model

EPOCHS = 10

mnist = tf.keras.datasets.mnist
fashion_mnist = tf.keras.datasets.fashion_mnist

(x_train, y_train), (x_test, y_test) = fashion_mnist.
load_data()
x_train, x_test = x_train / 255.0, x_test / 255.0

# Add a channels dimension e.g. (60000, 28, 28) => (60000,
28, 28, 1)
x_train = x_train[..., tf.newaxis]
x_test = x_test[..., tf.newaxis]
```

```python
train_ds = tf.data.Dataset.from_tensor_slices(
    (x_train, y_train)).shuffle(10000).batch(32)
test_ds = tf.data.Dataset.from_tensor_slices((x_test, y_test)).
batch(32)

class CustomModel(Model):
    def __init__(self):
        super(CustomModel, self).__init__()
        self.conv1 = Conv2D(32, 3, activation='relu')
        self.flatten = Flatten()
        self.d1 = Dense(128, activation='relu')
        self.d2 = Dense(10, activation='softmax')

    def call(self, x):
        x = self.conv1(x)
        x = self.flatten(x)
        x = self.d1(x)
        return self.d2(x)

model = CustomModel()

loss_object = tf.keras.losses.SparseCategoricalCrossentropy()
optimizer = tf.keras.optimizers.Adam()

train_loss = tf.keras.metrics.Mean(name='train_loss')
train_accuracy = tf.keras.metrics.SparseCategoricalAccuracy(nam
e='train_accuracy')

test_loss = tf.keras.metrics.Mean(name='test_loss')
test_accuracy = tf.keras.metrics.SparseCategoricalAccuracy(name
='test_accuracy')

@tf.function
def train_step(images, labels):
    with tf.GradientTape() as tape:
        predictions = model(images)
```

```
    loss = loss_object(labels, predictions)
  gradients = tape.gradient(loss, model.trainable_variables)
  optimizer.apply_gradients(zip(gradients, model.trainable_
  variables))

  train_loss(loss)
  train_accuracy(labels, predictions)

@tf.function
def test_step(images, labels):
    predictions = model(images)
    t_loss = loss_object(labels, predictions)

    test_loss(t_loss)
    test_accuracy(labels, predictions)

for epoch in range(EPOCHS):
    for images, labels in train_ds:
        train_step(images, labels)

    for test_images, test_labels in test_ds:
        test_step(test_images, test_labels)

    template = 'Epoch {}, Loss: {}, Accuracy: {}, Test Loss:
{}, Test Accuracy: {}'
    print(template.format(epoch + 1,
                          train_loss.result(),
                          train_accuracy.result() * 100,
                          test_loss.result(),
                          test_accuracy.result() * 100))

# Save the weights
model.save_weights('fashion_mnist_weights')

tf.saved_model.save(model, export_dir="c://Users//banua//
Downloads/MNIST/models")
```

The key is `tf.saved_model.save(model, export_dir="c://Users//banua//Downloads/MNIST/models")`.

This will save the model so that any model server can use it.

Step 3: Run the project.

Execute `main.py` from the IDE. See Figure 5-12.

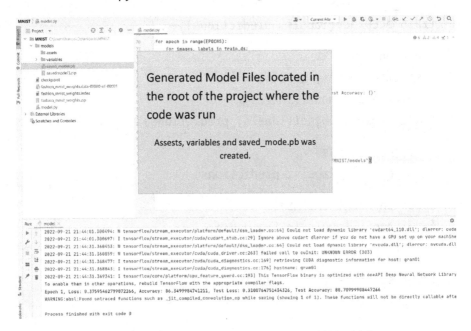

Figure 5-12. *Successful run of MNIST and model building*

Zip the assets, variables, and the `saved_model.pb.` file as `Savedmodel3.zip` and upload it to the Google Cloud Storage.

Step 4: Upload the models into Cloud Storage. Navigate to your Google Cloud Console and subscribe to Cloud Storage. It is available at `cloud.google.com`.

Create a storage bucket in Google Cloud Storage and upload the two files into the storage bucket. Use the defaults for this example. If you are using free credits from Google, this storage should be covered.

I created a bucket called `mnist-soc`. You will use the bucket name in the Cloud Functions call. See Figure 5-13.

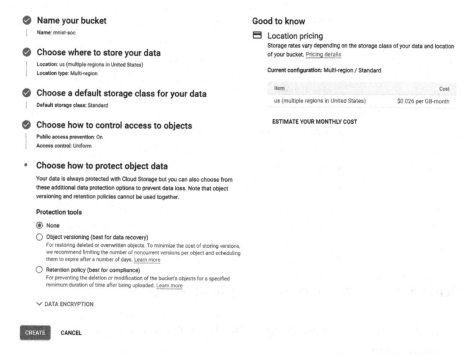

Figure 5-13. *Google Cloud Storage Bucket creation steps*

Name your bucket `mnist-soc` and leave the others set to the defaults; then click Create.

Upload the `savedmodel3.zip` file to this folder by clicking Upload Files. See Figure 5-14.

mnist-soc

⚠   Public to internet: This bucket is publicly accessible because all

Location	Storage class	Public acces
us (multiple regions in United States)	Standard	⚠ Public to

OBJECTS   CONFIGURATION   PERMISSIONS   PRO

Buckets > mnist-soc

UPLOAD FILES   UPLOAD FOLDER   CREATE FOLDER   TRA

Filter by name prefix only ▼   ≡ Filter   Filter objects and folders

Name	Size	Type
fashion_mnist_weights.data-000...	10.6 MB	appli
fashion_mnist_weights.index	515 B	appli
fashion_mnist_weights.zip	9.9 MB	appli
saved_model.zip	366 MB	appli
saved_model2.zip	32.7 KB	appli
savedmodel3.zip	9.9 MB	appli
test.png	391 B	imag

Figure 5-14. Models deployed into Cloud Storage

Click the file to get the details of the URL you need to connect to, as shown in Figure 5-15.

Buckets > mnist-soc > savedmodel3.zip

LIVE OBJECT	VERSION HISTORY

⬇ DOWNLOAD   ✎ EDIT METADATA   ✦ EDIT ACCESS   🗑 DELETE

Overview

Type	application/x-zip-compressed
Size	9.9 MB
Created	Sep 21, 2022, 9:47:45 PM
Last modified	Sep 21, 2022, 9:47:58 PM
Storage class	Standard
Custom time	—
Public URL ❓	https://storage.googleapis.com/mnist-soc/savedmodel3.zip
Authenticated URL ❓	https://storage.cloud.google.com/mnist-soc/savedmodel3.zip?authuser=1
gsutil URI ❓	gs://mnist-soc/savedmodel3.zip

Permissions

Public access	⚠ Public to internet

Protection

Hold status	None ✎
Version history ❓	—
Retention policy	None
Encryption type	Google-managed key

Figure 5-15. *URL for the savedmodel3.zip*

The URL you use for testing this example is https://storage.
googleapis.com/mnist-soc/savedmodel3.zip.

The test image you use for this example is https://storage.
googleapis.com/mnist-soc/test.png.

Note that the function that you created in Section 5.2 will be deployed
in Step 5. If you use savedmodel3.zip and test.png, it will fail. But you will
know that the function is working because you will get an error message
that the model could not be loaded. This is an acceptable outcome for the
model you created.

<u>Step 5:</u> Deploy the Spring Cloud Function to Google Functions. In this step, you take the function you created in Section 5.2 and deploy it into the Google Cloud Functions environment. The prerequisites and steps are the same as discussed in Chapter 2.

Prerequisites:

- Google account

- Subscription to Google Cloud Functions

- Google CLI (This is critical, as it is a more efficient way than going through the Google Portal)

- Code from GitHub at `https://github.com/banup-kubeforce/DJLXRay-GCP.git`

Modify the Spring Cloud Function to fit the Google Cloud Functions environment. See Listing 5-5.

Listing 5-5. Dependencies for GCP Added

```
<dependency>
    <groupId>org.springframework.cloud</groupId>
    <artifactId>spring-cloud-function-adapter-gcp</artifactId>

</dependency>

<dependencyManagement>
        <dependencies>
          <dependency>
              <groupId>org.springframework.cloud</groupId>
              <artifactId>spring-cloud-dependencies
              </artifactId>
              <version>${spring-cloud.version}</version>
              <type>pom</type>
              <scope>import</scope>
```

```xml
            </dependency>
            <dependency>
                <groupId>com.google.cloud</groupId>
                <artifactId>spring-cloud-gcp-dependencies
                </artifactId>
                <version>3.3.0</version>
                <type>pom</type>
                <scope>import</scope>
            </dependency>
        </dependencies>
    </dependencyManagement>
<build>
        <plugins>
            <plugin>
                <groupId>org.springframework.boot</groupId>
                <artifactId>spring-boot-maven-plugin</artifactId>
                <configuration>
                    <outputDirectory>target/deploy
                    </outputDirectory>
                </configuration>
                <dependencies>
                    <dependency>
                        <groupId>org.springframework.cloud
                        </groupId>
                        <artifactId>spring-cloud-function-
                        adapter-gcp</artifactId>
                        <version>3.2.7</version>
                    </dependency>
                </dependencies>
            </plugin>
```

```
<plugin>
    <groupId>com.google.cloud.functions</groupId>
    <artifactId>function-maven-plugin</artifactId>
    <version>0.9.1</version>
    <configuration>
        <functionTarget>org.springframework.cloud.
        function.adapter.gcp.GcfJarLauncher
        </functionTarget>
        <port>8080</port>
    </configuration>
</plugin>
    </plugins>
</build>
```

Deploy the Spring Cloud Function to Google Cloud Functions. Make sure that you build and package before you run the following command. A JAR file must be present in the target/deploy directory in the root of your project.

The saved model that you are going to test with is 400MB, so you have to accommodate this by increasing the memory to 4096 and setting the timeout to 540 seconds:

```
gcloud functions deploy DJLXRay-GCP --entry-point org.
springframework.cloud.function.adapter.gcp.GcfJarLauncher
--runtime java11 --trigger-http --source target/deploy
--memory 4096MB --timeout 540
```

Once this runs successfully, you will get the output shown in Figure 5-16.

```
C:\Users\banua\Downloads\djl-spring-boot-xray-master\DJLXRay-GCP>gcloud functions deploy DJLXRay-GCP --entry-point org.s
pringframework.cloud.function.adapter.gcp.GcfJarLauncher --runtime java11 --trigger-http --source target/deploy --memory
 4096MB --timeout 540
Allow unauthenticated invocations of new function [DJLXRay-GCP]? (y/N)?  y

Deploying function (may take a while - up to 2 minutes)...-
For Cloud Build Logs, visit: https://console.cloud.google.com/cloud-build/builds;region=us-central1/24dfea91-04e7-4fdf-a
300-2161dc3cdabf?project=908641329416
Deploying function (may take a while - up to 2 minutes)...done.
availableMemoryMb: 4096
buildId: 24dfea91-04e7-4fdf-a300-2161dc3cdabf
buildName: projects/908641329416/locations/us-central1/builds/24dfea91-04e7-4fdf-a300-2161dc3cdabf
dockerRegistry: CONTAINER_REGISTRY
entryPoint: org.springframework.cloud.function.adapter.gcp.GcfJarLauncher
httpsTrigger:
  securityLevel: SECURE_ALWAYS
  url: https://us-central1-springcf-348721.cloudfunctions.net/DJLXRay-GCP
ingressSettings: ALLOW_ALL
labels:
  deployment-tool: cli-gcloud
name: projects/springcf-348721/locations/us-central1/functions/DJLXRay-GCP
runtime: java11
serviceAccountEmail: springcf-348721@appspot.gserviceaccount.com
sourceUploadUrl: https://storage.googleapis.com/uploads-889412668576.us-central1.cloudfunctions.appspot.com/4a1bb299-0d0
d-4db3-9e30-09a865919e09.zip
status: ACTIVE
timeout: 540s
updateTime: '2022-09-22T12:12:43.759Z'
versionId: '1'
```

Figure 5-16. *Successfully deployed function with the specifed memory and timeout*

Navigate to your Google Cloud Functions console to verify and to get the URL to test. See Figure 5-17.

(··) Cloud Functions	Functions	➕ CREATE FUNCTION	↻ REFRESH				⬚
≡ Filter Filter functions							
	Environment	Name ↑	Last deployed	Region	Trigger	Runtime	Memory allocated
☐ ✓	1st gen	DJLXRay-GCP	Sep 22, 2022, 6:31:46 AM	us-central1	HTTP	Java 11	512 MB

Figure 5-17. *Function shows up in the console*

You now test in the Cloud Function console by providing input (see Figure 5-18). Note that you have to increase the memory to 4096MB with a timeout set to 540s just to be safe:

```
{"url":"https://djl-ai.s3.amazonaws.com/resources/images/chest_
xray.jpg",
"savedmodelpath":"https://storage.googleapis.com/mnist-soc/
saved_model.zip"}
```

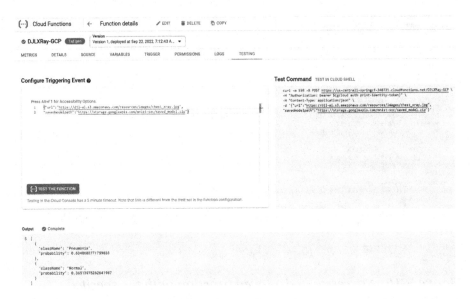

Figure 5-18. *Successful execution of the test*

If you scroll down the test console, you get the execution times. This shows that the function execution took 16392ms, as shown in Figure 5-19. This is 16s for execution, which is phenomenal. This is faster because you stored the saved model in Google Cloud Storage, which is closer to the function.

Figure 5-19. *Logs show the execution times*

This section explored the capabilities of TensorFlow and explained how you can use DJL and Spring Cloud Function together to access a saved TensorFlow model. DJL makes it easy for Java programmers to access any of the saved models generated using Python frameworks, such as PyTorch (pytorch.org) and TensorFlow.

240

You also found that you have to set the memory and timeout based on the saved model size and store the model closer to the function, such as in Google's storage offerings.

5.5. Model Serving with Spring Cloud Function with AWS Lambda and TensorFlow

This section emulates what you did in Chapter 2 for Lambda. It is best to finish that exercise before trying this one.

The prerequisites are the same as in Chapter 2. Here they are for your reference:

- AWS account

- AWS Lambda function subscription

- AWS CLI (optional)

- Code from GitHub at `https://github.com/banup-kubeforce/DJLXRay-AWS.git`

Step 1: Prep your Lambda environment. Ensure that you have access and a subscription to the AWS Lambda environment.

Step 2: Modify the Spring Cloud Function to fit the AWS Lambda environment. You need to add the DJL dependencies to the `pom.xml` file that you created in Chapter 2; see Listing 5-6.

Listing 5-6. DJL Dependencies

```
<dependency>
        <groupId>ai.djl</groupId>
        <artifactId>api</artifactId>
        <version>0.12.0</version>
```

```
</dependency>
<dependency>
    <groupId>ai.djl.tensorflow</groupId>
    <artifactId>tensorflow-api</artifactId>
    <version>0.12.0</version>
</dependency>
<dependency>
    <groupId>ai.djl.tensorflow</groupId>
    <artifactId>tensorflow-engine</artifactId>
    <version>0.12.0</version>
</dependency>
<dependency>
    <groupId>ai.djl.tensorflow</groupId>
    <artifactId>tensorflow-native-auto</artifactId>
    <version>2.4.1</version>
    <scope>runtime</scope>
</dependency>

<dependency>
    <groupId>org.projectlombok</groupId>
    <artifactId>lombok</artifactId>
    <optional>true</optional>
</dependency>
```

Step 3: Deploy the Spring Cloud Function to Lambda. You should follow the process outlined in Chapter 2 to build and package the Spring Cloud Function and deploy it to Lambda.

Step 4: Test. Once you deploy the function to Lambda, test it with Postman. You should get the result shown in Figure 5-20.

Figure 5-20. *Successful execution*

5.6. Spring Cloud Function with AWS SageMaker or AI/ML

This section explores the offering from AWS called SageMaker and shows how you can use Spring Cloud Function with it.

AWS SageMaker (`https://aws.amazon.com/sagemaker/`) is a comprehensive platform for AI/ML activities. It is like a one-stop shop for creating and deploying ML models. Figure 5-21 shows AWS SageMaker's flow.

Figure 5-21. *AWS SageMaker flow*

SageMaker allows you to build and deploy models with Python as the language of choice, but when it comes to endpoints, there are Java SDKs much like AWS Glue that create prediction APIs or serve models for further processing. You can leverage Lambda functions for these APIs.

So, as you saw in TensorFlow, you have to work in Python and Java to model and expose models for general-purpose use.

Let's run through a typical example and see if you can then switch to exposing APIs in Spring Cloud Function.

Note   This example uses the same sample to build, train, and deploy as in this hands-on tutorial in AWS.

```
https://aws.amazon.com/getting-started/hands-
on/build-train-deploy-machine-learning-model-
sagemaker/
```

Step 1: Create a notebook instance. Log on to SageMaker and create a notebook instance, as shown in Figure 5-22. Note: It is assumed that you have walked through the tutorial that Amazon provided.

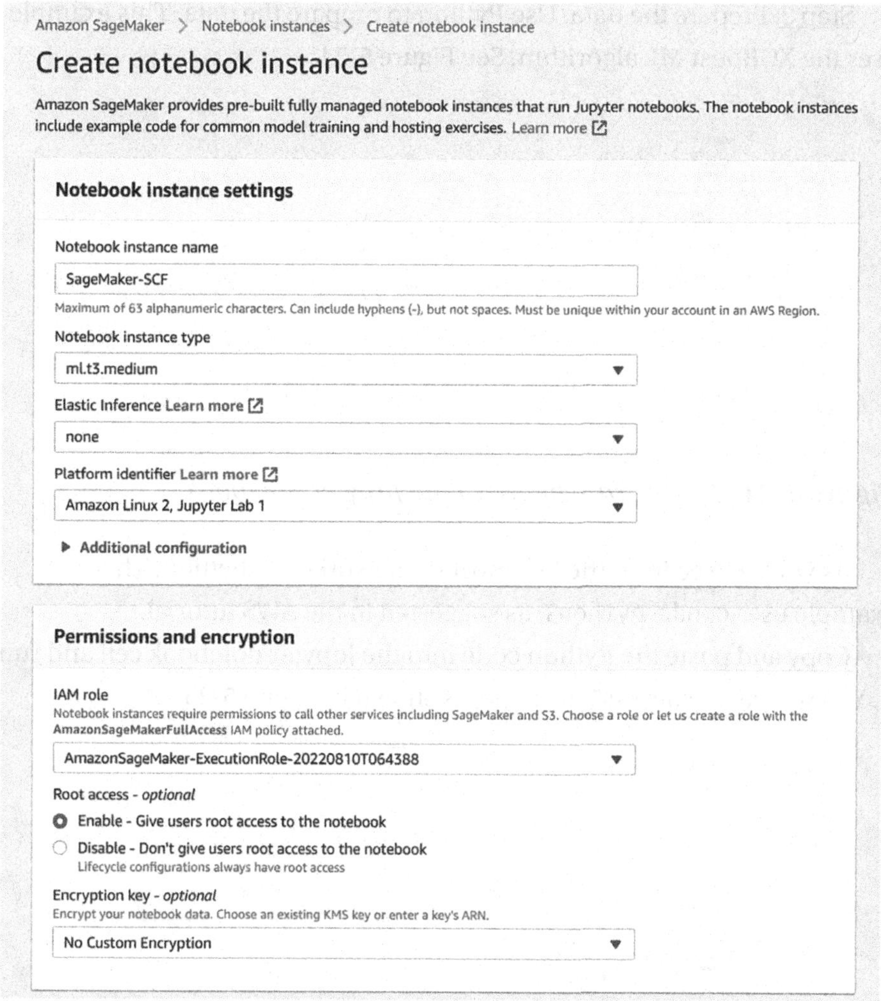

Amazon SageMaker > Notebook instances > Create notebook instance

Create notebook instance

Amazon SageMaker provides pre-built fully managed notebook instances that run Jupyter notebooks. The notebook instances include example code for common model training and hosting exercises. Learn more 🗗

Notebook instance settings

Notebook instance name

SageMaker-SCF

Maximum of 63 alphanumeric characters. Can include hyphens (-), but not spaces. Must be unique within your account in an AWS Region.

Notebook instance type

ml.t3.medium ▼

Elastic Inference Learn more 🗗

none ▼

Platform identifier Learn more 🗗

Amazon Linux 2, Jupyter Lab 1 ▼

▶ Additional configuration

Permissions and encryption

IAM role
Notebook instances require permissions to call other services including SageMaker and S3. Choose a role or let us create a role with the **AmazonSageMakerFullAccess** IAM policy attached.

AmazonSageMaker-ExecutionRole-20220810T064388 ▼

Root access - *optional*
- ⦿ Enable - Give users root access to the notebook
- ○ Disable - Don't give users root access to the notebook
  Lifecycle configurations always have root access

Encryption key - *optional*
Encrypt your notebook data. Choose an existing KMS key or enter a key's ARN.

No Custom Encryption ▼

Figure 5-22. *Notebook instance in SageMaker with properties set*

Your notebook instance will be created, as shown in Figure 5-23.

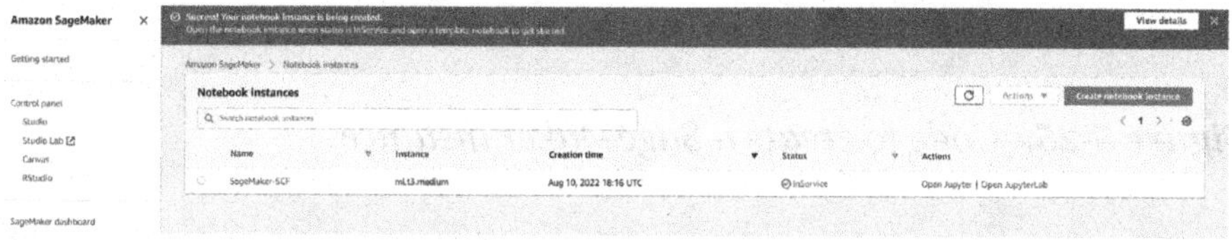

Figure 5-23. *Successful deployment of the notebook*

Step 2: Prepare the data. Use Python to prepare the data. This example uses the XGBoost ML algorithm. See Figure 5-24.

Figure 5-24. *Pick a framework in the Jupyter notebook*

As you can see from the list, most frameworks use Python. This example uses conda_python3, as suggested in the AWS tutorial.

Copy and paste the Python code into the Jupyter notebook cell and run it. You will get a "success" message, as shown in Figure 5-25.

Figure 5-25. *Code to create a SageMaker instance*

Copy and paste the code to create the s3 bucket to store your model, as shown in Figure 5-26.

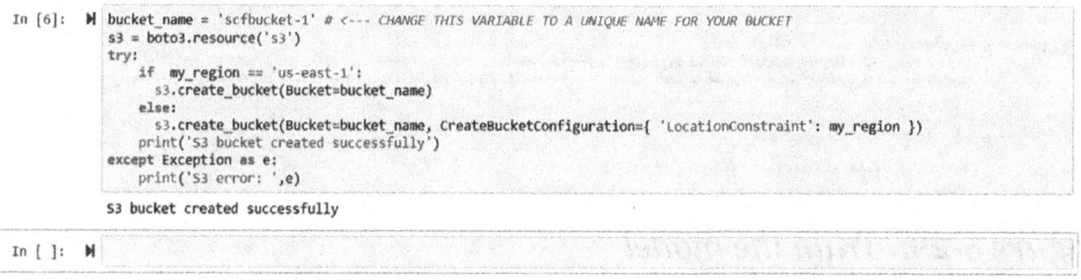

```
In [6]:  bucket_name = 'scfbucket-1' # <--- CHANGE THIS VARIABLE TO A UNIQUE NAME FOR YOUR BUCKET
         s3 = boto3.resource('s3')
         try:
             if my_region == 'us-east-1':
                 s3.create_bucket(Bucket=bucket_name)
             else:
                 s3.create_bucket(Bucket=bucket_name, CreateBucketConfiguration={ 'LocationConstraint': my_region })
             print('S3 bucket created successfully')
         except Exception as e:
             print('S3 error: ',e)

         S3 bucket created successfully

In [ ]:
```

Figure 5-26. *Create a bucket*

Now copy and paste the code to download data into a dataframe, as shown in Figure 5-27.

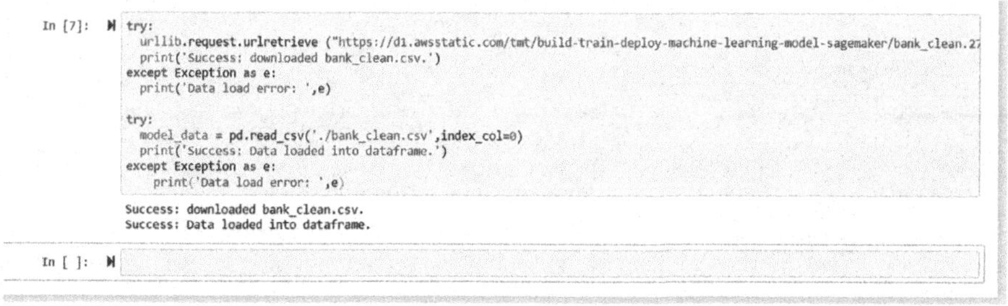

```
In [7]:  try:
             urllib.request.urlretrieve ("https://d1.awsstatic.com/tmt/build-train-deploy-machine-learning-model-sagemaker/bank_clean.27
             print('Success: downloaded bank_clean.csv.')
         except Exception as e:
             print('Data load error: ',e)

         try:
             model_data = pd.read_csv('./bank_clean.csv',index_col=0)
             print('Success: Data loaded into dataframe.')
         except Exception as e:
             print('Data load error: ',e)

         Success: downloaded bank_clean.csv.
         Success: Data loaded into dataframe.

In [ ]:
```

Figure 5-27. *Download the data into a dataframe*

Scuffle and split the dataset, as shown in Figure 5-28.

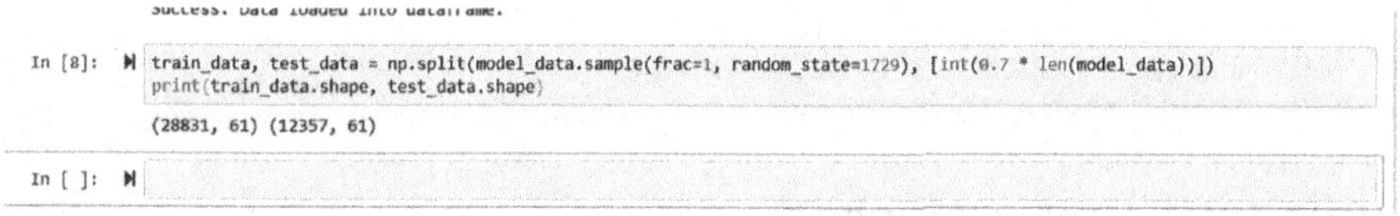

```
         Success: Data loaded into dataframe.

In [8]:  train_data, test_data = np.split(model_data.sample(frac=1, random_state=1729), [int(0.7 * len(model_data))])
         print(train_data.shape, test_data.shape)

         (28831, 61) (12357, 61)

In [ ]:
```

Figure 5-28. *Work on the dataset*

Step 3: Train the model. See Figure 5-29.

```
In [9]:  ▶ pd.concat([train_data['y_yes'], train_data.drop(['y_no', 'y_yes'], axis=1)], axis=1).to_csv('train.csv', index=False, header=
            boto3.Session().resource('s3').Bucket(bucket_name).Object(os.path.join(prefix, 'train/train.csv')).upload_file('train.csv')
            s3_input_train = sagemaker.inputs.TrainingInput(s3_data='s3://{}/{}/train'.format(bucket_name, prefix), content_type='csv')

In [10]: ▶ aker.Session()
            ker.estimator.Estimator(xgboost_container,role, instance_count=1, instance_type='ml.m4.xlarge',output_path='s3://{}/{}/output
            rparameters(max_depth=5,eta=0.2,gamma=4,min_child_weight=6,subsample=0.8,silent=0,objective='binary:logistic',num_round=100)

In [*]:  ▶ xgb.fit({'train': s3_input_train})
            2022-08-10 18:40:39 Starting - Starting the training job.
```

Figure 5-29. *Train the model*

You have to wait for Step 3 to finish before deploying the model; see Figure 5-30.

```
In [11]: ▶ xgb.fit({'train': s3_input_train})
            [93]#011train-error:0.094169
            [18:44:31] src/tree/updater_prune.cc:74: tree pruning end, 1 roots, 14 extra nodes, 28 pruned nodes, max_depth=5
            [94]#011train-error:0.094169
            [18:44:31] src/tree/updater_prune.cc:74: tree pruning end, 1 roots, 10 extra nodes, 14 pruned nodes, max_depth=5
            [95]#011train-error:0.094204
            [18:44:31] src/tree/updater_prune.cc:74: tree pruning end, 1 roots, 0 extra nodes, 28 pruned nodes, max_depth=0
            [96]#011train-error:0.094204
            [18:44:31] src/tree/updater_prune.cc:74: tree pruning end, 1 roots, 26 extra nodes, 20 pruned nodes, max_depth=5
            [97]#011train-error:0.093927
            [18:44:31] src/tree/updater_prune.cc:74: tree pruning end, 1 roots, 0 extra nodes, 38 pruned nodes, max_depth=0
            [98]#011train-error:0.093927
            [18:44:31] src/tree/updater_prune.cc:74: tree pruning end, 1 roots, 0 extra nodes, 32 pruned nodes, max_depth=0
            [99]#011train-error:0.093892

            2022-08-10 18:45:04 Completed - Training job completed
            ProfilerReport-1660156839: NoIssuesFound
            Training seconds: 137
            Billable seconds: 137
```

Figure 5-30. *Training is complete*

Step 4: Deploy the model. Make a note of the compute sizes used. This will impact your billing. See Figure 5-31.

```
In [12]: ▶ xgb_predictor = xgb.deploy(initial_instance_count=1,instance_type='ml.m4.xlarge')
            -------!
```

Figure 5-31. *Deploy the model*

Step 5: Make a note of the endpoints. See Figures 5-32 and 5-33.

Figure 5-32. *Endpoint of the deployment*

Figure 5-33. *Details of the endpoint*

<u>Step 6:</u> Create the Spring Cloud Function code to access the endpoint.
Listing 5-7 shows the POM dependencies.

Listing 5-7. AWS SDK Dependencies

```
<dependency>
    <groupId>com.amazonaws</groupId>
    <artifactId>aws-java-sdk-sagemakerruntime</artifactId>
    <version>1.11.979</version>
    <exclusions>
        <exclusion>
            <groupId>com.amazonaws</groupId>
            <artifactId>aws-java-sdk-core</artifactId>
        </exclusion>
    </exclusions>
</dependency><dependency>
    <groupId>com.amazonaws</groupId>
    <artifactId>aws-java-sdk-core</artifactId>
    <version>1.11.979</version>
</dependency>
```

Create a `Supplier` class to call and get the result from the SageMaker endpoint. The `SupplierFunction`, unlike discussed in Section 5.3, will invoke an endpoint URL and provide the results. Here, you use SageMaker's own model-serving capabilities. The Spring Cloud Function acts as a client for SageMaker. See Figure 5-34.

```java
@Component
public class SageMakerSupplier implements Supplier<String>
{
    public static final Logger LOGGER = LoggerFactory.getLogger(SageMakerSupplier.class);

    //usage
    @Autowired
    private AmazonSageMakerRuntime amazonSageMakerRuntime;


    @Override
    public String get ()
    {
        ByteBuffer bodyBuffer = ByteBuffer.wrap(SageMaker_EP.getData().getBytes());
        InvokeEndpointRequest request = new InvokeEndpointRequest()
                .withEndpointName("xgboost-2022-08-10-18-48-54-620") //xgboost-2022-08-10-18-48-54-620
                .withContentType("application/json")
                .withBody(bodyBuffer);

        InvokeEndpointResult invokeEndpointResult = amazonSageMakerRuntime.invokeEndpoint(request);

        return new String(invokeEndpointResult.getBody().array());
    }
}
```

Figure 5-34. *SageMakerSupplier.java*

Deploy the function in Lambda, as shown in Chapter 2.

This section explained how to create and deploy a model in AWS SageMaker. You then called the SageMaker endpoint using the SageMaker JDK client in the Spring Cloud Function, which was deployed in AWS Lambda.

The Java-based Lambda function can be tuned to be more responsive and have a shorter cold startup time by using mechanisms such GraalVMs.

5.7. Summary

As you learned in this chapter, you can serve models using Spring Cloud Function. But you also learned that serving models using Spring Cloud Function and Java is a stretch because the AI/ML models are written in Python. While Python may be popular, it is also important to note that in an enterprise, Java is king. Finding ways to leverage Java in AI/ML is the key to having an integrated environment within your enterprise. Cold starts of Python-based functions take a long time. This is where using Java and frameworks such as GraalVM speeds up the startup times.

The next chapter explores some real-world use cases of IoT and Conversation AI and explains how Spring Cloud Function can be used.

CHAPTER 6

Spring Cloud Function and IoT

This chapter covers Spring Cloud Function implementations with IoT. You'll see some real-world examples from manufacturing and logistics. You explore how Spring Cloud Function can operate with existing IoT platforms on the cloud and in datacenters. You also explore some specific implementations in Penske, which is interesting, as they can be applied to nearly all IoT-related scenarios.

Before you explore the solutions, you need to dive a bit into IoT and understand the status of the IoT market. You'll also look at some surveys on why Java is the preferred enterprise language for IoT development.

6.1. The State of IoT

IoT (Internet of Things) has been growing and is expected to grow 22 percent in 2022. This phenomenal growth has led to a plethora of data that needs to be acquired and processed.

According to a study by IoT Analytics Research in September 2021, the IoT device market is expected to grow phenomenally and by 2025 it is predicted to reach 25 billion devices. More about the study is available at https://iotbusinessnews.com/2021/09/23/13465-number-of-connected-iot-devices-growing-9-to-12-3-billion-globally-cellular-iot-now-surpassing-2-billion/.

With this growth potential, you can safely assume that the supporting technologies will also grow. These technologies not only include hardware sensors and IoT gateways, but also technologies such as microservices and functions. The IoT industry is best suited to implement these technologies, as they are highly distributed and rely heavily on the software components to be small and efficient.

Serverless function-based environments that are triggered on demand are perfectly suited to IoT, as they can save significant cost. Traditional approaches to IoT relied on dedicated applications running 24/7. They used up a lot of resources, adding to the cost of operation. With the nearly ephemeral nature of serverless functions, this cost can be moved to the "pay per use" approach.

Before you start working on some of the examples of IoT and Spring Cloud Function, it is best to understand why you need to code in Java. There are many alternative languages you can code in, but Java is the best for IoT and here is why:

- Java was designed with IoT in mind. If you look at early Java examples from Sun Microsystems, you will see that synchronization of digital clocks was referred to often.

- Java has been ported to many microcontrollers.

- Java is designed to run in a resource-constrained environment such as sensors.

- JVM makes code portable across platforms; you write once run anywhere.

As per the IoT survey done by `iot.eclipse.org`, which is available at `https://iot.eclipse.org/community/resources/iot-surveys/assets/iot-developer-survey-2020.pdf`, you can see that Java is the preferred language, both in the edge and in the cloud. Implementations on the edge are moving to containerization, per the study. This is great for Knative on Kubernetes installations on the edge.

Furthermore, the Spring Framework has been the platform of choice for many IIoT (Industrial IoT) projects. You can review a presentation at a SpringOne event in 2017 at `https://youtu.be/MReQD9tXQuA`.

Components like Spring Cloud Streams, Spring Cloud Data Flow, Spring Integration, Spring MQTT, Spring Data, and Spring XD play a significant role in IoT data acquisition, storing, and the transformation pipeline.

6.1.1. Example Spring Implementation

Consider this example implementation of Spring and its components in a connected fleet scenario.

The team at Penske leveraged Spring-based microservices, Spring Cloud Streams in combination with Spring Cloud Data Flow, to acquire data from sensors that were installed on Penske trucks. This application allowed Penske to monitor the trucks, do predictive maintenance, and manage the trucks in real-time. See Figure 6-1.

More information is available on the SpringOne website at `https://springone.io/2020/sessions/iot-scale-event-stream-processing-for-predictive-maintenance-at-penske`.

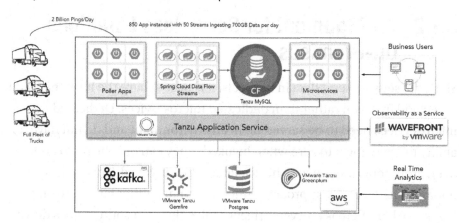

Figure 6-1. *Penske connected fleet implementation with Spring Cloud*

Let's dig a little more into the IoT process; see Figure 6-2.

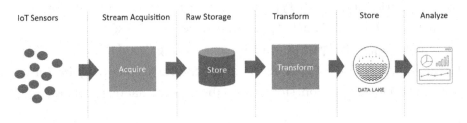

Figure 6-2. *IoT Process flow*

As in any data pipeline process, the IoT process includes acquiring data from sensors in the field. This data is then stored, transformed, and loaded into data lakes for further analysis.

Depending on the type of application, sensors send data either through a trigger event such as a repair or collision or via regular intervals. These intervals are 30 seconds to a minute in the case of logistics tracking or every few hours in the case of maintenance data. The data usually comes in as streams that need to be acquired. The most popular mechanism for acquisition is Apache Kafka.

6.1.2. An Argument for Serverless Functions On-Premises

Since the sensors send data in intervals, it is best to have the input handled by a cloud function rather than dedicated microservices. Dedicated microservices need to be served up in an environment and do not have the ability to scale down to zero when invoked. They can only be provisioned in environments that need to be available when invoked. This makes microservices a costly approach. Functions, on the other hand, are only invoked when there is an event trigger. Utilization of resources goes down to zero if they are not invoked. This is because the underlying serverless infrastructure such as Lambda and Knative can be scaled down to zero when not invoked.

This makes it a more cost-effective alternative. This applies to both on-premises and on the cloud. If it is on-premises, the argument against cloud functions on a serverless environment would be that the infrastructure cost has already been accounted for. Therefore, a dedicated microservice that is always on would be feasible. Wasting resources because you have them is not a prudent way to efficiently use IT. With functions running on serverless environments, such as Knative running on OpenShift or VMware Tanzu, on-premises would help save resources that could be used to run other activities. The on-premise resources are finite, so it's prudent to make the best use of them.

6.2. Spring Cloud Function on the Cloud with AWS IoT

Consider a use case where an automotive assembly plant wants to ensure that its robots are performing well. The engineers want to ensure that each of the robot's data is monitored for any anomalies and, in an event of a breakdown, the engineers are alerted. The assembly plant is firewalled and any data that needs to be analyzed can be sent to the cloud.

The solution is a hybrid cloud environment that isolates the assembly plant floor but connects to the cloud to send data from the plant floor. Figure 6-3 shows a solution that is implemented with AWS products that can be deployed on-premises and connect to the cloud to synchronize the data with the rest of the systems involved in decision-making.

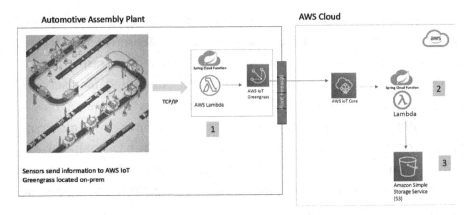

Figure 6-3. *Manufacturing plant process flow with AWS and Spring Cloud Function*

Solution components:

- AWS IoT Greengrass on-premises

- Prebuilt AWS Lambda functions that capture the sensor data

- AWS IoT core on cloud

- Spring Cloud Function running on AWS Lambda

- S3 storage to store the data

Components	Description
AWS IoT Greengrass on-prem	This solution from AWS allows you to bring the AWS capabilities such as Functions closer to where the IoT devices are. This can be deployed within for example a Manufacturing plant to collect data and connect with AWS IoT core on the AWS cloud. Additional information can be found here. https://aws.amazon.com/greengrass/
Prebuilt AWS Lamdba functions that capture the sensor data	These are functions that are provided by AWS Greengrass to act as event triggers and collect data through MQTT
AWS IoT core on cloud	This offering from AWS is hosted on the cloud and helps in the management of IoT devices. More information can be found here https://aws.amazon.com/iot-core/
Spring Cloud Function running on AWS Lambda	These are functions that we create to interact with devices as triggers or data aggregators
AWS S3	AWS S3 allows you to store the device data

You can build the solution using AWS IoT Greengrass and leverage a Spring Cloud Function that is deployed on Lambda. The point of this exercise is to understand the capabilities of Spring Cloud Function as a component that is integral to the solution.

The AWS IoT Greengrass implementation extends AWS Cloud to on-premises. You can run Lambda functions on Greengrass's edge.
Step 1: Install AWS IoT Greengrass. Install AWS IoT Greengrass on a device (`https://docs.aws.amazon.com/greengrass/v1/developerguide/install-ggc.html`). To test it, I installed the software on Windows. I used the tutorial at `https://aws.amazon.com/blogs/iot/aws-iot-greengrass-now-supports-the-windows-operating-system/` to get my first Greengrass implementation.

Once you have AWS IoT up and running, you need to create a function to connect to devices and collect data. Let's create a sample function.
Step 2: Spring Cloud Function to publish an MQTT message. You can clone the project from GitHub at `https://github.com/banup-kubeforce/AWSIots3-V2.git`.

Devices communicate with MQTT, so you need to leverage MQTT as a protocol. Create a Spring Cloud Function that publishes an MQTT message and create a consumer function to call MQTT publish.

This consumer will publish data using the MqttPublish class and will be the function that is exposed by Lambda; see Listing 6-1.

Listing 6-1. MqttConsumer.java

```java
package com.kubeforce.awsgreengrassiot;

import org.hibernate.cache.internal.
StandardTimestampsCacheFactory;
import org.slf4j.Logger;
import org.slf4j.LoggerFactory;
import org.springframework.beans.factory.annotation.Autowired;

import java.util.Map;
import java.util.function.Consumer;

public class MqttConsumer  implements
Consumer<Map<String,String>> {
    public static final Logger LOGGER = LoggerFactory.
    getLogger(MqttConsumer.class);

    @Autowired
    private MqttPublish mqttPublish;

    @Override
    public void accept (Map<String, String> map )
    {
        LOGGER.info("Adding Device info", map);
        MqttPublish mqttPublish= new MqttPublish();
    }

}
```

Next, create a publish class to publish messages to MQTT.

The MqttPublish class sends data using the IoTDataClient that is provided by AWS Greengrass SDK, to construct and send data. See Listing 6-2.

Listing 6-2. MqttPublish.java

```java
import java.nio.ByteBuffer;
import java.util.Timer;
import java.util.TimerTask;

import com.amazonaws.services.lambda.runtime.Context;
import com.amazonaws.greengrass.javasdk.IotDataClient;
import com.amazonaws.greengrass.javasdk.model.*;

public class MqttPublish {
    static {
        Timer timer = new Timer();
        // Repeat publishing a message every 5 seconds
        timer.scheduleAtFixedRate(new PublishDeviceInfo(),
        0, 5000);
    }

    public String handleRequest(Object input, Context
context) {
        return "Here is the device info";

    }
}
    class PublishDeviceInfo extends TimerTask {
        private IotDataClient iotDataClient = new
        IotDataClient();
```

```java
        private String publishMessage = String.format("Device
        info sent from device running on platform: %s-%s
        using Java", System.getProperty("os.name"), System.
        getProperty("os.version"));
        private PublishRequest publishRequest = new
        PublishRequest()
                .withTopic("device/info")
                .withPayload(ByteBuffer.wrap(String.
                format("{\"message\":\"%s\"}", publishMessage).
                getBytes()))
                .withQueueFullPolicy(QueueFullPolicy.
                AllOrException);

    public void run() {
        try {
            iotDataClient.publish(publishRequest);
        } catch (Exception ex) {
            System.err.println(ex);
        }
    }
}
```

Step 3: Deploy the Spring Cloud Function on AWS Greengrass locally.

AWS provides a great guide for deploying Lambda function on Greengrass at Run Lambda functions on the AWS IoT Greengrass core - AWS IoT Greengrass (amazon.com).

As described in Chapter 2, you will bundle the Spring Cloud Function and publish it to Lambda. Alternatively, you can also use these CLI commands:

```
aws lambda create-function \
--region aws-region \
--function-name  MqttConsumer \
```

```
--handler executable-name \
--role role-arn \
--zip-file fileb://Application_Name.zip \
--runtime arn:aws:greengrass:::runtime/function/executable
```

Navigate to the AWS IoT management console, and then click Greengrass, followed by Deployments. You can see the deployed components. Figure 6-4 shows a sample of the management console.

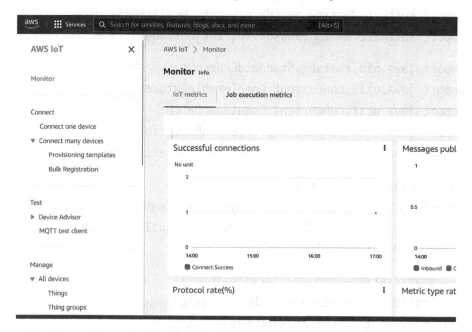

Figure 6-4. *AWS IoT Management console with some successful connections*

Step 4: Create a Spring Cloud Function to get data from the IoT core. Create a class to subscribe and get messages from Mqtt.

If you want to access the data that you published, you can run MqttSubscriber.java from the command line. You can use MqttSubscriber.java. This subscribes to a specific topic, device/info for example, and gets the messages. See Listing 6-3.

Listing 6-3. MqttSubscriber.java with Command-Line Utilities to Publish to AWS IoT

```
import software.amazon.awssdk.crt.CRT;
import software.amazon.awssdk.crt.CrtRuntimeException;
import software.amazon.awssdk.crt.mqtt.MqttClientConnection;
import software.amazon.awssdk.crt.mqtt.
MqttClientConnectionEvents;
import software.amazon.awssdk.crt.mqtt.QualityOfService;
import software.amazon.awssdk.iot.iotjobs.model.RejectedError;

import java.nio.charset.StandardCharsets;
import java.util.concurrent.CompletableFuture;
import java.util.concurrent.CountDownLatch;
import java.util.concurrent.ExecutionException;
import java.util.concurrent.atomic.AtomicReference;

public class MqttSubscriber  {
    static String ciPropValue = System.getProperty("aws.crt.ci");
    static boolean isCI = ciPropValue != null && Boolean.
    valueOf(ciPropValue);

    static String topic = "device/info";
    static String message = "Device Info";
    static int     messagesToPublish = 10;

    static CommandLineUtils cmdUtils;

    static void onRejectedError(RejectedError error) {
        System.out.println("Request rejected: " + error.code.
        toString() + ": " + error.message);
    }
```

```
/*
 * When called during a CI run, throw an exception that
   will escape and fail the exec:java task
 * When called otherwise, print what went wrong (if
   anything) and just continue (return from main)
 */
static void onApplicationFailure(Throwable cause) {
    if (isCI) {
        throw new RuntimeException("BasicPubSub execution
        failure", cause);
    } else if (cause != null) {
        System.out.println("Exception encountered: " +
        cause.toString());
    }
}

public String MqttSubscribe(){
    final String[] payload = {""};
    cmdUtils = new CommandLineUtils();
    cmdUtils.registerProgramName("PubSub");
    cmdUtils.addCommonMQTTCommands();
    cmdUtils.addCommonTopicMessageCommands();
    cmdUtils.registerCommand("key", "<path>", "Path to your
    key in PEM format.");
    cmdUtils.registerCommand("cert", "<path>", "Path to
    your client certificate in PEM format.");
    cmdUtils.registerCommand("client_id", "<int>", "Client
    id to use (optional, default='test-*').");
    cmdUtils.registerCommand("port", "<int>",
    "Port to connect to on the endpoint (optional,
    default='8883').");
    cmdUtils.registerCommand("count", "<int>", "Number of
    messages to publish (optional, default='10').");
```

```java
topic = cmdUtils.getCommandOrDefault("topic", topic);
message = cmdUtils.getCommandOrDefault("message",
message);
messagesToPublish = Integer.parseInt(cmdUtils.
getCommandOrDefault("count", String.
valueOf(messagesToPublish)));

MqttClientConnectionEvents callbacks = new
MqttClientConnectionEvents() {
    @Override
    public void onConnectionInterrupted(int errorCode) {
        if (errorCode != 0) {
            System.out.println("Connection
            interrupted: " + errorCode + ": " + CRT.
            awsErrorString(errorCode));
        }
    }

    @Override
    public void onConnectionResumed(boolean
    sessionPresent) {
        System.out.println("Connection resumed: " +
        (sessionPresent ? "existing session" : "clean
        session"));
    }
};

try {

    MqttClientConnection connection = cmdUtils.buildMQT
    TConnection(callbacks);
    if (connection == null)
    {
```

```java
    onApplicationFailure(new RuntimeException("MQTT
    connection creation failed!"));
}

CompletableFuture<Boolean> connected = connection.
connect();
try {
    boolean sessionPresent = connected.get();
    System.out.println("Connected to " +
    (!sessionPresent ? "new" : "existing") + "
    session!");
} catch (Exception ex) {
    throw new RuntimeException("Exception occurred
    during connect", ex);
}

CountDownLatch countDownLatch = new CountDownLatch(
messagesToPublish);

CompletableFuture<Integer> subscribed = connection.
subscribe(topic, QualityOfService.AT_LEAST_ONCE,
(message) -> {
    payload[0] = new String(message.getPayload(),
    StandardCharsets.UTF_8);
    System.out.println("MESSAGE: " + payload[0]);
    countDownLatch.countDown();
});

subscribed.get();

countDownLatch.await();

CompletableFuture<Void> disconnected = connection.
disconnect();
disconnected.get();
```

```
        // Close the connection now that we are completely
            done with it.
        connection.close();

    } catch (CrtRuntimeException | InterruptedException |
    ExecutionException ex) {
        onApplicationFailure(ex);
    }

  return payload[0];
  }

}
```

Create a class to upload the message to an S3 bucket. You can use the S3Upload.java provided; see Listing 6-4.

Listing 6-4. S3upload.java

```java
package com.kubeforce.awsiots3;

import software.amazon.awssdk.core.sync.RequestBody;
import software.amazon.awssdk.regions.Region;
import software.amazon.awssdk.services.s3.model.
PutObjectRequest;
import software.amazon.awssdk.services.s3.S3Client;

public class S3Upload {

    public String S3upload(String payload) {
        //set-up the client
        Region region = Region.US_WEST_2;
        S3Client s3 = S3Client.builder().region(region).
        build();

        String bucketName = "greengrass";
```

```
    String key = "IoT";

    s3.putObject(PutObjectRequest.builder().
    bucket(bucketName).key(key)
                    .build(),
            RequestBody.fromString(payload));
    s3.close();
    return ("success");
  }

}
```

Finally, create a Spring Cloud Function called Consumer that calls the MqttSubscriber and S3Upload classes. See Listing 6-5.

Listing 6-5. IoTConsumer.java

```
import java.util.Map;
import java.util.function.Consumer;

public class IoTConsumer implements
Consumer<Map<String,String>> {
    @Override
    public void accept (Map<String, String> map)
    {

        MqttSubscriber mqttSubscriber = new MqttSubscriber();
        S3Upload s3Upload = new S3Upload();
        s3Upload.S3upload(mqttSubscriber.MqttSubscribe());

    }
}
```

This function can be deployed as a Lambda function, as shown in Chapter 2.

You can find a sample execution and the outcomes on GitHub at `https://github.com/banup-kubeforce/AWSIots3-V2.git`.

In this section, you were able to deploy AWS IoT Greengrass locally, deploy a local Lambda function with Spring Cloud function code, publish data to the cloud, and store the data into S3 with another Spring Cloud function.

This is straightforward, as AWS has Java-based SDKs to help build the Spring Cloud Function clients. You also learned that you can deploy Lambda functions locally.

6.3. Spring Cloud Function on the Cloud with Azure IoT

This is the same use case as in the prior example, where an automotive assembly plant wants to ensure that its robots are performing well. The data from the sensors needs to be collected and analyzed for anomalies. Each assembly plant is walled off from the public Internet through firewalls.

The solution with Azure is very similar to the one you saw with AWS Greengrass. You need a way to get the device information from the plant floor, analyze it, and respond to it with an action within the plant floor, and then send the data to the cloud for further processing. Actionable insights are made closer to the devices.

Components:

- Azure IoT Edge Device

- Azure IoT hub

- Spring Cloud Function running on Azure Functions environment and deployed on the Azure IoT Edge

- Azure Blob store to store data in the cloud

6.3.1. Azure IoT Edge Device

The IoT Edge device manages communications between downstream leaf devices and the IoT hub. In this case, the leaf devices are robots with sensors. The IoT Edge device has a runtime that enables cloud logic on the devices. It supports Azure Functions to run on the edge device. See Figure 6-5.

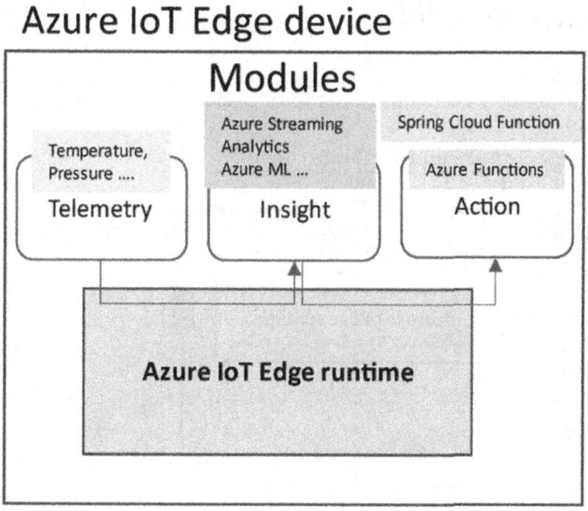

Figure 6-5. *Azure IoT Edge Device implementation*

6.3.2. Azure IoT Hub

This hub is a managed service offering from Azure that allows you to collect data from IoT devices and send them to other Azure services for further processing. This is an IoT gateway where you can connect and manage your devices through a single portal. More information can be found at https://docs.microsoft.com/en-us/azure/architecture/reference-architectures/iot.

6.4. Spring Cloud Function on Azure IoT Edge

Spring Cloud Function will be deployed on the Azure IoT Edge devices. Azure IoT Edge allows for deployment of containerized functions. More information can be found at https://learn.microsoft.com/en-us/azure/iot-edge/tutorial-deploy-function?view=iotedge-1.4.

Figure 6-6 shows this solution.

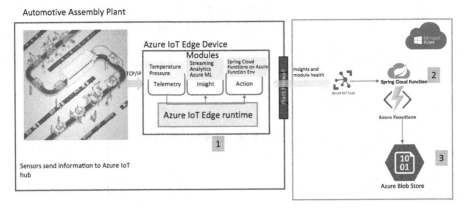

Figure 6-6. *Manufacturing plant processing using Azure and Spring Cloud Function*

Let's implement this solution.

Prerequisites:

- VS Studio Code configured for Spring Boot, as this has a very good integration with Azure IoT

- Azure Container Registry to store your containerized Spring Cloud Function

- Code from GitHub at https://github.com/banup-kubeforce/AzureIoTSimulator.git

- Azure IoTEdge and Azure IoTHub set up and configured

<u>Step 1:</u> Install an Azure IoT Edge device. You can follow the instructions at https://docs.microsoft.com/en-us/azure/iot-edge/quickstart-linux?view=iotedge-2020-11 to enable either a Windows or Linux device.

<u>Step 2:</u> Connect the device to Azure IoT. Since you cannot deploy the Azure Stack hub, it is best to use an Azure IoT hub on the web.

You can enable it on the Azure Portal. More information on how to configure your edge devices to connect to the IoT hub is available at https://docs.microsoft.com/en-us/azure/iot-edge/quickstart-linux?view=iotedge-2020-11.

You also have to register your device on the hub. See Figure 6-7.

Here is an example command line:

```
az iot hub device-identity create --device-id myEdgeDevice
--edge-enabled --hub-name {hub_name}
az iot hub device-identity connection-string show --device-id
myEdgeDevice --hub-name {hub_name}
```

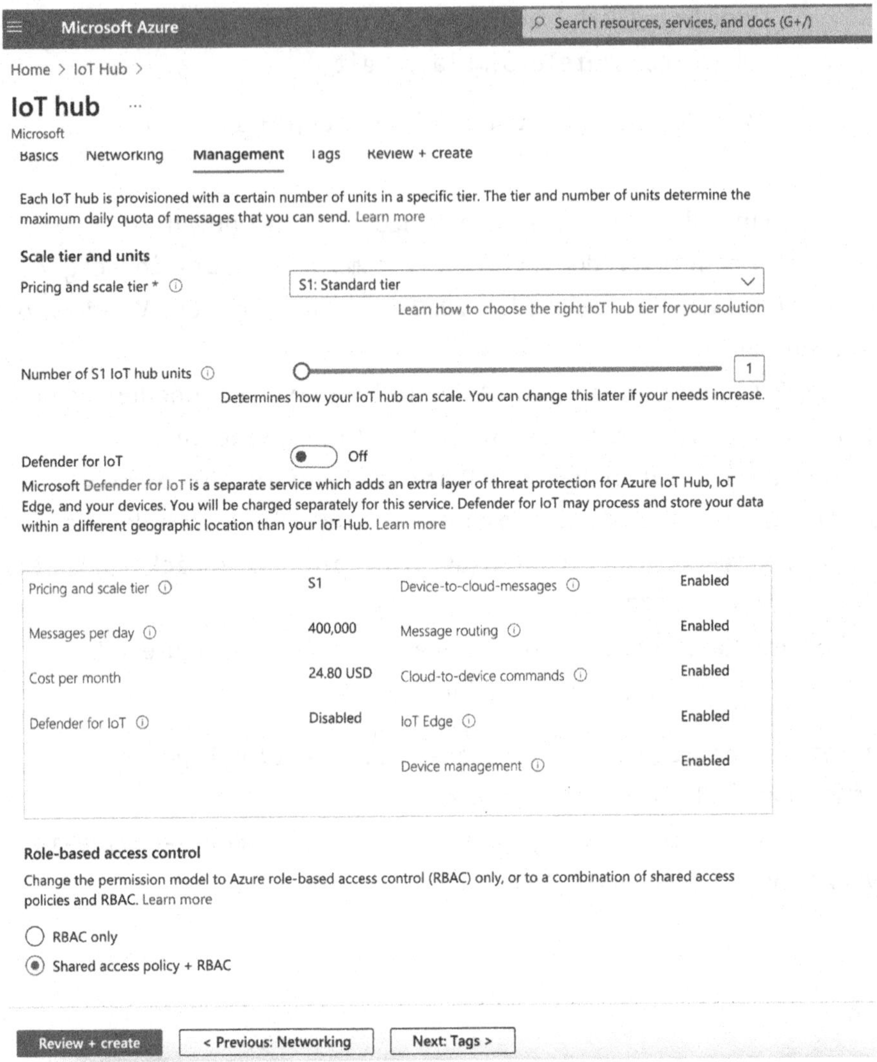

Figure 6-7. *IoT hub subscription in Azure Portal*

<u>Step 3:</u> Create a Spring Cloud Function and deploy it on Azure IoT Edge.

This code is available at `https://github.com/banup-kubeforce/` `AzureIoTSimulator.git`.

You can create a Spring Cloud Function that sends information from the edge device to the IoT hub. Make sure you have the connection string that you created in Step 1.

Dependencies:

```
<dependency>
    <groupId>com.microsoft.azure.sdk.iot</groupId>
    <artifactId>iot-device-client</artifactId>
    <version>2.1.1</version>
</dependency>
```

Write the code to connect to the IoT hub. The iot.connection.string variable is where you store the connection string you got in Step 1.

```
import com.microsoft.azure.sdk.iot.device.DeviceClient;
import com.microsoft.azure.sdk.iot.device.IotHubClientProtocol;
import org.springframework.beans.factory.annotation.Value;
import org.springframework.context.annotation.Bean;
import org.springframework.context.annotation.Configuration;

import java.net.URISyntaxException;

@Configuration
public class IOTConfiguration {

    @Bean
    public DeviceClient deviceClient(@Value("${iot.connection.
    string}") String connString) throws URISyntaxException {
        return new DeviceClient(connString,
        IotHubClientProtocol.HTTPS);
    }

}
```

Create a payload entity to construct the message:

```
package com.kubeforce.azureiotsimulator;

import java.time.LocalDateTime;

public class PayloadEntity {

    private final LocalDateTime timestamp;
    private final String message;

    public PayloadEntity(LocalDateTime timestamp, String
    message) {
        this.timestamp = timestamp;
        this.message = message;
    }

    public LocalDateTime getTimestamp() {
        return timestamp;
    }

    public String getMessage() {
        return message;
    }
}
```

Create the function to send the message:

```
package com.kubeforce.azureiotsimulator;
import com.microsoft.azure.sdk.iot.device.DeviceClient;

import com.microsoft.azure.sdk.iot.device.Message;
import com.microsoft.azure.sdk.iot.device.MessageSentCallback;
import com.microsoft.azure.sdk.iot.device.exceptions.
IotHubClientException;
```

```java
import org.slf4j.Logger;
import org.slf4j.LoggerFactory;
import org.springframework.beans.factory.annotation.Autowired;

import java.lang.invoke.MethodHandles;

import java.util.function.Function;

public class SendtoIoTFunction implements
Function<PayloadEntity, String> {
    public static final Logger LOGGER = LoggerFactory.
    getLogger(MethodHandles.lookup().lookupClass());
    @Autowired
    private DeviceClient deviceClient;
    Message message=null;
    @Override
    public String apply(PayloadEntity payloadEntity) {
        try {
            deviceClient.open(false);
            deviceClient.sendEventAsync(message, new
            MessageSentCallback() {
                @Override
                public void onMessageSent(Message message,
                IotHubClientException e, Object o) {
                    LOGGER.info("IOT Response || STATUS CODE ||
                    {}",message.toString());
                }
            }, null);
            deviceClient.close();
```

```
    } catch (IotHubClientException e) {
        throw new RuntimeException(e);
    }

    return null;
  }
}
```

<u>Step 4:</u> Deploy the function into Azure Function on the edge devices.

You will have to containerize the function as discussed in Chapter 2. Instead of pushing to Dockerhub, you have to push it to Azure Container Registry. Information on Azure Container Registry is available at `https://azure.microsoft.com/en-us/products/container-registry/`.

Use the VS Studio Code features. Additional information is provided on GitHub:

1) Create a deployment for a single device.

2) Select `deployment.amd64.jso` in the `config` folder. Click Select Edge Deployment Manifest.

3) Expand the modules to see a list of deployed and running modules. See Figure 6-8.

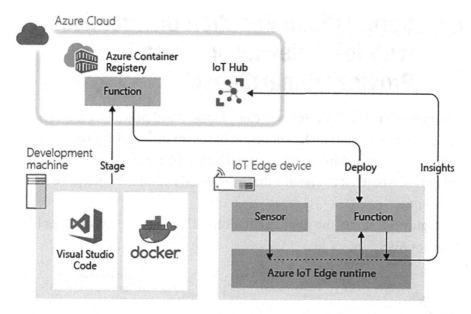

Figure 6-8. *Azure function deployment on the IoT edge devices using Azure IoT Edge runtime*
Source: https://learn.microsoft.com/en-us/azure/iot-edge/media/
tutorial-deploy-function/functions-architecture.png?view=i
otedge-1.4

This section showed that you can take the same use case of the manufacturing assembly plant and sensors and apply an Azure IoT solution to it.

You created a Spring Cloud Function and deployed it to Azure IoTEdge using the Azure Function. Detailed information is provided on GitHub at https://github.com/banup-kubeforce/AzureIoTSimulator.git.

You also learned that you can use the Azure IoT Edge devices with Azure IoT Edge runtime to collect data from sensors. This is very similar to how it is done in AWS.

6.5. Spring Cloud Function On-Premises with IoT Gateway on a SaaS Provider (SmartSense)

Enterprises that do not want to use any of the cloud provider's IoT components can offload the collection of sensor data to third-party companies. These third-party companies can then send the data as streams or a batch it to systems that are hosted within the enterprise's datacenter.

Figure 6-9 shows the implementation without using a hyperscaler like Azure or AWS.

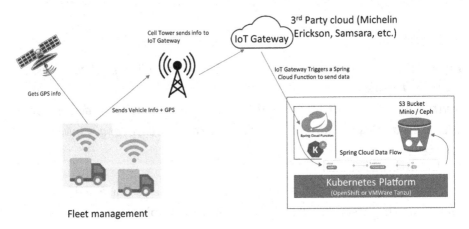

Figure 6-9. *Fleet management example*

For this use case, a company wants to manage its fleet of vehicles and provide data to its consumers about the vehicle's health, location, maintenance, repair info, driver info, and so on, to enable visibility of its fleet and cargo. The vehicle data needs to be collected and processed in its own datacenter. See Table 6-1.

Solution:

- Third-party IoT gateway providers such as Michelin, Erickson, Samsara, and so on

- Kubernetes platform on-premises such as OpenShift or VMware Tanzu

- Spring Cloud Data Flow

- S3 bucket hosted in the datacenter, like Minio or Ceph

- Spring Cloud Function on Knative

Table 6-1. *Components Description*

Components	Description
3rd party IoT gateway providers such as Michelin, Erickson, Samsara etc..	Provides the ability for sensors to send data
Kubernetes platform on-prem such as OpenShift or VMWare Tanzu	Provides as environment to deploy serverless functions in the datacenter
Spring Cloud Data Flow	A datapipeline that can be deployed in a datacenter on Kubernetes
Spring Cloud Functions on Knative	As Serverless Function environment to provide event triggers and interfaces
S3 bucket hosted in the datacenter like Minio or Ceph	A datacenter hosted S3 environment for storing data that is coming in from sensors

Step 1: Contact your third-party provider to get the information about their IoT hub. Since the work of acquiring the sensor data is offloaded to third-party providers, you can assume that data will be accumulated and routed to the third-party cloud from the vehicles.

Once the data is accumulated at the third-party gateway, it gets routed to the company's datacenter via an invocation of a function.

Step 2: Set up Spring Cloud Data Flow in your environment.

- Install Spring Cloud Data Flow in a Kubernetes
  environment like OpenShift or VMware Tanzu

- Create a Spring Cloud Data Flow data pipeline.

Installation of Spring Cloud Data Flow is discussed in Chapter 4.

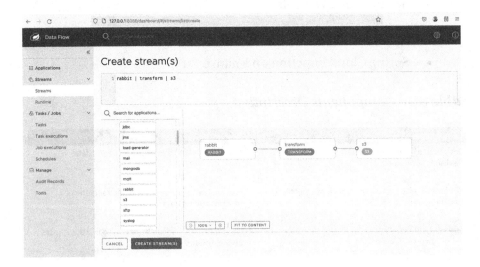

Figure 6-10. *Spring Cloud Data Flow*

This example uses RabbitMQ as the source and S3 Minio/Ceph as
the sink.

Step 3: Publish to RabbitMQ. See Chapter 4 for details of publishing to
RabbitMQ.

Step 4: Deploy the Spring Cloud Function on Knative, as you did in
Chapter 2, and expose a public endpoint for the IoT gateway to connect.

This completes the implementation of an on-premises solution that uses
a third-party IoT gateway. You can leverage the serverless environment, just
like AWS Lambda or Azure Functions. Knative on Kubernetes provides that
serverless environment to run the Spring Cloud Function.

You leveraged Spring Cloud Data Flow as the data pipeline to collect and process the sensor data.

More information on the project is available at `https://github.com/banup-kubeforce/onpremIoT.git`.

6.6. Summary

As you learned in this chapter, you can build IoT-based solutions using Spring Cloud Function, both in an on-premises environment, and as well as in AWS and Azure.

Spring Cloud Function is one of the most versatile frameworks in the Java world. It can be deployed on proprietary cloud-based serverless environments and on Knative, making it a very portable component.

Whether it is a manufacturing plant walled off from the public Internet or on the road with fleet management, you can build secure and reliable solutions with Spring Cloud Function.

CHAPTER 7

Industry-Specific Examples with Spring Cloud Function

This chapter explores some of the industry-specific implementations of Spring Cloud Function.

It leverages the IBM Cloud offering to demonstrate that Spring Cloud Function is supported on any cloud offering.

Some of the examples in this chapter are real-world scenarios in which functions play a critical role. For example, a function that sends alarms about pipeline leaks and a chat function that helps customers solve problems.

7.1. Oil/Natural Gas Pipeline Tracking with Spring Cloud Function and IOT

This section looks at how Spring Cloud Function can be used in the context of natural gas pipelines.

Miles and miles of gas pipelines need to be constantly monitored for leaks, cracks, temperature fluctuations, and pressure issues in order to avoid costly breakdowns in the transmission of gas and to avoid explosions.

© Banu Parasuraman 2023
B. Parasuraman, *Practical Spring Cloud Function*,
https://doi.org/10.1007/978-1-4842-8913-6_7

This solution leverages IBM Cloud and its IoT platform offerings along with smart gateways to capture sensor data and provide analysis and visualizations. You'll see how to deploy Spring Cloud Function and integrate it with IBM Event streams to store the streaming data into IBM Cloudant DB. See Figure 7-1.

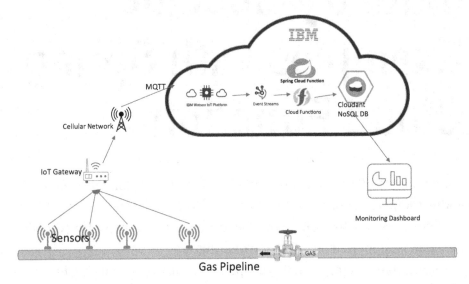

Figure 7-1. *Gas pipeline IoT implementation*

The required components are outlined in Table 7-1.

Table 7-1. *Components for an Example Solution*

Sensor	The Preferred Sensor
IoT Gateway	Your preferred gateway product
IBM Cloud Functions	`https://cloud.ibm.com/functions/`
IBM Watson IoT Platform	`https://www.ibm.com/cloud/watson-iot-platform`
IBM Watson IoT Platform – Message Gateway	`https://www.ibm.com/docs/en/wip-mg`
IBM Event Streams	`https://www.ibm.com/cloud/event-streams`
IBM Cloudant DB	`https://www.ibm.com/cloud/cloudant`

7.1.1. Sensors

There are multiple parameters that need to be measured and tracked when monitoring the health of a pipeline. This data can be categorized into asset and external data.

Asset data can include pressure, flow rate, wall thickness, and cracks. External data can include temperature, humidity, pH levels, and soil resistivity. Smart sensors can be installed along the length of the pipeline to transmit information to a nearby IoT gateway.

7.1.2. IoT Gateway

These devices act as sensor data aggregators and send the acquired data to receiving systems like the Watson IoT platform. They also allow the Watson IoT platform to connect and manage sensor devices. There are many cloud-ready gateways in the market.

These cloud-ready gateways allow for connectivity to different cloud platforms, including Azure, AWS, the Watson IoT platform, and so on.

7.1.3. IBM Cloud Functions

IBM Cloud offers serverless cloud functions that can be either scripted on the web-based console or deployed on Docker containers. If you are developing in Java and dotnet, you need to use the Docker option. Alternatively, Knative on Kubernetes is offered as a way to deploy Spring Cloud Function with Docker images. More information is available at `https://www.ibm.com/cloud/functions`.

7.1.4. IBM Watson IoT Platform

This product from IBM also allows you to set up and manage connected devices. It has a dashboard that offers device management, MQTT support, data lifecycle management, and secure communication with TLS for MQTT. More information is available at `https://www.ibm.com/cloud/internet-of-things`.

7.1.5. IBM Watson IoT Platform: Message Gateway

IBM Message Gateway receives the message that IoT sensors send and sends it to platforms such as IBM Event Streams.

More information is available at `https://www.ibm.com/docs/en/wip-mg`.

7.1.6. IBM Event Streams

This is based on Apache Kafka and allows for managing streaming event data coming from the IBM Watson IoT platform. More information is available at https://www.ibm.com/cloud/event-streams.

7.1.7. IBM Cloudant DB

This is a fully managed distributed database that allows for storing data from the IBM Watson IoT platform. You can find more information at https://www.ibm.com/cloud/cloudant.

Now you'll see how to realize the flow shown in Figure 7-2, where the IoT sensors send information to the IBM Event Stream through the message gateway. The message is then received from IBM event streams through a Spring Cloud Function and stored in Cloudant DB. It is suggested you explore the integration between sensors and the message gateway at https://www.ibm.com/docs/en/wip-mg/5.0.0.1?topic=os-imaserver-rpm.

Figure 7-2 shows the flow that this example plans to achieve.

Figure 7-2. *Use case for sensor data consumption flow*

The focus is on creating a Spring Cloud Function that receives the message published to a topic called "Sensor-topic" in event streams and stores it into the Cloudant DB.

Step 1: Register with IBM Cloud and subscribe to Watson IoT platform.

You can start at https://www.ibm.com/cloud/internet-of-things and click Get Started to start the process.

If you are just this trying out, you can use the free tier (lite). See Figure 7-3.

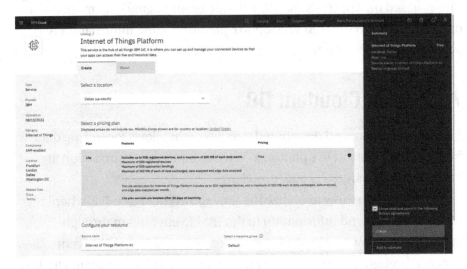

Figure 7-3. *IBM Cloud Watson IOT*

Step 2: Add devices that need to be monitored.

To get to the Add Device page, click your name on the top right and click the IoT resource that was created in Step 1; see Figure 7-4.

Figure 7-4. *Add Device page*

The Add Device page takes you to a step-by-step process to configure your device. You have to select your device type and device ID, and then provide the device information such as serial number, model, and so on. Then you can enter an optional token. Preview all the information you entered by clicking the Finish button. This will create the device, as shown in the Figure 7-5.

Figure 7-5. *Add devices on the Watson IoT platform*

Step 3: Subscribe to the IBM event streams.

Here again, you have the option of using a free tier (Lite). See Figure 7-6.

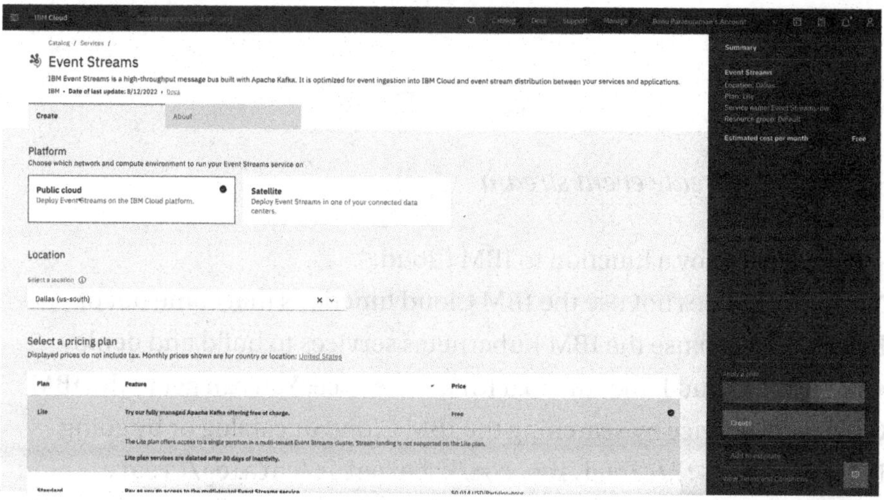

Figure 7-6. *IBM Cloud event streams*

You then stipulate where you want to run the event stream—on a public cloud or satellite, as well as the cloud instance location. Then select your pricing plan (the Lite option is free), give it a name, and assign a resource group. You can also provide some identification tags. This will create the event stream.

Step 4: Create a topic with the required parameters.

Within your event streams dashboard, click the Create Topic button and enter the name of the topic, as well as any partitions and message retention parameters. This will create a topic, which you can see on the Event Streams page, as shown in Figure 7-7.

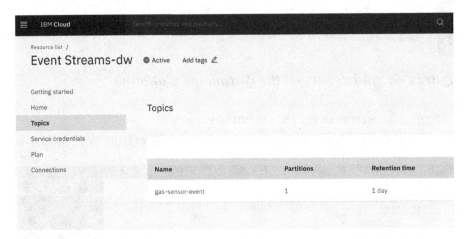

Figure 7-7. *Create event stream*

Step 5: Deploy a function to IBM Cloud.

This step does not use the IBM Cloud functions that come out of the box. You can use the IBM Kubernetes services to build and deploy your Spring Cloud Function on a Knative service. You can get to the IBM Kubernetes service by searching the IBM Cloud or catalog or by going directly to `https://cloud.ibm.com/kubernetes/catalog/create`.

Now create a bare minimum cluster that is free. This is what I like about the IBM Cloud; you are really getting a free service even for a Kubernetes cluster. This is unlike other cloud providers, where you must pay for the underlying compute and storage.

If you are creating a free cluster, be aware that this cluster will be deleted after 30 days.

Once on the Kubernetes cluster page, pick the pricing plan and a Kubernetes cluster will be created for you. With Lite, you do not have the option to name the cluster. You can subscribe to the standard tier to get more control. See Figure 7-8.

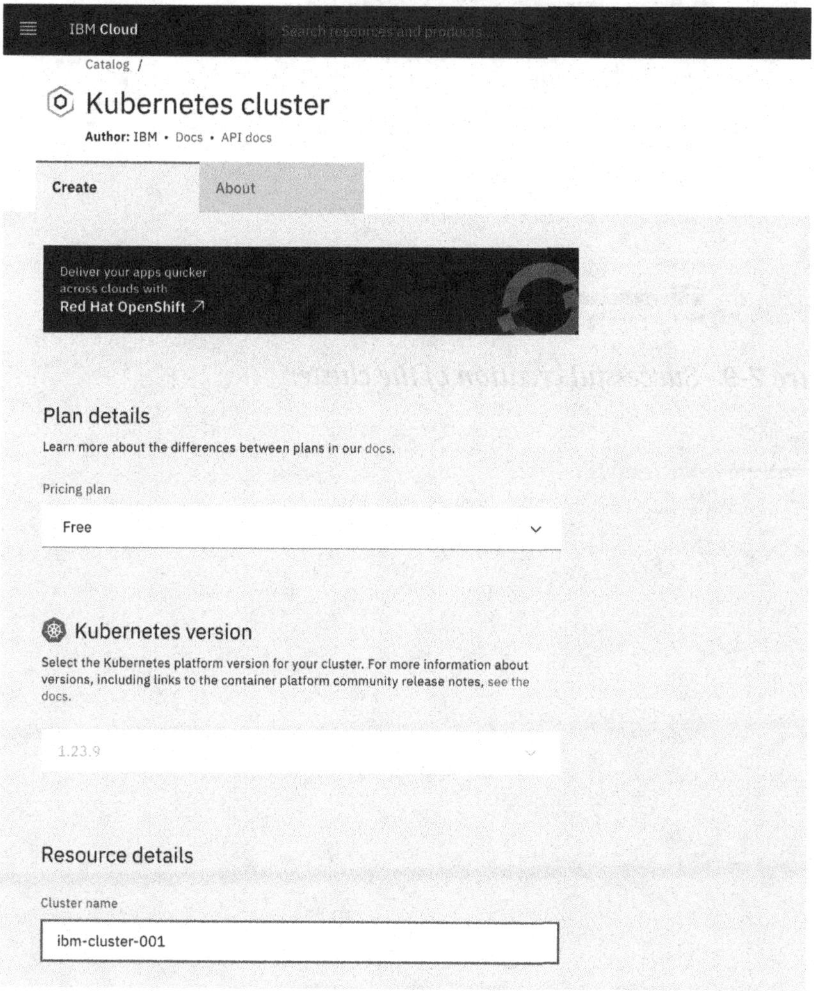

Figure 7-8. *Subscribe to IBM Kubernetes*

IBM Cloud will go through the process of creating the cluster and bring you to the page shown in Figure 7-9.

Figure 7-9. *Successful creation of the cluster*

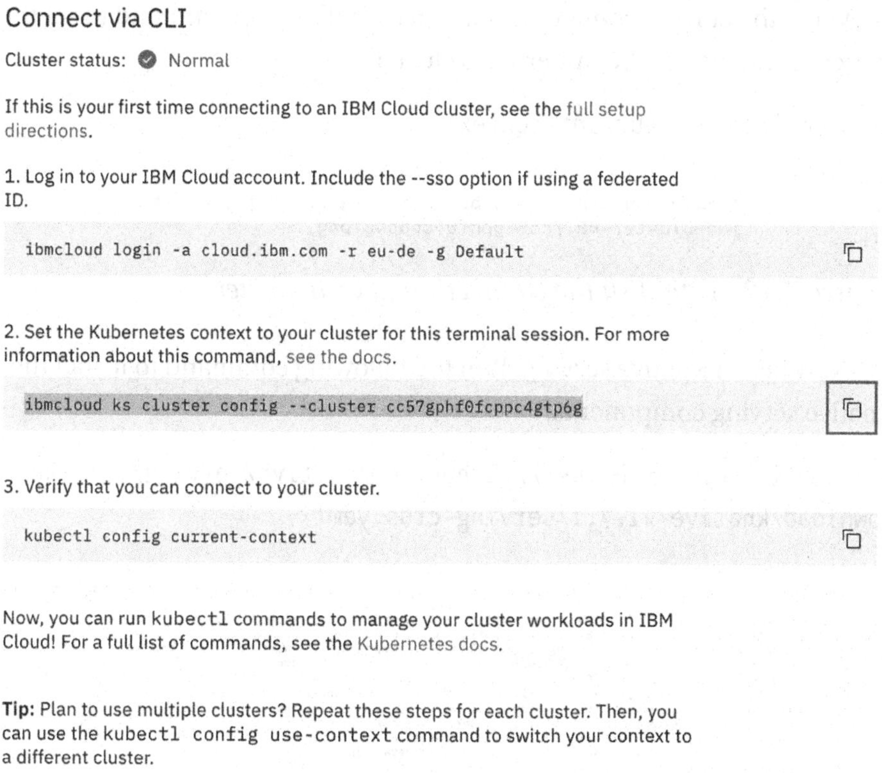

Connect via CLI

Cluster status: ✔ Normal

If this is your first time connecting to an IBM Cloud cluster, see the full setup directions.

1. Log in to your IBM Cloud account. Include the --sso option if using a federated ID.

```
ibmcloud login -a cloud.ibm.com -r eu-de -g Default
```

2. Set the Kubernetes context to your cluster for this terminal session. For more information about this command, see the docs.

```
ibmcloud ks cluster config --cluster cc57gphf0fcppc4gtp6g
```

3. Verify that you can connect to your cluster.

```
kubectl config current-context
```

Now, you can run kubectl commands to manage your cluster workloads in IBM Cloud! For a full list of commands, see the Kubernetes docs.

Tip: Plan to use multiple clusters? Repeat these steps for each cluster. Then, you can use the kubectl config use-context command to switch your context to a different cluster.

Figure 7-10. *Some boilerplate instructions after creating the cluster*

Connect to the cluster by running the following command to get the cluster information:

```
$ ibmcloud ks cluster config --cluster cc57gphf0fcppc4gtp6g
```

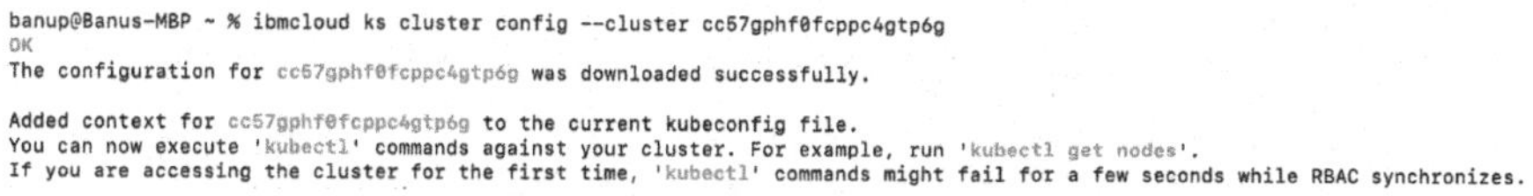

```
banup@Banus-MBP ~ % ibmcloud ks cluster config --cluster cc57gphf0fcppc4gtp6g
OK
The configuration for cc57gphf0fcppc4gtp6g was downloaded successfully.

Added context for cc57gphf0fcppc4gtp6g to the current kubeconfig file.
You can now execute 'kubectl' commands against your cluster. For example, run 'kubectl get nodes'.
If you are accessing the cluster for the first time, 'kubectl' commands might fail for a few seconds while RBAC synchronizes.
```

Figure 7-11. *Your kubectl is configured to connect to the cluster*

Verify the current configuration. Run the following command to set the context of Kubectl to the Kubernetes cluster:

```
$ kubectl config current-context
```

```
banup@Banus-MBP ~ % kubectl config current-context
ibm-cluster-001/cc57gphf0fcppc4gtp6g
```

Figure 7-12. *Establish the connection to your cluster*

Now install Knative serving. Run the following command to install the Knative serving components:

```
$ kubectl apply -f https://github.com/knative/serving/releases/
download/knative-v1.7.1/serving-crds.yaml
```

```
banup@Banus-MBP ~ % kubectl apply -f https://github.com/knative/serving/releases/download/knative-v1.7.1/serving-crds.yaml
customresourcedefinition.apiextensions.k8s.io/certificates.networking.internal.knative.dev created
customresourcedefinition.apiextensions.k8s.io/configurations.serving.knative.dev created
customresourcedefinition.apiextensions.k8s.io/clusterdomainclaims.networking.internal.knative.dev created
customresourcedefinition.apiextensions.k8s.io/domainmappings.serving.knative.dev created
customresourcedefinition.apiextensions.k8s.io/ingresses.networking.internal.knative.dev created
customresourcedefinition.apiextensions.k8s.io/metrics.autoscaling.internal.knative.dev created
customresourcedefinition.apiextensions.k8s.io/podautoscalers.autoscaling.internal.knative.dev created
customresourcedefinition.apiextensions.k8s.io/revisions.serving.knative.dev created
customresourcedefinition.apiextensions.k8s.io/routes.serving.knative.dev created
customresourcedefinition.apiextensions.k8s.io/serverlessservices.networking.internal.knative.dev created
customresourcedefinition.apiextensions.k8s.io/services.serving.knative.dev created
customresourcedefinition.apiextensions.k8s.io/images.caching.internal.knative.dev created
```

Figure 7-13. *Knative crds are created*

Run the following command to install the Knative serving core:

```
$ kubectl apply -f https://github.com/knative/serving/releases/
download/knative-v1.7.1/serving-core.yaml
```

```
banup@Banus-MBP ~ % kubectl apply -f https://github.com/knative/serving/releases/download/knative-v1.7.1/serving-core.yaml

namespace/knative-serving created
clusterrole.rbac.authorization.k8s.io/knative-serving-aggregated-addressable-resolver created
clusterrole.rbac.authorization.k8s.io/knative-serving-addressable-resolver created
clusterrole.rbac.authorization.k8s.io/knative-serving-namespaced-admin created
clusterrole.rbac.authorization.k8s.io/knative-serving-namespaced-edit created
clusterrole.rbac.authorization.k8s.io/knative-serving-namespaced-view created
clusterrole.rbac.authorization.k8s.io/knative-serving-core created
clusterrole.rbac.authorization.k8s.io/knative-serving-podspecable-binding created
serviceaccount/controller created
clusterrole.rbac.authorization.k8s.io/knative-serving-admin created
clusterrolebinding.rbac.authorization.k8s.io/knative-serving-controller-admin created
clusterrolebinding.rbac.authorization.k8s.io/knative-serving-controller-addressable-resolver created
customresourcedefinition.apiextensions.k8s.io/images.caching.internal.knative.dev unchanged
customresourcedefinition.apiextensions.k8s.io/certificates.networking.internal.knative.dev unchanged
customresourcedefinition.apiextensions.k8s.io/configurations.serving.knative.dev unchanged
customresourcedefinition.apiextensions.k8s.io/clusterdomainclaims.networking.internal.knative.dev unchanged
customresourcedefinition.apiextensions.k8s.io/domainmappings.serving.knative.dev unchanged
customresourcedefinition.apiextensions.k8s.io/ingresses.networking.internal.knative.dev unchanged
customresourcedefinition.apiextensions.k8s.io/metrics.autoscaling.internal.knative.dev unchanged
customresourcedefinition.apiextensions.k8s.io/podautoscalers.autoscaling.internal.knative.dev unchanged
customresourcedefinition.apiextensions.k8s.io/revisions.serving.knative.dev unchanged
customresourcedefinition.apiextensions.k8s.io/routes.serving.knative.dev unchanged
customresourcedefinition.apiextensions.k8s.io/serverlessservices.networking.internal.knative.dev unchanged
customresourcedefinition.apiextensions.k8s.io/services.serving.knative.dev unchanged
secret/serving-certs-ctrl-ca created
secret/knative-serving-certs created
image.caching.internal.knative.dev/queue-proxy created
configmap/config-autoscaler created
configmap/config-defaults created
configmap/config-deployment created
```

Figure 7-14. *Knative serving core is deployed*

Install Istio. Istio creates an ingress for the cluster. Run the following code to install it:

```
$ kubectl apply -l knative.dev/crd-install=true -f https://
github.com/knative/net-istio/releases/download/knative-v1.7.0/
istio.yaml
```

```
customresourcedefinition.apiextensions.k8s.io/authorizationpolicies.security.istio.io created
customresourcedefinition.apiextensions.k8s.io/destinationrules.networking.istio.io created
customresourcedefinition.apiextensions.k8s.io/envoyfilters.networking.istio.io created
customresourcedefinition.apiextensions.k8s.io/gateways.networking.istio.io created
customresourcedefinition.apiextensions.k8s.io/istiooperators.install.istio.io created
customresourcedefinition.apiextensions.k8s.io/peerauthentications.security.istio.io created
customresourcedefinition.apiextensions.k8s.io/proxyconfigs.networking.istio.io created
customresourcedefinition.apiextensions.k8s.io/requestauthentications.security.istio.io created
customresourcedefinition.apiextensions.k8s.io/serviceentries.networking.istio.io created
customresourcedefinition.apiextensions.k8s.io/sidecars.networking.istio.io created
customresourcedefinition.apiextensions.k8s.io/telemetries.telemetry.istio.io created
customresourcedefinition.apiextensions.k8s.io/virtualservices.networking.istio.io created
customresourcedefinition.apiextensions.k8s.io/wasmplugins.extensions.istio.io created
customresourcedefinition.apiextensions.k8s.io/workloadentries.networking.istio.io created
customresourcedefinition.apiextensions.k8s.io/workloadgroups.networking.istio.io created
namespace/istio-system created
serviceaccount/istio-ingressgateway-service-account created
serviceaccount/istio-reader-service-account created
serviceaccount/istiod created
serviceaccount/istiod-service-account created
clusterrole.rbac.authorization.k8s.io/istio-reader-clusterrole-istio-system created
clusterrole.rbac.authorization.k8s.io/istio-reader-istio-system created
clusterrole.rbac.authorization.k8s.io/istiod-clusterrole-istio-system created
clusterrole.rbac.authorization.k8s.io/istiod-gateway-controller-istio-system created
clusterrole.rbac.authorization.k8s.io/istiod-istio-system created
clusterrolebinding.rbac.authorization.k8s.io/istio-reader-clusterrole-istio-system created
clusterrolebinding.rbac.authorization.k8s.io/istio-reader-istio-system created
clusterrolebinding.rbac.authorization.k8s.io/istiod-clusterrole-istio-system created
clusterrolebinding.rbac.authorization.k8s.io/istiod-gateway-controller-istio-system created
clusterrolebinding.rbac.authorization.k8s.io/istiod-istio-system created
role.rbac.authorization.k8s.io/istio-ingressgateway-sds created
role.rbac.authorization.k8s.io/istiod created
role.rbac.authorization.k8s.io/istiod-istio-system created
rolebinding.rbac.authorization.k8s.io/istio-ingressgateway-sds created
rolebinding.rbac.authorization.k8s.io/istiod created
rolebinding.rbac.authorization.k8s.io/istiod-istio-system created
customresourcedefinition.apiextensions.k8s.io/authorizationpolicies.security.istio.io unchanged
customresourcedefinition.apiextensions.k8s.io/destinationrules.networking.istio.io unchanged
customresourcedefinition.apiextensions.k8s.io/envoyfilters.networking.istio.io unchanged
customresourcedefinition.apiextensions.k8s.io/gateways.networking.istio.io unchanged
customresourcedefinition.apiextensions.k8s.io/istiooperators.install.istio.io unchanged
customresourcedefinition.apiextensions.k8s.io/peerauthentications.security.istio.io unchanged
customresourcedefinition.apiextensions.k8s.io/proxyconfigs.networking.istio.io unchanged
customresourcedefinition.apiextensions.k8s.io/requestauthentications.security.istio.io unchanged
customresourcedefinition.apiextensions.k8s.io/serviceentries.networking.istio.io unchanged
customresourcedefinition.apiextensions.k8s.io/sidecars.networking.istio.io unchanged
customresourcedefinition.apiextensions.k8s.io/telemetries.telemetry.istio.io unchanged
customresourcedefinition.apiextensions.k8s.io/virtualservices.networking.istio.io unchanged
customresourcedefinition.apiextensions.k8s.io/wasmplugins.extensions.istio.io unchanged
customresourcedefinition.apiextensions.k8s.io/workloadentries.networking.istio.io unchanged
customresourcedefinition.apiextensions.k8s.io/workloadgroups.networking.istio.io unchanged
configmap/istio created
configmap/istio-sidecar-injector created
deployment.apps/istio-ingressgateway created
deployment.apps/istiod created
service/istio-ingressgateway created
service/istiod created
Warning: autoscaling/v2beta2 HorizontalPodAutoscaler is deprecated in v1.23+, unavailable in v1.26+; use autoscaling/v2 HorizontalPodAutoscaler
horizontalpodautoscaler.autoscaling/istiod created
Warning: policy/v1beta1 PodDisruptionBudget is deprecated in v1.21+, unavailable in v1.25+; use policy/v1 PodDisruptionBudget
poddisruptionbudget.policy/istio-ingressgateway created
poddisruptionbudget.policy/istiod created
mutatingwebhookconfiguration.admissionregistration.k8s.io/istio-sidecar-injector created
validatingwebhookconfiguration.admissionregistration.k8s.io/istio-validator-istio-system created
envoyfilter.networking.istio.io/stats-filter-1.11 created
envoyfilter.networking.istio.io/stats-filter-1.12 created
envoyfilter.networking.istio.io/stats-filter-1.13 created
envoyfilter.networking.istio.io/stats-filter-1.14 created
envoyfilter.networking.istio.io/stats-filter-1.15 created
envoyfilter.networking.istio.io/tcp-stats-filter-1.11 created
envoyfilter.networking.istio.io/tcp-stats-filter-1.12 created
envoyfilter.networking.istio.io/tcp-stats-filter-1.13 created
envoyfilter.networking.istio.io/tcp-stats-filter-1.14 created
envoyfilter.networking.istio.io/tcp-stats-filter-1.15 created
```

Figure 7-15. *Istio is successfully deployed*

Now run the following command to configure the network components:

```
$ kubectl apply -f https://github.com/knative/net-istio/
releases/download/knative-v1.7.0/net-istio.yaml
```

```
banup@Banus-MBP ~ % kubectl apply -f https://github.com/knative/net-istio/releases/download/knative-v1.7.0/net-istio.yaml

clusterrole.rbac.authorization.k8s.io/knative-serving-istio unchanged
gateway.networking.istio.io/knative-ingress-gateway created
gateway.networking.istio.io/knative-local-gateway created
service/knative-local-gateway unchanged
configmap/config-istio created
peerauthentication.security.istio.io/webhook created
peerauthentication.security.istio.io/domainmapping-webhook created
peerauthentication.security.istio.io/net-istio-webhook created
deployment.apps/net-istio-controller created
deployment.apps/net-istio-webhook created
secret/net-istio-webhook-certs created
service/net-istio-webhook created
mutatingwebhookconfiguration.admissionregistration.k8s.io/webhook.istio.networking.internal.knative.dev unchanged
validatingwebhookconfiguration.admissionregistration.k8s.io/config.webhook.istio.networking.internal.knative.dev unchanged
```

Figure 7-16. *Network components of Istio are created*

Now install Magic DNS. It allows you to call the service from an FQDN rather than an IP address.

```
$ kubectl apply -f https://github.com/knative/serving/releases/
download/knative-v1.7.1/serving-default-domain.yaml
```

```
banup@Banus-MBP ~ % kubectl apply -f https://github.com/knative/serving/releases/download/knative-v1.7.1/serving-default-domain.yaml

job.batch/default-domain created
service/default-domain-service created
```

Figure 7-17. *Default domain (Magic DNS) created*

Run the following command to get the status of the services:

```
$ kubectl get pods --namespace knative-serving
```

```
NAME                                          READY   STATUS    RESTARTS   AGE
activator-54cdf744fb-4qplb                    1/1     Running   0          4m16s
autoscaler-684495f859-gj8pb                   1/1     Running   0          4m15s
controller-865d96c97f-tdt78                   1/1     Running   0          4m14s
default-domain-wq7sf                          1/1     Running   0          38s
domain-mapping-5d488c9654-bmw7c               1/1     Running   0          4m13s
domainmapping-webhook-54d46d9b6c-29b2j        1/1     Running   0          4m13s
net-istio-controller-665674d95b-gmb7p         1/1     Running   0          87s
net-istio-webhook-5858ddf6f5-qkshr            1/1     Running   0          86s
webhook-65984d8585-bc92v                      1/1     Running   0          4m11s
```

Figure 7-18. *Knative components are running*

Once the status is Running, you can deploy Spring Cloud Function.

Step 6: Create a Cloudant database. Navigate to your subscription on the IBM Cloud and click Create Resource. Search for Cloudant.

You can also get to the Cloudant page at `https://cloud.ibm.com/catalog/services/cloudant`.

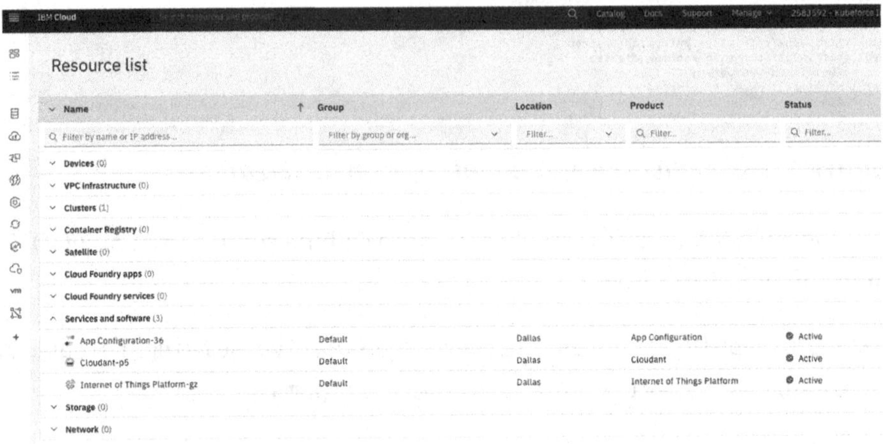

Figure 7-19. *IBM Cloud resources*

Choose the Cloudant instance listed in Services and Software to start configuring your instance. Set up the Cloudant configuration as per your specification. See Figure 7-20.

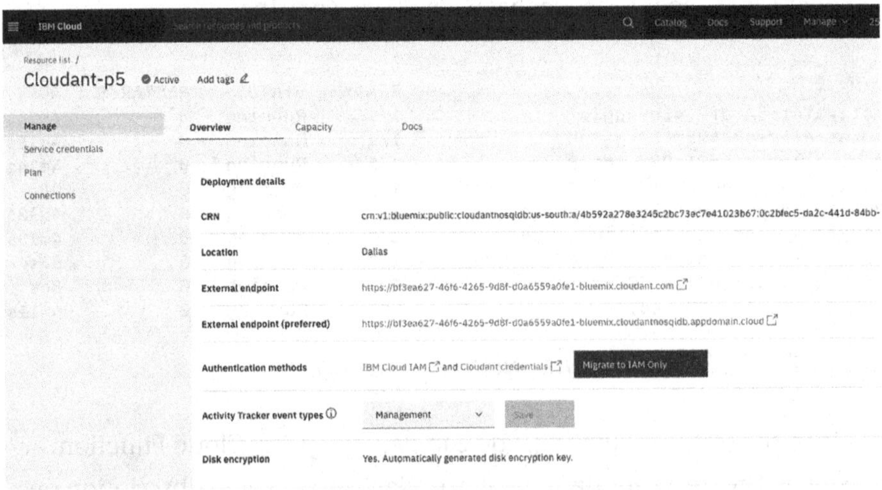

Figure 7-20. *IBM Cloud Cloudant specs*

You can use Create Database on the top of the screen. Provide the name and partition information to create the database. Once this process is complete, you can see the database, as shown in Figure 7-21.

Figure 7-21. *Cloudant DB*

<u>Step 7:</u> Create a Spring Cloud Function to connect to the event streams and Cloudant DB. You can download it at `https://github.com/banup-kubeforce/IBMIoTV2`.

You use the Spring Kafka and Cloudant for the Maven dependency, as shown in Listing 7-1.

Listing 7-1. Dependencies

```
<dependencies>
  <dependency>
    <groupId>com.ibm.cloud</groupId>
      <artifactId>cloudant</artifactId>
        <version>0.3.0</version>
  </dependency>
```

```
<dependency>
    <groupId>com.cloudant</groupId>
    <artifactId>cloudant-client</artifactId>
    <version>2.20.1</version>
</dependency>

</dependencies>
```

Listing 7-2 shows the application.properties.

Listing 7-2. Cloudant and IBM Event Streams Configuration

```
spring.cloud.function.definition=iotCloudantSupplier
cloudant.db=sensordb

cloudant.url="https://apikey-v2-w2z4fgix9dlpw626eihi4g4n9w
20ntyekk7jknbyrio:1d012fa20433d315b899a2ed90f3fefb@23204
af3-2c33-4bfb-bbc4-f55bbe1902ea-bluemix.cloudantnosqldb.
appdomain.cloud"
cloudant.apikey="Service credentials-1"

spring.datasource.url=jdbc:h2:mem:employee
spring.datasource.driverClassName=org.h2.Driver
spring.datasource.username=sa
spring.datasource.password=
spring.h2.console.enabled=true
spring.jpa.database-platform=org.hibernate.dialect.H2Dialect
spring.jpa.defer-datasource-initialization=true

#EventStreams
#Connection
spring.kafka.jaas.enabled=true
spring.kafka.jaas.login-module=org.apache.kafka.common.
security.plain.PlainLoginModule
```

```
spring.kafka.jaas.options.username=token
spring.kafka.jaas.options.password=NhZ7i_
IHpf3piG99jQpIMGtZTT3tRggmfj7UhaztdNFx
spring.kafka.bootstrap-servers=broker-2-2068cxqswxtbl1kv.kafka.
svc09.us-south.eventstreams.cloud.ibm.com:9093,broker-1-2068cx
qswxtbl1kv.kafka.svc09.us-south.eventstreams.cloud.ibm.com:909
3,broker-0-2068cxqswxtbl1kv.kafka.svc09.us-south.eventstreams.
cloud.ibm.com:9093,broker-5-2068cxqswxtbl1kv.kafka.svc09.us-
south.eventstreams.cloud.ibm.com:9093,broker-3-2068cxqswxtbl1
kv.kafka.svc09.us-south.eventstreams.cloud.ibm.com:9093,broker-
4-2068cxqswxtbl1kv.kafka.svc09.us-south.eventstreams.cloud.ibm.
com:9093
spring.kafka.properties.security.protocol=SASL_SSL
spring.kafka.properties.sasl.mechanism=PLAIN

#Producer
spring.kafka.template.default-topic=sensor-topic
spring.kafka.producer.client-id=event-streams-kafka
spring.kafka.producer.key-serializer=org.apache.kafka.common.
serialization.StringSerializer
spring.kafka.producer.value-serializer=org.apache.kafka.common.
serialization.StringSerializer

#Consumer
listener.topic=sensor-topic
spring.kafka.consumer.group-id=sensor-topic
spring.kafka.consumer.auto-offset-reset=earliest
spring.kafka.consumer.key-deserializer=org.apache.kafka.common.
serialization.StringDeserializer

spring.kafka.consumer.value-deserializer=org.apache.kafka.
common.serialization.StringDeserializer
```

You have to provide the device ID, protocol, data, and status of the device into a JSON object for Cloudant to store. See Listings 7-3 through 7-5.

Listing 7-3. CloudantConsumer.java

```java
import com.cloudant.client.api.ClientBuilder;
import com.cloudant.client.api.CloudantClient;
import com.cloudant.client.api.Database;
import org.json.JSONObject;
import org.slf4j.Logger;
import org.slf4j.LoggerFactory;
import org.springframework.beans.factory.annotation.Autowired;

import java.util.Map;
import java.util.function.Consumer;

/*
{
"deviceid":"gas-sensor1",
"protocol":"mqtt",
"data":"{temp:25,pressure:35}",
"status":"Warning"
}
 */
public class IotCloudantConsumer implements
Consumer<Map<String,String>> {
    public static final Logger LOGGER = LoggerFactory.
    getLogger(IotCloudantConsumer.class);

    @Autowired
    private IotRepository iotRepository;
```

```java
CloudantClient client = ClientBuilder.
account("23204af3-2c33-4bfb-bbc4-f55bbe1902ea-bluemix")
        .iamApiKey("B2DtIBIPIP1qhFt6swrl-OnbQZcY6ZB1SVti
        _9zKX832")
        .build();

Database db = client.database("sensordb",false);
@Override
public void accept (Map<String, String> map)
{
    LOGGER.info("Creating the Iot sensor info", map);
    JSONObject iotdata = new JSONObject();
    iotdata.put("deviceid","gas-sensor1");
    iotdata.put("protocol","mqtt");
    iotdata.put("data","{temp:25,pressure:35}");
    iotdata.put("status","Warning");

    IotSensor sensorinfo = new IotSensor (map.
    get("deviceid"), (map.get(
            "protocol")), map.get("data"), map.
            get("protocol"));
    db.save(iotdata);

}


}
```

Listing 7-4. CloudantConnector.java

```java
import com.cloudant.client.api.ClientBuilder;
import com.cloudant.client.api.CloudantClient;
import com.cloudant.client.api.Database;
```

```
public class CloudantConnector {
    CloudantClient client = ClientBuilder.
    account("23204af3-2c33-4bfb-bbc4-f55bbe1902ea-bluemix")
            .iamApiKey("B2DtIBIPIP1qhFt6swrl-OnbQZcY6ZB1SVti
            _9zKX832")
            .build();
    Database db = client.database("sensordb",false);
}
```

Listing 7-5. EventStreamsSupplier.java (See GitHub for the Latest)

```
package com.kubeforce.ibmiotv2;

import org.json.JSONObject;
import org.springframework.kafka.core.KafkaTemplate;

import java.util.List;
import java.util.concurrent.CopyOnWriteArrayList;
import java.util.function.Supplier;

public class EventStreamsSupplier implements Supplier {

    CloudantConnector cloudantConnector = new
    CloudantConnector();
    private KafkaTemplate<String, String> template;
    private List<String> messages = new
    CopyOnWriteArrayList<>();
    @Override
    public String get() {
        String result = messages.toString();
        JSONObject iotdata = new JSONObject();
        iotdata.put("message",result);
        cloudantConnector.db.save(iotdata);
        messages.clear();
```

```
    return result;

    }
}
```

The `EventStreamsSupplier` function connects to the IBM event streams and gets the data in the `sensors-topic`. It then stores this data in the Cloudant `sensordb`.

Step 8: Deploy the Spring Cloud Function to Knative on the Kubernetes cluster. Refer to Chapter 2 for deploying Spring Cloud Function on Knative.

Step 9: Integrate event streams to invoke Spring Cloud Function. Invoke the `EventStreamSupplier` function. When running the function locally, you will get the output in Figure 7-22.

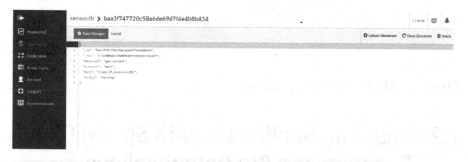

Figure 7-22. *Running the EventStreamsSupplier locally*

Figure 7-23 shows the information that is stored in Cloudant DB.

Figure 7-23. *IoT data stored in CloudantDB*

This section explored the world of IoT from an IBM Cloud and IBM Watson IoT perspective. Figure 7-24 shows the various components of the IoT platform that were covered.

You also saw that you can build functions with Spring Cloud Function and deploy them on IBM Cloud on Kubernetes.

You subscribed to IBM Cloud, created a device in the IoT platform, created a Kubernetes cluster, created a Cloudant database, created a function to post the data into the Cloudant database, connected event streams to the function, and connected the Cloudant database to the IoT platform. There are lots of things to configure in order to set up an end-to-end flow. See Figure 7-24.

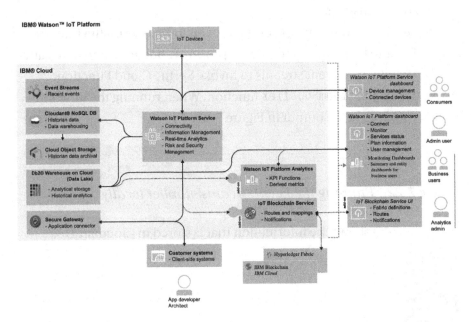

Figure 7-24. *Watson IoT context*

7.2. Enabling Healthcare with Spring Cloud Function and Big Data Pipelines

Healthcare is dependent on data. Be it patient records, image recognition, genomics, tracking wearables, and using sensors, a healthcare system is bombarded with data. Figure 7-25 conceptualizes Big Data in healthcare.

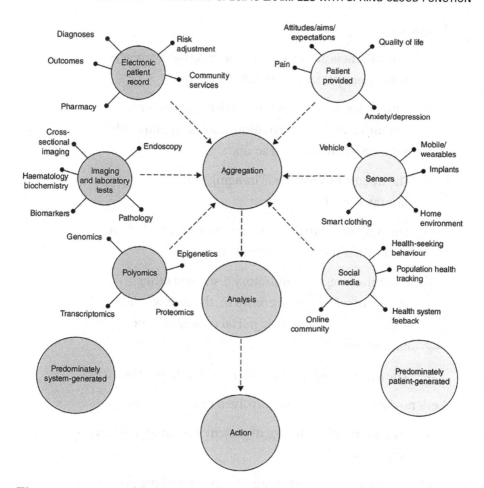

Figure 7-25. *Healthcare context*
Source: *https://www.researchgate.net/publication/330249318/*
figure/fig1/AS:713182909829120@1547047464835/
Conceptualizing-big-data-in-healthcare-Health-system-data-
are-aggregated-with-data.png (*Creative commons license*
https://creativecommons.org/licenses/by/4.0/)

The use case here is that a patient walks into a hospital complaining of
a pain in the back, near the spine. The pain has been persistent and they
want a quick diagnosis.

The process:

1) The patient is admitted into the hospital by means of a patient portal and check-in process.

2) Initial patient analysis is done using EHRs and patient-provided information, such as quality of life, pain, expectations, and so on.

3) The doctor recommends imaging and laboratory tests.

4) The patient is provided with a smart wearable that tracks their movement in the hospital.

5) Once the imaging, laboratory tests, and other pertinent information comes in, the doctors use their smart AI diagnostic portal to diagnose possible conditions.

6) The doctor informs the patient of the diagnosis.

Let's now look at the systems involved in this process:

- Patient portal for intake of patient information (data acquisition)

- Intake and aggregate patient surveys and patient history (data aggregation)

- Labs and imaging (image data)

- Diagnosis (data analysis and AI recommendations)

- Smart wearables (IoT streaming data)

Translating this processes into a cloud architecture view, you can see that Spring Cloud Function plays an important role in all these processes. It is therefore essential for the functions to be portable so that the best cloud providers can be used in each case. See Figure 7-26.

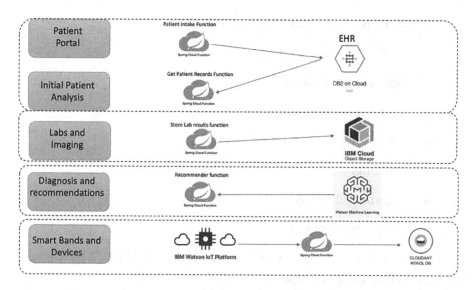

Figure 7-26. *Applications of Spring Cloud Function in the various healthcare flows*

7.3. Conversational AI in Retail Using Spring Cloud Function

AI and retail are inextricably tied at the hip. Humans enjoy shopping, mall strolling, online shopping, and just online browsing. They constantly encounter AI by way of targeted advertising, product recommendations, and product placements. Many of these features are run by robots. This means that AI and retail are converging.

Based on Fortune business insights, the retail AI market is expected to reach $19.9 billion by 2027, with a growth rate of 34.4 percent from 2020 to 2027 (Source: https://www.meticulousresearch.com/product/artificial-intelligence-in-retail-market-4979).

Some of the top ways that AI is used in retail include:

- Predictive analytics using Big Data

- Demand forecasting

- Visual searching

- Recommender systems

- Chatbots

- Augmented reality

- Brand management

COVID-19 changed the way that AI interacted with retail. AI powered by chatbots rose to prominence.

Chatbots—or conversational AI—in fact became the AI interface for retail. Most communication with a product or support team is initiated using an AI interactive session. Better customer experience through these chatbots is of paramount importance to retailers. If the chatbots were bad, the customer would move on to another retailer. So brand management, recommendations, predictions, and forecasting all relied on how the chatbot interacted with the customers and if it extracted the right information to provide the customers with the best experience.

IBM, AWS, Azure, Google, and other cloud providers focused their attention on capturing the conversational AI market, as every retailer was clamoring for an edge with these customer interactions.

You will look at how IBM approached conversational AI and at how Spring Cloud Function plays a role in connecting systems with people.

The IBM conversational AI offering includes a wide array of products on the IBM Cloud and on cloud paks. Cloud paks are software that can be deployed to any cloud.

IBM Cloud provides both generic Kubernetes and Red Hat OpenShift Kubernetes, while the cloud paks are offered on Red Hat OpenShift. Spring Cloud Function can be deployed on any Kubernetes offering.

Figure 7-27 shows a conceptual representation of conversational AI.

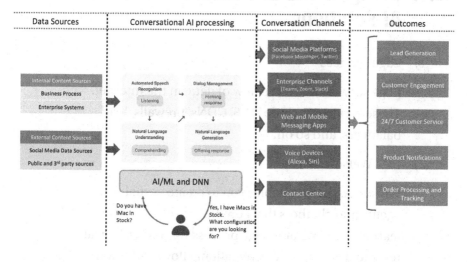

Figure 7-27. *Conversational AI concept*

By translating this concept into an IBM Cloud-based architecture, you get Figure 7-28.

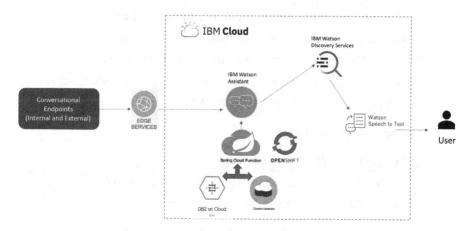

Figure 7-28. *Conversational AI systems view*

7.3.1. Components of Conversational AI Solutions

1) Edge services

   Edge services allow the flow of data on the Internet. These services include DNS, CDNs, firewalls, load balancers, and so on.

2) IBM Watson Assistant

   Watson Assistant enables you to create virtual agents and chatbots that combine machine learning, natural language processing, and graphical tools to design your conversational flows. Additional information is available at `https://www.ibm.com/products/watson-assistant`.

3) IBM Watson Discovery Services

   Watson Discovery Services helps you ingest, parse, index, and annotate content. The ingested data can come from internal and external data sources. Additional information is available at `https://www.ibm.com/cloud/watson-discovery`.

4) Watson Speech to Text

   Watson Speech to Text converts voice to text. Additional information is available at `https://www.ibm.com/cloud/watson-speech-to-text`.

5) Spring Cloud Function deployed on Knative on OpenShift (IBM Cloud)

Spring Cloud Function can be deployed on OpenShift in the IBM Cloud. Knative has to be configured on OpenShift. This process is outlined in the Knative deployment discussion throughout this book.

6)   DB2 on cloud

This is a fully managed SQL database on the cloud. Information about DB2 on cloud can be found at `https://www.ibm.com/cloud/db2-on-cloud`.

7)   Cloudant DB

This is a fully managed distributed database ideal for web and mobile apps and storing IoT or mobile data. More information can be found at `https://www.ibm.com/cloud/cloudant`.

7.3.2. Watson Assistant Webhooks and Spring Cloud Function

Once you create and deploy a Spring Cloud Function, you need to be able to call it from the Watson Assistant. This can be done by means of Webhooks.

The following requirements need to be met for Webhooks:

- The call must be a POST HTTP request. You can use your consumer function here.

- The request body must be a JSON object (`Content-Type: application/json`).

- The response must be a JSON object (`Accept: application/json`).

- The call must return in eight seconds or fewer. This is
  an important requirement and can easily be met with
  Spring Cloud Function.

7.3.3. Implementing the Watson Assistant with Spring Cloud Function

Step 1: Write the Spring Cloud Function code. The Watson Assistant
requires an OpenAPI specification. Add the code in this section to your
Pom.xml file.

Listing 7-6 shows the dependencies.

Listing 7-6. Open API Dependencies to Connect to the Watson
Assistant

```
<dependency>
    <groupId>org.springdoc</groupId>
    <artifactId>springdoc-openapi-ui</artifactId>
    <version>1.6.11</version>
</dependency>
```

Now you need to create Spring Cloud Function code for iMac
inventory. The model allows Watson to connect to and get a response. See
Listing 7-7.

Listing 7-7. inventory.java

```
package com.kubeforce.watsonimacs;

import javax.persistence.Entity;
import javax.persistence.GeneratedValue;
import javax.persistence.Id;
import javax.persistence.Table;
```

```java
@Entity
@Table(name= "inventory")
public class Inventory {

        @Id
        @GeneratedValue(generator = "UUID")
        private Long id;

        private String name;

        private int inventoryid;

        private String description;

        private String quantity;

    public Inventory(String name, int invid, String
    description, String quantity)
    {
        this.name = name;
        this.inventoryid = invid;
        this.description = description;
        this.quantity = quantity;
    }

    public Inventory() {

    }

    public String getName ()
        {
            return name;
        }
```

```java
public void setName (String name)
{
    this.name = name;
}

public int getEmployeeIdentifier ()
{
    return inventoryid;
}

public void setCustomerIdentifier (int invid)
{
    this.inventoryid = invid;
}

public String getEmail ()
{
    return description;
}

public void setEmail (String email)
{
    this.description = description;
}

public String getSalary ()
{
    return quantity;
}

public void setSalary (String salary)
{
    this.quantity = quantity;
}
```

```java
public Long getId ()
{
    return id;
}

public void setId (Long id)
{
    this.id = id;
}
}
```

Listing 7-8 shows the InventoryConsumer file.

Listing 7-8. InventoryConsumer.java

```java
import org.slf4j.Logger;
import org.slf4j.LoggerFactory;
import org.springframework.beans.factory.annotation.Autowired;

import java.util.Map;
import java.util.function.Consumer;

public class InventoryConsumer implements
Consumer<Map<String,String>> {
    public static final Logger LOGGER = LoggerFactory.
    getLogger(InventoryConsumer.class);

    @Autowired
    private InventoryRepository InventoryRepository;

    @Override
    public void accept (Map<String, String> map)
    {
        LOGGER.info("Creating the inventory", map);
```

```
        Inventory inventory = new Inventory (map.get("name"),
        Integer.parseInt(map.get(
                "inventoryid")), map.get("description"), map.
                get("quantity"));
        InventoryRepository.save(inventory);
    }

}
```

Listing 7-9 shows the InventoryFunction file.

Listing 7-9. InventoryFunction.java

```
package com.kubeforce.watsonimacs;

import org.springframework.beans.factory.annotation.Autowired;

import java.util.Optional;
import java.util.function.Function;

public class InventoryFunction implements
Function<Long,Inventory>  {
    @Autowired
    private InventoryRepository inventoryRepository;

    @Override
    public Inventory apply (Long s)
    {
        Optional<Inventory> inventoryOptional =
        inventoryRepository.findById(s);
        if (inventoryOptional.isPresent()) {
            return inventoryOptional.get();
        }
        return null;
    }
}
```

Listing 7-10 shows the InventorySupplier file.

Listing 7-10. InventorySupplier.java

```java
package com.kubeforce.watsonimacs;

import org.slf4j.Logger;
import org.slf4j.LoggerFactory;
import org.springframework.beans.factory.annotation.Autowired;
import org.springframework.stereotype.Component;

import java.util.List;
import java.util.function.Supplier;

@Component
public class InventorySupplier implements Supplier
{
    public static final Logger LOGGER = LoggerFactory.
    getLogger(InventorySupplier.class);

    @Autowired
    private InventoryRepository InventoryRepository;

    @Override
    public Inventory get ()
    {
        List <Inventory>inventories = InventoryRepository.
        findAll();
        LOGGER.info("Getting the computer of our choice - ",
        inventories);
        return inventories.get(0);
    }
}
```

Deploy this code into an IBM Kubernetes Knative instance, as shown in Chapter 2 for Knative.

This code will now have an OpenAPI definition. This will allow the Watson Assistant to communicate with your function You can use this to configure the custom extensions in the Watson Assistant.

Step 2: Configure the Watson Assistant.

1) Define the scope of the chatbot:

   a. Example use cases

      i. Tell the user what Apple products are available.

      ii. Tell them how many iMacs are in stock.

2) Log in to the IBM Cloud (`http://cloud.ibm.com`).

Figure 7-29. *IBM Cloud dashboard*

3) Sign up for the Watson Assistant and create an instance.

   You can arrive at the Watson Assistant dashboard by searching the IBM Cloud portal or using this link `https://cloud.ibm.com/catalog/services/watson-assistant`.

Pick your plan and choose a location, as shown in Figure 7-30.

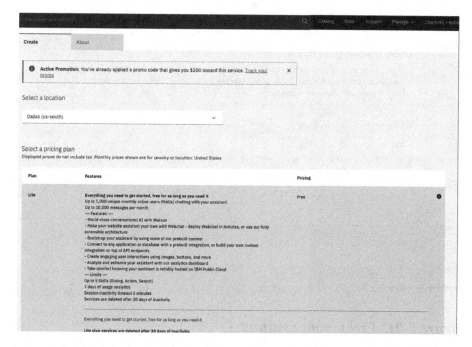

Figure 7-30. *The Watson Assistant signup page*

Click the Create button to proceed to the next step of personalizing your assistant.

4) Create and personalize your assistant.

Choose the name you want for your assistant and click Next. See Figure 7-31.

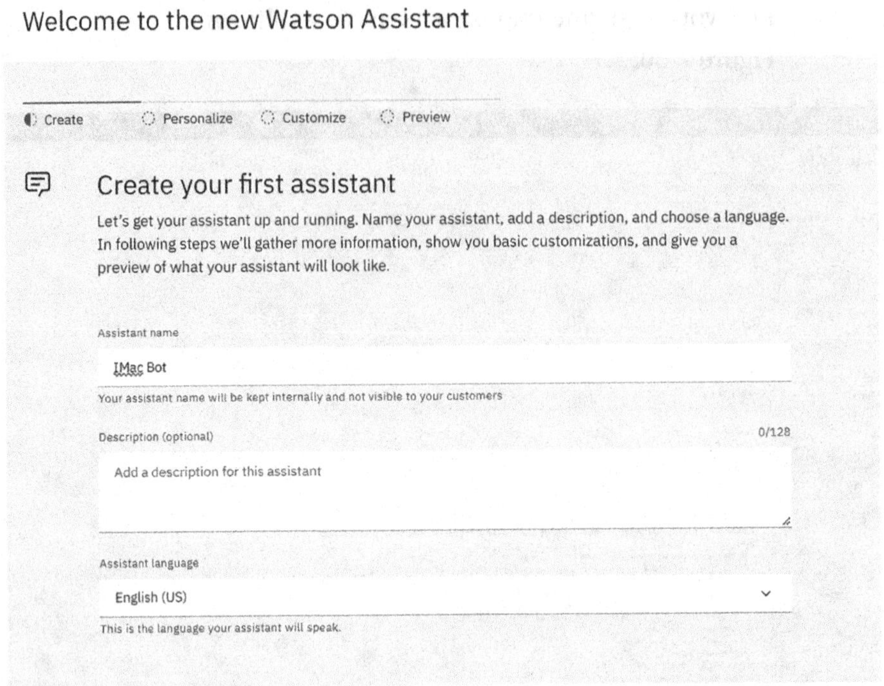

Welcome to the new Watson Assistant

Figure 7-31. *Create your assistant*

Choose your options. You will be provided a preview of the chat window.

You can choose the type of deployment you prefer. This example uses Facebook, as it provides a nice interface. See Figure 7-32.

Welcome to the new Watson Assistant

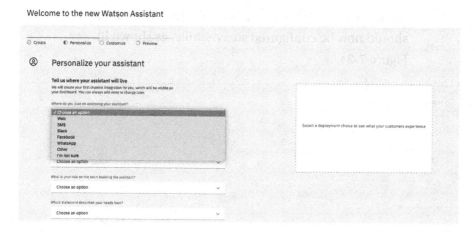

Figure 7-32. Create an assistant with a template

Fill in the Tell Us About Yourself section to your liking.
See Figure 7-33.

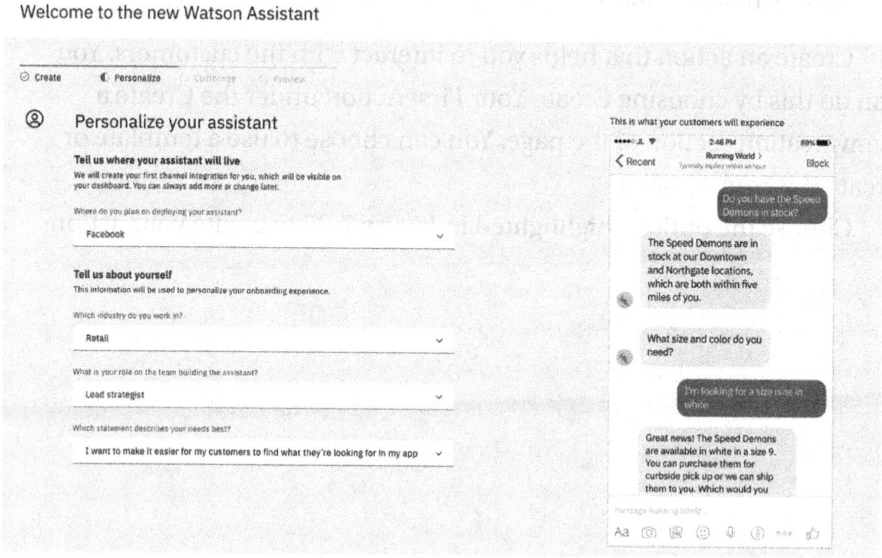

Welcome to the new Watson Assistant

Figure 7-33. Assistant with a Facebook template

Click Create to arrive at the next window. The assistant should now be configured successfully, as shown in Figure 7-34.

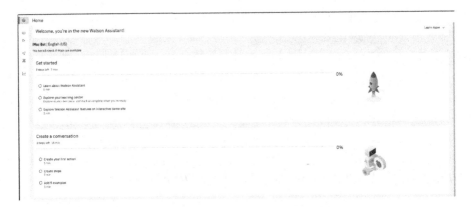

***Figure 7-34.** The assistant has been created successfully*

    5)   Create an action.

Create an action that helps you to interact with the customers. You can do this by choosing Create Your First Action under the Create a Conversation section of the page. You can choose to use a template or create this from scratch.

Choose the options highlighted in Figure 7-35 to create your action.

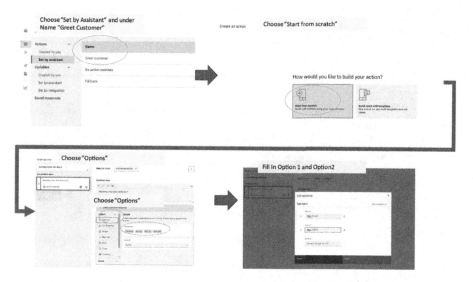

Figure 7-35. *Flow of activities to create your action*

Continue following the instructions to complete the action. You can click Preview to look at how the conversation flows and modify it to fit your needs. You now need to tie this to the Inventory function you created in Step 1 to let the bot search the inventory and respond. See Figure 7-36.

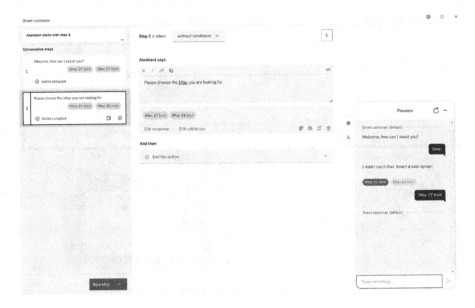

Figure 7-36. *Create an action*

You now have to create an integration using the Integrations button shown at the bottom-left side of the screen in Figure 7-37. This is available on the Home button.

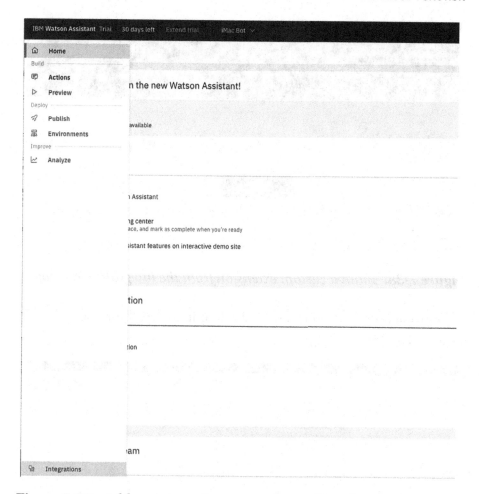

Figure 7-37. *Add an integration to support calling the Spring Cloud Function*

   6)   Build a custom extension.

   The Integrations button will take you to the Build Custom Integrations dashboard, as shown in Figure 7-38.

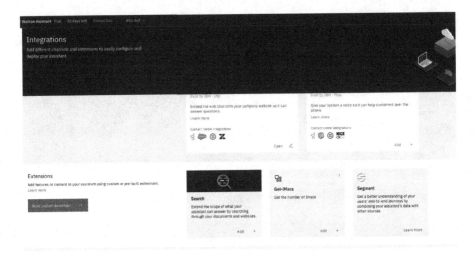

Figure 7-38. *Build a custom extension from the integration catalog*

Provide your extension name and a description, as shown in Figure 7-39.

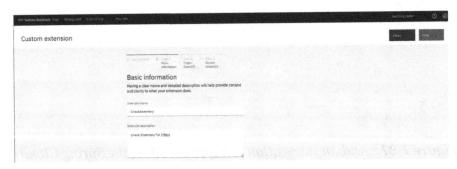

Figure 7-39. *Provide the custom extension information*

Pick the function that you deployed. Once you provide the URL, it will give you some options to choose from, as shown in Figure 7-40.

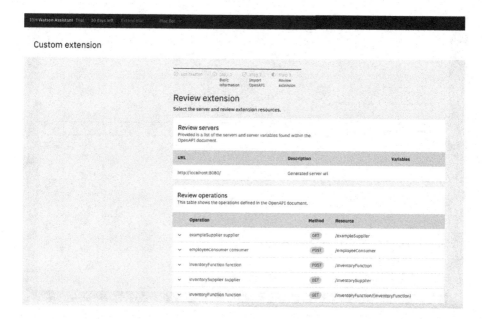

Figure 7-40. *Add Open API URL for the deployed Spring Cloud Function*

Apply the custom extension, as shown in Figure 7-41.

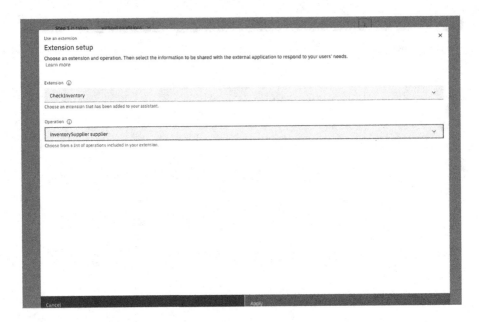

Figure 7-41. *Apply the custom extension*

The custom extension is now available for the action, as shown in Figure 7-42.

Figure 7-42. *The custom extension is available for the action*

You can now can retest your chat interface by going back to the chat that you created.

See GitHub at `https://github.com/banup-kubeforce/Watson-imacs.git` for additional information. Deploy the code in your environment and integrate. This is a fun exercise.

7.4. Summary

This chapter looked at some real-world use cases and deployed Spring Cloud Function in IBM Cloud.

This demonstrates the true "write once, deploy anywhere" capability of Spring Cloud Function.

The chapter also looked at what IBM Cloud has to offer. IBM Cloud is versatile and has many products that have been built and optimized over the years. You saw how IBM Cloud can be used in the oil and gas, healthcare, and retail markets.

There are many other use cases in which you can apply Spring Cloud Function, and it can be an alternative to a microservices architecture or can coexist with one. The decision to use functions over microservices needs to be carefully analyzed for cost, scalability, and performance before deciding on an approach.

Index

A

Printed in the United States
by Baker & Taylor Publisher Services